P E R F E C

To Kenneth McCandless Gregg,
both past and present

The PERFECT Holiday

ANNE GREGG

BBC BOOKS

My grateful thanks to Rob Neillands, Bill Buckley, Kathy Tayler, Gillian Thomas, David Tennant and Andrew Eames for their invaluable contribution and help in areas where my own knowledge was thin; to Anne Jenkins for her dexterity on the word processor and creative encouragement; to Nina Shandloff and Julian Flanders at BBC Books for their gentle guidance; and to my nearest and dearest for their patience and understanding when in the writing this book achieved the status of a four-letter word.

Published by BBC Books,
a division of BBC Enterprises Limited,
Woodlands, 80 Wood Lane, London W12 0TT

First published 1989

© Anne Gregg and BBC Enterprises 1989

Illustrations © Ian Dicks

ISBN 0 563 20645 4

Set in 10/12pt Garamond by Goodfellow and Egan Ltd, Cambridge
Printed and bound in Great Britain by Richard Clay Ltd, Bungay, Suffolk
Cover printed by Fletchers of Norwich

CONTENTS

CHAPTER ONE

The Perfect Holiday

What's your idea of the perfect holiday? Camping, cruising, island hopping? Pounding the cobbles of some medieval city? Seeing the far side of the world or enjoying the fish-chips-and-candy-floss fun of a traditional British seaside? Do you like a bit of action, learning to do something different? Or do you simply want to lie back on some palm-fringed beach somewhere under the sun and not think of England, as most of us do?

Everyone's idea of a perfect holiday is different. That's why those of us who work on the *Holiday* programme can never give a straight answer when we are asked, as we often are, 'What's the best holiday of all?' It depends on what you like to do, with whom, and whether you prefer things to be lively or laid back.

'Perfect' is a high target to aim for. After all, life isn't perfect, so why should holidays be? In the complicated chess game of moving people from one place to another, the board is governed by Murphy's Law – 'If things can go wrong, they will'. We're all pawns at the mercy of surcharges by tour companies, strikes by air traffic controllers or seamen, Fawlty hotels, temperamental taxi drivers and overwrought waiters – not to mention the weather, the water, foreign plumbing or our own personal plumbing! And we all know that real disasters can ruin lives as well as holidays.

But let's keep a sense of proportion. Despite the impression given by the media, only a very small percentage of holidays go seriously wrong. The figure, surprisingly, is somewhere between 3 and 4 per cent. That's the rate of complaint registered by the Association of British Travel Agents (ABTA). Nor do all the holidays that misfire do so because a tour company, airline or some other outside force is at fault. Quite a large number turn out to be disappointing because people have chosen badly in the first place.

The trouble is, we set off with such high hopes. Holidays are dreams-for-sale, with glossy brochures hammering the glamour, accentuating the positive and playing down the negative. So the build-up of anticipation from the time of booking to the point of departure is almost bound to be eroded by anticlimax.

A national newspaper once carried out a survey on holiday-makers leaving a major airport for their annual summer holiday abroad. They were categorised, among other things, as advance bookers or last minuters. Two weeks later, the reporter checked out the same group arriving home and discovered that a high proportion of the people who had had months to look forward to their holiday were dissatisfied, whereas almost all of those who had slipped away on the spur of the moment had had a marvellous time.

Mind you, it's not easy to draw a moral from that. Many of us *have* to plan well ahead. In any case, if a lot of us didn't book those inclusive holidays in advance, the whole industry would be thrown into a state of flux and package holiday prices would soar. But there is a great deal to be said for keeping a rein on your excitement, especially the children's, for doing a bit of extra research about where you are going and how you are getting there, for preparing for take-off as wisely and efficiently as you can – and then for remembering to pack that vital ingredient, the holiday spirit. In other words, be practical in the run up, then relax. Successful holidays aren't necessarily the ones that go exactly to plan. Leave room for surprises, for often the unexpected adds to the fun. Be open to doing things spontaneously. Take minor hitches in your stride.

There's an amusing anecdote about Charles Dickens in Edmund Swinglehurst's book *The Romantic Journey* (Epic Editions), a history of Thomas Cook, one of the longest established names in travel. It tells of the author's dismay on discovering that his stateroom on the steam-packet *Britannia* bound for America bore little resemblance to 'the highly varnished lithographic plan hanging up in the agent's counting house in the city of London' – the kind of reaction many of us have had on seeing our hotel room after admiring a wide-angled picture of it in the holiday brochure. But Dickens made a good story of it:

> By very nearly closing the door, and twining in and out like serpents, and by counting the little washing stand as standing room we could manage to insinuate four people into it, all at one time; and entreating each other to observe how very airy it was (in dock), and how there was a beautiful porthole which could be kept open all day (weather permitting), and how there was quite a large bull's eye just over the looking-glass which would render shaving a perfectly easy and delightful process (when the ship didn't roll too much); we arrived, at last, at the conclusion that it was rather spacious than otherwise!

Interestingly, on hearing the title of this book before I began to write it, the director of a travel company remarked drily, 'What you need to achieve the perfect holiday is the perfect holidaymaker.' Well he would, wouldn't he? But there's more than a kernel of truth in that. There are people who will find something to complain about when everything is perfect, and people who will enjoy themselves when nothing is perfect.

It's one thing to scream with justification about being double booked in the honeymoon suite on your first night of wedded bliss (this actually happened to a pair of unhappy couples in the hands of the country's biggest travel company), but another to whinge about picky details like rust on your balcony chairs.

If after a few days, a week or a fortnight you come home with a glow, having had a rest and a laugh, enjoyed the food and the scenery, made new friends and discoveries, and not fallen ill or out with your nearest and dearest, then your holiday has been as close to perfection as makes no difference.

This book is about choosing the holiday that's right for you, which is halfway towards making the whole exercise a success. It is packed with holiday ideas and thumbnail sketches of destinations the *Holiday* programme has reported on in recent series, and places that are personal favourites of mine. It's also prefaced with a bit of practical advice to help you in the planning stages and en route.

What it isn't is a vast reference book covering every conceivable resort. Indeed, some of the more obvious ones aren't listed since they are so well known that you can get the lowdown on them from every other brochure, as well as from every other friend who has been there.

It's a book to dip into, to steer you in the direction of places you might not have thought of, to give you fresh inspiration for a family holiday, to suggest ways to resolve a conflict of interests and, at the very least, to supply you with a few good tips for making the going smoother.

DECISIONS, DECISIONS

Every year before the Christmas turkey's cold, the newspapers thicken with travel supplements, commercial TV ads cajole us to book now for faraway sun and fun, and the high street travel agents begin to bulge with new brochures, posters and special offers. Even before the bird is stuffed, the *Holiday* team are popping up on your screens to remind you to watch us in the New Year.

Leaving aside the hype, there's a lot of helpful information about. Yet travel agents maintain that more than half their customers don't know where they want to go when they come in to buy a holiday. Obviously, it helps! Some travel agents are extremely knowledgeable and willing to take time to advise and guide, but it's asking rather a lot if you expect them to choose your holiday for you. To begin with, travel agents are in business to sell and have a vested interest in persuading you to buy inclusive holidays from the travel companies or tour operators who give them the most favourable commission. They also have to handle an increasing range of holidays and, with the best will in the world, cannot keep tabs on all there is to know about every one. Moreover, they don't deal with every travel company. Many sell direct to the public.

It's much wiser to do a bit of your own research first. A

travel agent operates best when you, the customer, know pretty much what you want, if not precisely how to achieve it. Once you've made an informed choice based on your family's fancies and finances, and decided on the where and the what, your travel agent can help on the how and the how-much. This applies whether you're a package holiday buyer or an independent traveller.

By all means pick up various brochures and useful information from them to take away and pore over in your own time. But there are other sources to tap before you make a decision. The Association of Independent Tour Operators (AITO) publishes a list of over 80 small specialist travel companies which you won't find on the shelves of every travel agent. Small companies need to be more efficient than their larger counterparts in order to survive and often offer better quality holidays – the kind you feel have been designed for you personally rather than mass produced. Their prices may not be

rock bottom, but in terms of value for money, they score high (see address list in appendix for AITO).

Tourist offices are a prime source of information, too. There's the English Tourist Board, no less than 12 regional tourist boards affiliated to it, and separate boards in Scotland, Wales, Northern Ireland, the Isle of Man, and the Channel Islands (see address list in appendix). Each in turn will be able to give you the addresses and telephone numbers of the small local tourist information centres in their domain. These are often a mine of invaluable help and advice, offering a bundle of marvellously detailed literature about sights, hotels, camp sites, activities and so on. For example, if you want to know more about Oban, write to the Scottish Tourist Board for the Oban Tourist Information Centre address. Alternatively, an envelope marked 'Tourist Information Centre, Oban' would almost certainly get there. The Post Office might not encourage this kind of short cut, but the local postman probably won't mind.

Every foreign country hoping to attract British tourists has a tourist office based in London, ready to hand out bales of bumf not only about the attractions of their country but also about which British travel companies arrange inclusive holidays there. A point to note. If at first you don't succeed in getting through on the telephone to any national tourist office, give up and write instead. As a general rule, they're equipped with too few lines to cope with the volume of enquiries they get – especially in the peak booking months early in the year – but you will usually get a comprehensive reply to any written request for information within a week, or two at the very most.

Another major source of inspiration about places is travel guides and travel books. Pop in to your local bookshop or have a browse around the travel section of your local library. The Automobile Association (AA) publishes masses of excellent guides, route planners, maps and atlases. Any AA travel shop or national chain of newsagents and stationers will have a good selection. But there are plenty of other splendid publishers of guides like Collins, Berlitz, Letts, Insight and so on. To my mind the most revealing of all books about places are novels in which the setting is well drawn. I remember reading *Tai Pan*, James Clavell's swashbuckling story of the founding of Hong

Kong, as I was actually in flight on the way to the colony. Although I arrived with my swash well and truly buckled, owing to jet lag, I had a vivid picture of the Hong Kong I wanted to get to know.

Whichever way you set about it, boning up before you make a decision on the destinations you short list for your holiday, or on the type of holiday you think your family might enjoy, will pay dividends. Only when you're thoroughly clued up about both the pleasures and possible pitfalls can you make the sort of choice that ensures a perfect holiday. Don't leave it all to someone else. Remember, after your mortgage, your holiday swallows the biggest single lump of your annual expenditure. It's worth giving a lot of careful thought to it in the planning stages.

BOOK NOW OR LATER?

Most of us don't have a great deal of leeway when it comes to plotting the dates for a summer holiday. They're dictated by the school holidays and/or the office rota – unless you're the boss. When you're restricted to going away during the peak months, you need to move fairly quickly – in January and February if not before – to make sure of being able to book what you want. If the timing doesn't matter, you can afford to be flexible, especially if you're making your own travel arrangements, as many of us do both for Britain and abroad.

It's not necessarily any more expensive to do it yourself, only more time consuming. Flight-only deals are worth bearing in mind if you tend to be a last-minuter. Ask your travel agent about these. They are seats on planes – mostly charter – to popular destinations, which tour operators haven't sold. You have to fix up your own hotel, but your travel agent can help with this, either by bleeping up the information about hotel room availability on the computer, or consulting the hotel gazetteers and phoning your booking direct. Recently, when we made a film about this on the *Holiday* programme, we followed the story through to a hotel in Majorca and found that out of five tour operators sending UK holidaymakers there, only two were offering an inclusive price that was cheaper than the flight-only deal plus normal hotel tariff.

By the way, one well-known chain of travel agents publishes a *Guide to Good Hotels* which is a collection of customers' comments – a very useful piece of literature to thumb through if you don't know your Miramars from your Bellavistas!

PARTICULAR PROBLEMS

Decisions about whether to travel by car or on trains, boats or planes depend on how fit you and yours are, and whether or not you have babies and small children in tow. Long journeys of any kind are anathema to tiny tots and a strain on parents – especially long flights. If yours are very young, try to make the getting there as easy as possible. If a car trip of several hours is inevitable, it's not a bad idea to drive during the night when little ones are likely to sleep through. If you're heading for the Mediterranean, it may pay to budget extra and put the car on the train overnight. You'll save on motorway tolls, meals en route and probably the price of an overnight stop, so the difference may not be significant.

Do ask yourself if it's wise to transport under-fives to sizzling heat. No matter how careful you are, their tender skins and constitutions can suffer under a strong sun – and at that age they couldn't care less about the weather as long as they're having fun. Holidaying in the temperate climates of northern Europe, including Scandinavia, is often a more comfortable option for everyone, with the added advantage that you can travel by road, rail and/or sea and avoid the potential hazard of being stranded at an airport because of delayed flights.

Something to remember about cross-Channel travel if you're older, liable to get breathless or a bit unsteady on your feet, is that most ferries have a lot of steep stairways to negotiate. Going by hovercraft is much less taxing. The North Sea cruise ships are better equipped with lifts between decks.

'Have wheelchair, will travel' is the admirable attitude of many disabled people who tackle infinitely more obstacles than the rest of us to go on holiday. They know that the fresh perspective gained after even a brief break from daily routine is almost always worth the effort. If you're handicapped in any way, or intending to travel with someone who is, make sure that everyone along the line from travel agent to tour operator, carrier to hotel, is made aware of your needs so that all the right arrangements can be made to smooth your passage. No one can deny the complications – particularly, for instance, when it comes to transporting battery power packs for wheelchairs aboard aircraft – but a great deal of support is available if you ask for it at the right time. There are also two excellent organisations to contact for advice and guidance. One is the Holiday Care Service which provides holiday information for disabled people, older travellers, single parents and anyone else with special needs. The other is Access to the Skies, an advisory committee of Radar which deals specifically with the difficulties of flying if you're not an able-passenger (see address list in appendix for both).

The 'Travel Wise' leaflets published by British Airways are also a boon: *Travelling as an Elderly Passenger, Incapacitated Passengers, Travelling with Babies and Children* are just three. There is also *Special Meals*, not about ordering a gourmet treat but rather for vegetarians or those on a strict diet for medical reasons. All airlines will accommodate people with problems so long as they get prior notice, but you can send for the BA leaflets any time.

BA can also help if you're afraid of flying. From time to time they put on familiarisation trips of an hour from regional airports. The captain talks you through takeoff and landing and invites you to have a look in the cockpit. This sort of initiation helps at least half of the frightened flyers get over their nerves.

A MONTH TO GO

Suddenly the calendar begins to smile at you as the time dwindles down to Departure Day. But there are some details you ought not to leave to the last minute.

One of the most boring aspects of holidaying abroad – in fact, probably the only bore – is insurance. And because it's boring, we're lazy about it. All that minute print couched in legalese is so off-putting. Boring or not, I must focus on a few vital points and urge you to spare more than a cursory glance at the forms and policies to make sure you're covered for the kind of holiday you're planning.

Happy motoring

If you're taking your own car to the Continent, fully comprehensive cover is better than third party. Although a Green Card is no longer compulsory in EEC countries except Greece, it's advisable because your insurance cover could prove inadequate without it. For Spain you also need a Bail Bond because your car and property can be impounded if you have a serious accident there. Both a Bail Bond and a Green Card are vital in Spain.

On a fly-drive deal, the insurance provided is usually adequate in Europe, but North America is another matter. Many of the companies offering fly-drive packages to the States and Canada give you minimum-liability cover starting at only $25 000. This is far from enough if you have a bad smash-up. Both the AA and RAC offer good top-up schemes for their members, and the AA also offers it to non-members (ask for their *Motoring Abroad* booklet).

Check up on the rules of the road for other countries. If you run into trouble, ignorance of the law will be no excuse any

more than it is at home. The national tourist offices of the country or countries you're heading for can supply you with a summary of the points you should be aware of.

Well and truly covered?

Look out for loopholes in any general holiday insurance that purports to cover life, health and belongings, especially those offered by a tour operator as part of, or in conjunction with, an inclusive package. Get out the magnifying glass and read every line, or get your insurance broker to check it for you and advise on whether you should take out additional cover. There can be nasty little get-out clauses which could at best leave you in the lurch and at worst in disastrous circumstances. For instance, you might injure yourself doing something that you might regard as a perfectly normal holiday activity, like windsurfing, but which turns out to be classified as a dangerous sport in your insurance. For the little extra it costs, taking out your own insurance may well be worth it.

To jab or not to jab

A month before you go is the time to find out which, if any, inoculations or immunisations you'll need for anywhere further flung than the EEC. Most travel agents have a list of what's compulsory and what's optional and will check to make sure there have been no changes because of a sudden outbreak of yellow fever or malaria. The tourist boards concerned will also advise you, and so will your local DHSS. The DHSS publishes two extremely helpful leaflets for overseas travellers: *Before You Go, the Traveller's Guide to Health* and *While You're Away*, which includes advice about AIDS.

Trouble spots and bovver

In the volatile world we live in, the chances of the natives getting restless in the very country you've set your sights on are not inconsiderable. Terrorist activity, political and geographical upheavals, artificial and natural disasters can suddenly turn a holiday paradise into a danger zone. Some countries, like Israel, learn to live with continual unrest and still sustain their tourist industry. We have our own example in Northern Ireland. But if you're worried about the risks you might be taking in going to places where trouble is festering or has recently flared up, the first checkpoint is, again, your travel agent who should be in touch with the Foreign Office Travel Advice Service. If you have any doubts, contact the FO yourself.

While you're at it, ask the FO to send you their booklet *Get It Right Before You Go*. It's about what a British Consulate abroad can and can't do for you. For example, it can't pay your hotel, medical or return travel bills if you run out of funds.

IT'S IN THE BAG

As one who always packs twice as much as she needs, frequently forgets her toothbrush, and once put an unwrapped dispenser of Evostick in her suitcase to repair a torn sandal and found the entire contents glued together on arrival, A Gregg is not the best person to give advice about packing! However, here are a few good tips I try to remember:

● Pack anything that might leak with extra care. Wrap in clingfilm or polythene bags any suspect containers with dicey screw tops.

● Transfer make-up, shampoo and other toiletries into smaller containers. It makes a big difference in weight.

● Take a small bar of soap in case it's not provided where you fetch up.

● Don't pack valuable jewellery or watches in your suitcase. Wear it all.

● Put together a mini medical kit: a pain killer like aspirin; a tube of antihistamine cream for insect bites (buy the repellent spray or the little tablets which burn on a plugged-in heater when you're there); antiseptic cream; something for sunburn; sticking plasters.

● Roll rather than fold clothes if you use a soft barrel-shaped bag; fold them in a suitcase. Pack loosely so they can move a little; tightly packed equals tightly creased on arrival.

● Take two medium-sized suitcases rather than one large one for easier balance as you carry.

● Invest in an adaptor plug for electric gadgets.

● Make room for a lightweight travel iron. Uncrushable fabrics have the disadvantage of being uncomfortable and sticky in hot climates. Pure cotton is best even if it needs a little smoothing now and then.

● Label your suitcases, but do so discreetly. You don't want to advertise that your home is going to be empty, but you may find it hard to claim compensation if your luggage goes AWOL and you haven't labelled it at all.

Protecting your bags from determined pilferers in transit is tricky. Locking doesn't stop them, but it deters them. One senior BBC cameraman maintains that a smart suitcase is an irresistible lure, so he puts his svelte job inside an extremely tatty old holdall for the journey, unveils the beautiful suitcase on landing and stuffs the holdall out of sight. This way he can still impress the doorman at posh hotels!

Just in case your luggage should go astray, it's a good ploy to pack a change of underwear in your cabin baggage. If you're a family, scatter belongings throughout each other's suitcases. Then if one of these goes missing, the unlucky member will at least have something clean to change into.

In all the nine years I've been travelling with the *Holiday* programme, only once has luggage failed to turn up on the airport carousel. It happened in Goa. Not one item, either of our personal belongings or the filming gear, made an appearance after an internal flight from Bombay. Luckily we had the camera, which always travels as cabin baggage, and half a roll of film, so we could go on working. But to stay cool we had to find something lighter to wear. We ended up in a funny old general store buying identical white T-shirts and shorts. For an entire day and evening we wandered around looking like a lost tennis team! Happily the bags and gear turned up the next day.

BEATING THE JET LAG

In order to film part of a home-swapping story in Los Angeles a few years ago, I had to fly out to California for just two days. The production team and camera crew were already there. It wasn't so much the outward leg that worried me as the return trip. How was I going to feel after two eight-hour time changes in the space of a weekend? The works were surely going to spring out of my body clock and go ping!

I asked the advice of a globetrotting friend. 'When you're flying,' he said, 'drink lots of non-fizzy soft drinks but no alcohol. Flying dehydrates you and so does alcohol. And don't eat. In the air, eating makes you swell up.'

It sounded like a load of laughs, but I did exactly as he suggested – and it worked. I arrived feeling sleepy and hungry but otherwise marvellous. On the way home, I repeated the experiment and, after one good eight-hour crash-out in my own nest, bounced back into UK time as if I'd never been away. On subsequent long haul trips I've never managed to be quite so abstinent, and have usually felt the worse for it.

Everyone has their own pet antidote to jet lag. Sir David Attenborough takes a different tack. As soon as he settles in, he switches his watch to the time of the country he's going to, then eats and sleeps accordingly. Some say walk about a lot. Joan Collins recommends a swift bottle of champagne, feet up and a big sleep, and she looks pretty good on it!

I think the real key to surviving jet lag, or any holiday journey for that matter, is to try to minimise the last-minute hassle before takeoff. When you're already overtired and overwrought, the stress of travelling just wipes you out. Pace out the preparation and the packing. Write lists if it helps, putting down even the things you think you won't forget but often do – like switching off the gas/electrics/boiler/iron and putting the neighbour's cat out. Whatever the hitches – and there are bound to be some – try to be calm and smile at your loved ones, for a knotted stomach and knitted brows don't help. Then, whether you're fastening a safety belt or a seat belt, staggering along a railway platform or up a gangplank, your exit will be smoother, the getting there easier and your landing happier.

CHAPTER TWO

Beautiful Beaches

The most traditional holiday of all – and still the one most of us want – is beside the seaside. The attraction starts right from the moment we're dangled as toddlers to dip unsuspecting toes in the freezing shallows of some chilly British bay, through the years of construction and demolition of sand castles, to the discovery that brown is beautiful and there is a delicious sensual pleasure in being a body on the beach. Then comes our first blissful exposure to Mediterranean sun and the revelation of resorts where the sweatshirts never get taken out of the suitcase. Eventually, if we're lucky, we make it to the tropics, to what Terry Wogan calls the great Bounty Bar beaches of the world.

Wherever it is, a beautiful beach by definition should be sandy, clean and safe for swimming. It can have the most picturesque setting imaginable and be a total write-off if you can't actually go in the water. I shall never forget Melville Island, at the top end of Down Under. As I gazed longingly at the Timor Sea curling tantalisingly over one of the loveliest shorelines I've ever seen, the tail of my eye caught a sign looming in the foreground: a big X across the image of a swimmer above the open jaws of a crocodile. There are some snaps you don't want to come home with!

The appeal of Melville, however, is a great deal more than beachcombing: it is one of the places you meet the Aborigines on their own ground (see chapter 11). But every good beach to my mind should have other distractions – in Britain and other temperate climates because you can never rely on the sun staying out, and in hotter spots because you can't rely on it ever going in. Undiluted sunbathing is not good for anyone.

Almost all the beaches in this chapter have interesting surroundings with plenty of things to see and do, with the possible exception of the Maldives. They are such tiny islands there isn't much going on except what's happening in, on or by the sea, but they are ravishingly beautiful – everyone's idea of a tropical paradise – and if you're a water sports addict, the action is non-stop.

Mention paradise to Kathy Tayler and her beach memories focus on an incident that livened up filming on the Greek island of Mykonos. She was interviewing an English couple on its well-known Paradise Beach when the girl started to giggle. Kathy ploughed on with her questions until both the interviewees totally corpsed, pointing helplessly over the cameraman's shoulder. Turning round, the whole crew were confronted by an interested onlooker standing there starkers!

How much or how little you wear on any beach depends on the custom of the country you're in, and it's as well to find out what the form is before you go so as not to shock the locals – or give yourself a shock. When *Holiday* films have included shots of topless tourists basking, we sometimes get irate phone calls from sensitive viewers. We feel, however, that when some degree of nudity is liable to be part of the scene, it's only fair to warn you.

A little research for a recent series revealed some surprising facts about nudity on the beach. While women can't go topless in risqué Rio, they can in elegant Acapulco – except that they don't because they'd probably be laughed at. On the Indonesian island of Lombok, next to liberal Bali, tourists have been stoned for stripping off, and in Monaco the police fine streakers on the spot – though the mind boggles as to where they keep their money. And did you know there are only six nudist beaches in the whole of the USA? If you aren't sure whether to bare all or nothing but your knees, contact the London-based tourist office of the country concerned and ask them about the sartorial code for the beach.

LOUNGING AROUND THE LIZARD

Prescribed reading for Cornwall's secretive and lovely Lizard peninsula is Daphne Du Maurier's *Frenchman's Creek* – because the creek really exists, a finger of tranquil water reaching in off the Helford river. Thickets of greenery creep to the water's edge and tree branches writhe across its muddy shores. It's not hard to imagine the novel's seventeenth-century heroine and her pirate lover meeting here by moonlight. A boat trip from Helford or the sailing centre of St Anthony will take you along the river and up the creek, and maybe you'll discover the tiny hidden chapel dedicated to St Francis which not a lot of people know about.

There are plenty of places to use as a base on the Lizard. These are not only within sniffing distance of some of the most seductive corners of Cornwall but also on or near terrific beaches. Kynance Cove and Mullion Cove are two of the most stunning – perfect hard sand with great rocky stacks threaded with the blue and purple mineral called serpentine, or Lizard stone, which is made into jewellery. From the cliffs above you can enjoy views of the whole coastline and listen to the sea rattling in the caves below. The scenery around the more sheltered Kennack Sands is gentler and so are the waves, just right for little ones, and there are any number of small unnamed coves to discover for yourself.

The charm of the Lizard is its immense variety of terrain within a limited radius. The headland of Lizard Point is dissected by miniature valleys where tiny streams tumble towards the sea and many rare plants thrive undisturbed. The National Trust protects part of the area. Then there are the working fishing villages of Coverack and Cadgwith with their picturesque thatched cottages and cheerful pubs, where tasty food is served and old salts tell smugglers' tales or ghost stories and may even burst into song.

Many delightful spots around the Helford river have inns and small eateries where a crab or lobster dinner won't cost you an arm and a leg. However, if you succumb to too many Cornish cream teas, you will almost certainly sacrifice your waistline, but try them at Rose Cottage in Helford village. This little tea shop is straight off the top of a chocolate box.

If there are drab days, a visit to the all-weather Aero Park at Helston should help distract the children with its exhibition of historic aircraft, Flambards life-size Victorian village and a Britain in the Blitz display. The Poldark Mine at Wendron is an intriguing museum piece and the Seal Sanctuary at Gweek better than any zoo.

Also within your orbit from the Lizard: the wonderful Minnack Theatre in its natural rocky setting; the remains of the old tin works on the northwestern tip of Cornwall in real Poldark country; and the popular haunts of St Ives, Mousehole, Land's End and St Mawes.

Although there are big posh hotels like the Polurrian and excellent small family ones like the Tregildry, you can have a very reasonable holiday at B&Bs in these parts – *The Best Bed*

& *Breakfast in the World*, an annual manual published by East Woods Press, is an invaluable source – or by renting one of the many charming, privately owned cottages. The local tourist office (see address list in appendix) will direct you to these.

THE NORTH NORFOLK COAST

The fact that Cromer usually scores high in the sunshine stakes – it had the most sunny hours in the entire kingdom a couple of years ago – is good enough reason to head for the beaches of north Norfolk. This coastline, which runs around the upper curve of East Anglia's bulge, has so many assets it's surprising more British holidaymakers don't veer in its direction. The sea is clean as a whistle, the bathing's safe, there are wide sandy bays backed by cliffs and there's plenty to do when it rains.

Cromer itself is a resort in the old-fashioned mould: an ancient fishing village with a Victorian seafront overlooking acres of pale sand. It's a place for families with young children rather than teenagers since the pace is fairly gentle. The great gourmet treat is Cromer crab. Cromer has no harbour, so you can watch the fishermen landing their catch on the beach from their odd little broad-beamed boats.

A few miles west, the flint village of Sheringham has its attractions too: the Little Theatre which goes flat out during the season; the North Norfolk Railway and its lovable steam trains; and the pottery, which pounds down pebbles from the beach for a glaze.

Further west as you turn into the Wash, there are more lovely beaches of which Hunstanton is the only one in East Anglia to enjoy sunsets over the sea. Old Hunstanton, arranged around its duck pond, is better than the main resort. Not far away at Sandringham, HM spends her hols. You can visit the 7000-acre royal estate and wander into its museum and the park church, where the organ given by Edward VII is still in excellent tune. Then there's the splendid old medieval market and port town of King's Lynn which has some pleasing historical bits to explore. The seventeenth-century Customs House is probably the most striking building, and nearby is a fascinating brass rubbing centre which has many original pieces to work on.

On any drive inland from the coast you'll find some of the most delightful villages in England nestling in the gentle dips of the softly undulating countryside – despite Noel Coward's put down, not all of Norfolk is totally flat. There are places with wonderful names, like Wells-next-the-Sea and Burnham Deepdale, and heavenly churches, like the one at Salle. Anne Boleyn's family helped build it and they say she was brought back from the Tower to be buried there. Unlikely as that may be, it's true that Pocahontas, the American Indian princess who married John Rolfe in 1614, settled in Heacham in 1616. Although she died soon after she is clearly remembered both on the village sign and in a church memorial. Another source of pleasure in Heacham is the Lavender Farm – fields of it stretch into the distance where you stop for tea at the old mill.

'If all else fails there's always the zoo' needn't be said with the usual resignation in Norfolk because Philip Wayre's zoo in the Norfolk Wildlife Park is unique. It is the largest collection of European animals in the world and more are actually bred here than taken from the wild.

Finally, don't forget Norwich, Norfolk's main city and as fine as the insurance ads proclaim. Its Norman cathedral is glorious, and its tight little cobbled streets are full of antique shops and oddities. The most intriguing emporium is the Mustard Shop. It not only sells Colman's famous condiment in a variety of guises but tells the history of the Norwich company in a small museum.

BONNY NORTH BERWICK

Where the wide Firth of Forth meets the North Sea, the neat and tidy township of North Berwick is an ideal family resort in Scotland. A firm favourite since Victorian times, it has a necklace of beaches with soft clean sand interspersed with rocky nooks and crannies that are sheer joy for children of all ages to potter in. It even has the bonus of a heated *outdoor* swimming pool, should the North Sea breezes make sea bathing seem a bit too spartan – but North Berwick, like north Norfolk, has often been at the top of the good weather charts.

Around its sheltered fishing and yacht harbour, where the sea food is always fresh, are a good range of hotels, guesthouses and places offering bed and breakfast – and a hearty one at that – plus plenty of shops, cafés and restaurants. There are also two good camping and caravan sites. The one at Yellowcraig is especially nice, pitched on springy grass within sand dunes that are covered in dog roses, and only five minutes' walk from the beach. In the main holiday weeks there is always a summer show with a recognisable TV name or two on the bill, while for the more serious minded, the local museum tells the history of North Berwick in a lively and quite unfusty way. Golfers have two fine 18-hole courses nearby and another half dozen within easy reach, all of which welcome visitors.

Two large lumps of land give North Berwick its identity and delightful setting. Just outside town is the 617-foot North Berwick Law, a rounded hill from whose top you get spectacular views – the coastline here is among the best in southern Scotland. The majestic ruins of Tantallon Castle on its rocky promontory invite exploration, but the real eye catcher is the Bass Rock, a massive 350-foot-high pile less than three miles off shore. This impressive islet is one of the UK's finest seabird sanctuaries with gulls, kittiwakes and gannets swirling on and off it in their tens of thousands. A boat trip to the Bass Rock is a wonderful experience as the birds wheel around and above you in speckled clouds, sending out their plaintive cries. It is an unforgettable trip for everyone.

Not least of North Berwick's attractions is its nearness to Edinburgh (see chapter 7), which is only 25 miles away. It's a pleasant drive on good roads or an easy trip by express bus or train, both of which offer frequent services. The resort also acts as a jumping-off point for touring the romantic Border country in your own car or on a coach tour. And that splendid border town of Berwick-on-Tweed is less than 40 miles away along one of the most scenic routes in southeast Scotland.

The best way to get the latest low-down on the myriad other good things North Berwick has to offer is to write to the local Tourist Information Office in the town itself. They'll send you booklets galore.

JUST TENBY

Wales has some lovely beaches, from the bracing sandscapes of the Gower peninsula to quiet strands like Criccieth at the foot of Snowdonia, but for all-round charm and friendly atmosphere, Tenby's are hard to beat.

Tenby is a gem: a small walled town perched on a rocky headland at the western end of Carmarthen Bay. It's everything a good old-fashioned family resort ought to be – not too big, not too dear (a town tour by horse-drawn wagonette will set you back little more than 70 pence) and not full of grand hotels looking down their noses at you. The three-star Imperial with its terraced gardens blends graciously into the foreground, while the bulk of holidaymakers are catered for in unpretentious small hotels and guesthouses. Most of these were formerly private homes so they have that cosy feeling which brings visitors back to the same one year after year. And Tenby blooms. Flowers burst out of window boxes and beds on street islands, tumble over garden walls and baskets hung in porches – and the grey stone buildings are a perfect foil for their colours.

The children, of course, will be more interested in the colour of the lollipops and the tooth-chipping sticks of rock with Tenby all-the-way-through – that is, when they aren't clamouring for another ice cream from Fecci's which probably has the largest selection of flavours in the entire land.

The beaches are sheltered, with the kind of soft golden sand that's perfect for sand castles, and when the youngsters get restless you can scoop them up and pile aboard one of the little excursion boats. These chug you past the fortress of St Catherine and towards St Margaret's Island to see the seals – or to Caldy to visit the monks.

Other summer happenings include the odd fair – spelled fayre, naturally – and medieval frolics in the thirteenth-century courtyard of the fortress. There they dress you in sackcloth, feed you stew, bread, fruit and mead, and lay on a minstrel or two to sing for your supper.

THE BEST IN BRITTANY

Jutting out like the spout of a teapot on the map of France, Brittany has the longest coastline of any region in the country and an abundance of beaches. Take your pick from the firm sweeps of blond sand bordering the channel from Dinard to Perros-Guirec and beyond, to the breezy Atlantic shores of Benodet and Beg Meil in Finistère, to the more sheltered southern beaches of Quiberon, Carnac and La Baule. In between are hundreds of little bays and coves, many almost deserted either side of July and August.

French sun may not be as predictable here as it is by the Mediterranean, but the sea is less polluted and this makes it the perfect choice for families with young children. Lots of coastline also means lots of lovely fresh fish to eat, and people guzzling huge platters of *fruits de mer* (shellfish, especially oysters) is a familiar sight in seaside restaurants. Breton pancakes are another speciality; *crêperies* abound, providing cheap filling snacks for those with several mouths to feed.

The Breton countryside is also rather special – rugged or rural and rambling – so the nicest way to holiday here is to take your car across the Channel and rent a gîte (see chapter 4) near a farm. You'll be treated with tremendous kindness by the local people. The Bretons like Britons – there's a Celtic link back in the mists of time. You'll also have the pleasure of shopping in country village markets, exploring some of the heavenly old towns with castles and medieval centres – Dinan, Josselin and Quimper are just three – and perhaps puzzling over the prehistoric standing stones (*menhirs*) which are a unique feature of the region.

Seaside action includes every kind of water-sport. Sea water and seaweed also provide thalassotherapy – a unique treatment for anyone who's rheumatic or just plain run down. Centres are dotted around the coast and you can pop in for a day or make this the focus of your holiday.

Golf is also a big thing in Brittany. It's well-stocked with courses which welcome day visitors and charge reasonable green fees, so those who get bored with helping to build sand castles can potter off with their putters.

ALL ALONG THE ALGARVE

Mile upon mile of superb golden beaches stretch along Portugal's southern tip – and they really are golden, powdered down from the distinctive ochre cliffs that rise behind. Here and there, the cliffs are indented with bays or *praias*, some wide arcs, others little hairpin coves. They all face south, the water's clean, and welcome breezes take the sting out of summer's highest temperatures.

It's easy to see why the Algarve has become such a popular destination for British families over the past 20 years or so and shows no sign of waning. The snowballing preference for self-catering coincided with the development of this holiday coast, so it is now a kind of villadom: the hills are alive with all-mod-cons Moorish style, and there are apartment complexes down to the sea which sometimes hide the view. Some small villages like Armação de Pera have been swallowed up completely by high-rise blocks, and there are a few new ones like Quarteira that have little aesthetic appeal; but don't let anyone tell you the Algarve is totally spoiled. A great deal of it retains its original charm. The centres of villages like Alvor, though surrounded by hotel developments, and Carvoeiro, despite its peppering of little white houses with pools and patios, are still delightful.

Ancient Lagos is the liveliest and most appealing larger town towards the western cape. Once the residence of Prince Henry the Navigator, it has a lovely eighteenth-century church, the Igrega de Santo Antonio, as well as many fine old streets and the arcaded square of Praça da Liberdade near the harbour.

The charm of the Portuguese themselves is a major contributor to the Algarve boom. They are among the gentlest and kindest of people. Many in this area have Arab origins, for it was held longest by the Moors. A sardine feast by the harbour at Portimão will soon have you rubbing shoulders with locals and other nationalities. This is great fun. You sit elbow-to-elbow at long tables while men in big shady sombreros grill shoals of the silvery fish over a brazier.

Local markets are marvellous for stocking up with other fish as well as fruit and vegetables – Portimão has one of the biggest and best. But the food in restaurants is so good and so inexpensive that most self-caterers don't bother to do much cooking for themselves in the end. Hotel guests on half board are well served, too.

The price of petrol is about the only thing that will raise your eyebrows and lower your budget in Portugal, but if you can run to hiring a car for even a day or two it will open up some lovely inland territory. You can visit Caldas de Monchique, an enchanting small spa town up in the hills; or Silves, where a cathedral outside the ruined walls of a Moorish citadel tells the town's history at a glance; or tiny out-of-the-way country places like Loule where restaurant menus may be in Portuguese only and a third of the price of any on the coast. Don't worry, the locals will shyly help you choose what to eat – perhaps a tasty *torta de bacalhau*, a kind of cod pizza.

The Algarve is also 'Sportugal', as the tourist office has dubbed it, for tennis and golf fanatics. There are courts and courses galore where you can have a game just to keep your hand in, take some serious tuition or enjoy a whole holiday based at one of the top-notch sporting complexes.

ANTIGUA'S 365

A beach for every day of the year is the boast of this small eastern Caribbean island. While not all of the 365 are easily accessible or safe, there are certainly enough to go round, and if you can imagine what it's like walking on talcum powder, that's what most of Antigua's sand is like.

The hotels have picked the prime sites – along the coastline with enough acreage in front to encompass all the paraphernalia of water sports and still leave room for sunbathers to spread theirs. Crowded it isn't. Frequented by Americans it is.

For more authentic bursts of island life, head for some of the public beaches – half empty most of the time. At Darkwood Beach on Sundays a ramshackle restaurant will be busy cooking up spicy fish and okra (just one dish on the menu) while townspeople from St John's, the main port and capital, mingle with a handful of pale and interested visitors. Someone's transistor will crackle into life and the rhythm soon drags everyone, locals and interlopers alike, out of the shade or the water to disco themselves silly on the dazzling shore.

Antigua is much less developed than Barbados. St John's is pink-and-purple pretty, with streets of clapboard cottages, small bars dispensing outsize piña coladas, and a harbour full of banana boats.

Nelson's Dockyard on the other side of the island is something else. For two years the famous British admiral holed up here with his forces awaiting an attack from the French that never came. The irony of it was that he lost many of his men through malaria and other diseases which were rife at a time when overdressed troops had to stick it out in humid and unhygienic conditions.

Today Nelson's Dockyard is much more salubrious. A few very up-market hotels cluster around the perfectly restored admiral's house and the old boatyards. Ritzy yachts fleck the harbour, and you need a fistful of dollars to pay for a dinner of spiny lobster in restaurants like The Lookout. However, anyone here for the day can economise by buying a snack of fresh mangoes from the sellers squatting on the shore. They pick them in Antigua's mini rain forest.

Drive around the island and you'll easily find your own patch of virgin sand to picnic on. But be prepared to give the locals a lift. They're not shy of asking!

GEORGEOUS IN GOA

The beaches, ah, the beaches of Goa – that ex-Portuguese state in the southwest of the Indian subcontinent. They seem to go on forever. Long, curving pathways of gold edged with tiny crescents of surf and, as far as the eye can see, backed by thickets of outsize palms bending seawards. There are reminders of the Portuguese here. The spires of old white wooden chapels stand like exclamation marks amid the swathes of rice paddies and clumps of jungle, and there are skin colours of the palest coffee, harking back to European origins, as well as the duskier complexions of South India. A point to remember if your stomach winces at the thought of a surfeit of highly spiced curries is that Goan cuisine is the least corrosive because of the Portuguese influence. Sauces are milder and fish dishes delicious.

Goa is a long way to go just for a beach holiday. Most people tack on a week here as the antidote to a fairly concentrated sightseeing tour of India. It is the perfect place to recover both from the pace of touring and from the onslaught of third world poverty, which can be very distressing. When Mother Theresa investigated Goa, she found little disease and no real hardship.

HUNDREDS AND THOUSANDS IN THE MALDIVES

If you hanker after the kind of shore Robinson Crusoe got washed up on, you'll find it in the Maldives. In fact, you'll find it thousands of times over, for there are 2000 islands altogether. Some of them are mere specks in the Indian Ocean, scattered from the toe of the Indian subcontinent to just below the equator. Virtually every one is ringed with cutlass-shaped bays of pale coral sand lapped by tepid water of an unbelievable turquoise.

The attraction of this archipelago is that it has little else but beaches. The government of the Maldives is deliberately trying to keep them as uncommercialised as possible, wary of the effect tourist overkill might have on the inhabitants. Only a few islands have been developed – if you can call the building of one hotel development – but many are so tiny there isn't room for shops, eateries and other signs of tourism. There may be no local village and no locals except for the hotel staff.

The main island, Male, has an airport of one runway to let the twentieth century in, but its old fishing harbour is in a total time warp, give or take a few outboard motors.

If you like a bit of shopping, a spot of history, the odd temple or two, forget the Maldives. There is just sailing in the traditional dhonis, surfing and waterskiing, fishing and picnicking on desert islets. It helps pass the time. Oh, and because the reefs around here are among the most spectacular in the world, there's a lot of snorkelling and scuba diving. If you've never tried it before, you can hire the gear and glean a little instruction – though for rather a lot of money.

All this seagoing action creates healthy appetites and you'll eat well – if you like fish, shellfish and curries. The food is beautifully cooked if lacking in variety.

Don't expect the height of luxury in your hotel. Accommodation is very basic – more by accident, one feels, than design, but you could argue that it helps preserve the islands' intrinsic character. Certainly when you step out of your little thatched cottage right on to one of those picture postcard beaches, it doesn't seem to matter much.

The emphasis is on getting back to nature – but not to the extent of peeling off the tiniest thread of your swimming gear. The Maldives have been Muslim for 800 years and modesty is the rule.

THE FAR EASTERN PROMISE OF PENANG

A long time ago, the intrepid Portuguese dropped anchor on Penang's famous Batu Feringi beach en route for China and Japan. And who could blame them? With its backdrop of Malaysian jungle, it is every bit as fabulous as the brochures promise.

The Portuguese traders didn't land on this 'pearl of the Orient' just to linger on its golden sands, of course, nor does anyone who goes to the island today. For it would be wasting the opportunity Penang offers to sample the exotic appeal of Malaysia in microcosm. In any case, it's hard to stew on the beach for long because of the humidity. For the first few days, before you adjust to it, you feel as if someone's trying to stuff hot cotton wool up your nostrils every time you leave your air-conditioned hotel room! This is the time to board an equally well air-conditioned coach and take a look at where you are.

Lush is the only word for the scenery. There's the watery flatness of the rice paddies, the dense groves of betel nut palm – the pinang tree which gave the island its name – and the sprawling rubber plantations. All the rubber trees in Penang were grown from just nine seeds sent out from Kew Gardens. In turn, the original seeds came from Brazil. You notice little pots tied near a gash in the tree trunks, and here and there a lone Malay worker inspecting them. Collecting the latex before the cup brimmeth over is a matter of perfect timing.

In the capital of Georgetown the best way to sightsee is by trishaw. These rickshaws drawn by bicycles pedal children to school, housewives to the shops and businessmen to their offices, and some are converted into 'snack'-shaws to provide meals on wheels. A few stately government buildings remind

you of colonial days, but far more interesting are the temples and palaces of old Malaysia dotted about the island – the Snake Temple, for instance, though it's not for the faint-hearted.

Getting your bearings on your coach tour, you'll spot other beaches deserted except for fishermen pottering in their picturesque junks. The reason they're empty is simple: even the local people don't stray from the popular beaches because the need to be near a constant supply of cool drinks overrides any desire to have the sands to themselves.

A string of top-class hotels share Batu Feringi. Each has beautiful pools set in spacious tropical gardens that are vivid with frangipani and hibiscus, so there's no claustrophobia. Each also has its beach stalls wafting filmy batik sarongs, while itinerant beach vendors try to press shell necklaces on recumbent sunbathers. They do it so charmingly that it's hard to send them away.

Since the population is a mix of Malay and Chinese, the food is a delectable blend of both cultures. Most packages here are B&B only, so you can please yourself as to how much else you eat. Prices are reasonable everywhere. There are coffee shops as well as main restaurants in the hotels and lively local eateries nearby. In the evenings it's pleasant to wander along the roadside and choose your dinner venue according to which cooking aroma tweaks your tastebuds. Entertainment is sometimes thrown in after supper in the shape of jugglers, paper lion dancers or fire-eaters, and it's not done just for tourists – Penang is one place where local people are as much in evidence as visitors.

There are more beautiful beaches around all of the Special Islands (next chapter) as well as the shores of many other places covered throughout this book.

CHAPTER THREE

Special Islands

To some, islands are claustrophobic and parochial. To others they are little worlds apart. This is certainly their appeal for me. Every island, whatever its shape, location or parent country, has its own character, and somehow you feel finding out what makes it tick is feasible within the space of a week or two. In contrast, getting to know a country when you're occupying a relatively small scrap of it seems beyond your grasp.

With a few exceptions like the Isle of Dogs in London and Ile-de-France, the French region in which Paris lies, islands are surrounded by water. That not only means a generous quota of beaches and seaside pleasures, but often a highly coloured history shaped by seaborne traders and invaders. Islands, particularly those in a cat's cradle of shipping lanes, tend to change hands more frequently than countries, so island people are often an intriguing mix of nationalities. They're generally tolerant and inwardly tough, adaptable, self-confident and courteous. They're proud of their survival and they know who they are – probably because throughout the centuries they've had more than their share of identity crises. The Shetlanders are insulted if you refer to them as Scots in the same way the Sicilians refuse to be called Italians. Even on groups of islands, there's a streak of rivalry between neighbours. On Guernsey they make car stickers that say 'Bergerac takes his holidays in Guernsey', and when I said I was going to put on a jersey, they positively twitched. 'You mean a Guernsey!' 'No, I don't. I simply mean a sweater!'

For some reason, things happen to me on islands. I fell in love on Mauritius, fell over an octopus on Orpheus, and almost fell down a volcano in Sicily!

The first is a story I shall keep to myself. The second was funny afterwards, though at the time the *Holiday* team thought they might have to send me home on a stretcher. We'd been filming aboard a small yacht around Orpheus Island off north Queensland, Australia. A scuba diver had caught an octopus and left it slithering on deck. Leaping to avoid the blob, I executed a perfect Tom-and-Jerry skid on the slime and went splat on the flat of my back! Luckily, I was merely dented and a couple of hot baths soon dispersed the bruising.

Working for the *Holiday* programme is often a great deal tougher than it looks – and sometimes a bit hairy. On Sicily we were determined to film an excursion up Mount Etna. Tourists can scale the summit whenever the boffins in the observatory reckon it is measurably safe. Having been delivered to about 600 feet below Europe's largest active crater by a red minibus, we set off in hooded orange anoraks, looking like gnomes going up a big black sand dune. From above, the monster roared and belched sulphur fumes that made the cameraman Chris Sadler's eyes stream, my mascara run and producer Patricia Houlihan wince as tiny particles of grit crept behind her contact lenses. We kept going, breathing into our sleeves to filter out the sulphur (they say it's good for catarrh!) while our two guides seemed totally unperturbed.

At the edge it was like looking into hell. There, staring back, were the insomniac monster's fiery red eyes. It was frightening and fascinating. I took a step forward and was conscious of a firm hand suddenly gripping my elbow. It was one of the guides. My right foot had gone an inch further than it ought and a gust of wind could have blown me over. Funnily enough, it was only after we'd all come down that we realised what a scary experience it had been – but I wouldn't have missed it for anything. It's one reason why Sicily is among my favourite islands. You can be sizzling on a beach one moment and exploring natural wonders the next.

In this chapter there are a few other favourites. Each has something special to offer: a certain something that makes it stand out.

SURPRISING SHETLAND

Shetland's not the first place that springs to mind when people plan their holidays. That's what's so good about it – you can virtually have it to yourself. That doesn't mean it's not used to catering for visitors. Its hotels are up to international standards with en suite bathrooms and top-class cuisine – everything you'd expect in London or Paris. If you're holidaying on a tighter budget, there are plenty of good quality B&Bs too.

Lerwick, the capital, is a bustling town of 8000 people with a cinema and two nightclubs. There are no traffic lights, parking meters or well-known chain stores. Most visitors go for the wild open spaces which look extremely bleak when the weather's dull but become breathtakingly beautiful the moment the sun pops out. Sunshine improves any place, of course, but it absolutely transforms Shetland. The locals say: 'If you don't like our weather, hang on a minute', and it's true. Rain, sleet, gales and blazing sunshine all in the space of an hour is nothing remarkable.

Shetlanders are exceptionally friendly, but two things get their goat. Never call their islands 'the Shetlands'. It's either 'Shetland' or 'the Shetland Islands'. And never label them Scottish. Their ancestors were Vikings and they are simply and proudly Shetlandic, no more Scottish than French or African. But British, of course.

Apart from Mainland, there are many smaller islands to explore and the nine tiny interisland car ferries get you there. Fair Isle, where the pullovers come from, is a must. You can buy these off-the-peg for £40 to £50, or have one designed and knitted for you for about £10 to £20 more. Fair Isle only measures 3 by 2 miles (5 by 4 km), has about 70 inhabitants and two churches. No pubs! You can stay at the Bird Observatory where the accommodation is somewhere between a hotel and a hostel, or at a couple of B&Bs.

On the island of Yell, track down Bobby Tullock, a world-famous naturalist who, for a very modest price, takes out parties in his boat for an expert guided tour of Shetlandic wildlife. He might take you to Hascosay, uninhabited by humans these days but teeming with skuas, otters, seals, puffins and occasionally dolphins. You can fish for brown trout, sea trout and a Shetlandic peculiarity called tusk, or make friends with a Shetland pony, or just walk through the strangely treeless countryside and along the stunning beaches.

In Lerwick in the evening, the massed violins of the Shetland Fiddlers are something to listen to. The town's tourist office will tell you where and when they're next performing. Or you could become a galley slave, rowing out to sea on the *Dim Riv*, a model of a Viking longboat built and operated by local enthusiasts. It's free although, understandably, they pass a hat round.

So don't think of Shetland as barren and boring. The people are great, the scenery's unusual and beautiful and there's plenty to do. Go soon before everyone else realises how lovely it is.

WHERE BERGERAC TAKES HIS HOLIDAYS?

When the sun shines on Guernsey, you can understand why Renoir came here to paint. The light is dazzling and throws everything into sharp focus. Beyond the bright bristle of yacht masts in St Peter Port harbour and the granite castle where a cannon booms at midday, you can often see in clear detail the green hills and quiet beaches of little Herm island, a 20-minute boat ride away.

The parts of Guernsey that refreshed Renoir's inspiration are those that tourists don't often reach. These are along the south coast where narrow lanes trundle down through the folds of headlands covered by gorse and bramble to tiny bays like Petit Bot and Moulin Huet. The windmill that gave its name to the latter has long since disappeared, but the ruins of the old cottage that features in Renoir's *Fog on Guernsey* are just visible through their overgrowth of greenery. In 1883 the great artist painted about 15 canvases of Moulin Huet's picturesque arrangement of rocks, sea and cliffs – scenes that have hardly altered, except that now there are banks of pale hydrangeas in the foreground edging the lawn of a small tea room.

Second largest of the Channel Islands, Guernsey is a bit of a paradox. On the tourist beat it is fairly uncommercialised, but in other ways it is commercially obsessed. Finance – offshore companies and all that – accounts for half the island's income because of low taxes and no VAT. The benefits for visitors are mixed. Price tags in shops aren't significantly lower as the no-VAT advantage is often offset by higher costs. But car hire is a real bargain at around £30 *a week* for a small saloon. Guernsey companies buy cars from the Continent to resell in the UK at a profit, so until there's 1000 miles on the clock, they hire them out cheaply. With inexpensive direct flights from over 20 UK airports, it's hardly worth taking your own car across the Channel.

Petrol is half the UK price, though you're unlikely to need more than a tankful a week on 24 square miles (62 sq km) of island! You do, however, have to take out collision insurance as many of the country roads are virtually single track. Traffic is light, other drivers are polite and the speed limit is 35 miles per hour, but road signs are pretty sparse and you can easily go round in circles without a good road map.

Guernsey on the whole offers an unstructured holiday in pleasant unspoiled surroundings. The countryside is strewn with pretty ginger-coloured Guernsey cattle, glints with green-houses (Guernsey toms and flowers) and, despite French place names, looks very English. The west coast beaches are good, interspersed with seaweedy rocks, and the resorts of Vazon and Cobo Bay are ultra simple – no more than sea fronts, really, with small hotels, guesthouses and a scattering of self-catering cottages. It was at Cobo that Prince Charles learned to windsurf – the prevailing on-shore winds and shallow waters make conditions ideal. Sailing enthusiasts are in heaven.

St Peter Port, the island's main port and only sizeable town, is charming – an old quarter toppling on the hill, a nineteenth-century market hall, classy boutiques and shops with duty-free signs. It also has lots of good restaurants, but not much in the way of entertainment: no cabarets or shows. In fact, apart from one leisure centre with an indoor swimming pool, cinema, disco and snooker tables, there's little to occupy children and young adults on a rainy day. The butterfly farm, where they breed pupae for export, is fun, and there's a tomato museum which is a curiosity for half-an-hour's visit. More interesting is the Occupation Museum which vividly depicts the difficulty and deprivation of the war years under the Germans with a wealth of weapons, clothes and artefacts, a reconstruction of a St Peter Port street and a country kitchen of 1944. The detail is fascinating, from newspapers of the time to a black market price list which has tea and coffee at £25 a pound. The ingenious Guerns made tea out of bramble leaves and coffee from parsnips. It therefore comes as no surprise when you discover that nowadays they make wine from tomatoes! Don't laugh. It's actually quite drinkable.

Guernsey is just the place for a couple wanting a quiet, up-market holiday. The best hotels – the Old Governor's House, the Duke of Richmond and the St Pierre Park – are exceptionally well run. It is also just right for a family with young children who are happy building sand castles, going on nature walks and messing about in boats.

THE BALEARICS

Majorca is not only the largest in the quartet of Spanish islands in the Mediterranean, but the most interesting. It has the greatest variety of resorts, the most spectacular terrain and the most fascinating capital.

It is, however, something of a curate's egg. There are stretches like Arenal where endless high-rise hotels have turned a flat strip of coastline into a mini concrete jungle. But there is also a wealth of unspoiled natural beauty. On the rugged western side, high-rise rocks give you the most stupendous views. If you climb to the top of the Torre de las Animas (Tower of Souls) you can see how, in days of yore, pirates could be spotted as they approached. Smugglers were harder to pick out as they pulled their small boats ashore beneath the intricately terraced hillsides of Banyalbufar.

It was on this wild and wonderful west coast that the composer Chopin and writer George Sand spent an unhappy winter. To this day Chopin concerts are held in the rooms where they stayed.

No one wants to squander precious sunbathing time steaming inside a car, but a day's trip into the mountains can be a real eye opener. The Cordillera de Poniente range slants along the northwest and the Sierra de Levante on the east. The roads through them are good, the scenery is breathtaking and the scents of wild thyme and pine are as invigorating as a Badedas bath.

Majorca's not very big, roughly 50 by 60 miles (80 by 95 km), so you'll have time to find a deserted bay for a swim before driving back again – perhaps some pebbly shore like Cala Tuent, between Puerto Soller and Cala San Vicente, with its one beach bar and restaurant tucked into a fold in the rocks.

The most appealing Majorcan resorts are those away from the crowded southwest. Particularly nice are those on the southeastern coast, from Porto Cristo, a well-established old fishing harbour, to the small Moorish-style custom-built villages of Porto Petro and Cala d'Or. A topography of rugged promontories, long inlets and tiny half-moon bays keeps these resorts from spreading. There are villas here, but in moderation. Other pleasant newish developments are on the northeastern tip and inland, where a little height helps keep you cooler.

The odd thing about Majorca is that often there are oases of peace only a few miles from the busiest, brashest places.

Twenty minutes by car from Magaluf and Palma Nova is the tiny port of Andraitx with its handful of hotels and apartments, a windsurfing school, and arguably the best fish restaurant on the island.

Whatever you do, don't miss a proper look at the old part of Palma, even if you save only a few hours before you leave for the airport. Its gorgeous cathedral, tiled squares, shady avenues and warren of narrow shopping streets are well worth exploring.

Ibiza, empty 20 years ago, is now almost unrecognisable. San Antonio Abad used to have two hotels and one bar. Now it is a fully fledged holiday playground, reputedly with more drinking places than any other European resort. At night the chatter of crickets is inaudible above the sounds of discos and the full-throated warblings of young Brits having a noisy, boozy time. But it's fun! Although there are few good beaches nearby, brief boat trips deliver you to the sands of Cala Bassa and other wilder shores, and most hotels take the trouble to make their pool areas especially attractive. The local ice cream in San Antonio, by the way, is out of this world!

While Santa Eulalia is similar to San Antonio, if not so loud, the old capital of Ibiza is quite different. It's still very attractive, even if it has sprouted a suburban sprawl of hotels and apartments. Within the walls of the citadel is a honeycomb of cafés, restaurants with *excellent* food, bars and shops. If you want to get the historical perspective, there's an old fortress to visit, an impressive cathedral and a museum which has relics of the Carthaginians who first-footed the island 2600 years ago.

Menorca, least commercialised of the Balearics apart from tiny Formentera, has a lot of charm. Around a soft green centre, its ragged coastline has hundreds of little sandy bays nestling among rocks and pinewoods. Some of the prettiest are inaccessible except by boat, so there are lots of water excursions. One well-known holiday company publishes the *Meon Book of Beaches in Menorca* explaining how to get to the real gems by road. Write to Meon House for it (see address list in appendix).

High-rise is minimal here. Good self-catering developments,

which share pools and gardens, are clustered around the main port and capital of Mahon and the older port and former capital of Ciudadela. Mahon has reminders of Nelson, who is rumoured to have brought Lady Hamilton to a splendid old manor house overlooking the harbour – since dubbed the English Farm. Ciudadela is quieter, full of cloisters and shady market places, an odd mix of architecture from the Middle Ages onwards. It's the kind of place where fishermen sit mending their nets by the harbour in the morning sun, and the tantalising whiff of prawns in garlic or Spanish omelette drift from waterside restaurants.

Another speciality of Menorca is 'the wind that sings', as the locals call it: an almost perpetual breeze that renders the highest temperatures more bearable and generously fills the sails of yachts and windsurfers.

CORSICA, THE SCENTED ISLE

This lovely French island is one of the few really unspoiled holiday destinations left in Europe. Imagine a chunk of the Alps dropped into the Mediterranean and you have Corsica: high peaks still snow-tipped in early summer, laricio pine forests from which Nelson chose his tall ship masts and, falling away to the coast, an ever-changing arrangement of escarpments and ravines, hills and valleys, fleeced with the tangled undergrowth of fragrant shrubs and wild herbs they call the *maquis*. Napoleon was born in Ajaccio, the island's capital, and apparently he used to sniff the breeze on homecoming voyages, impatient for the first scent of his native territory.

Corsica is for anyone who revels in beautiful scenery, nature, fishing, sailing, surfing, swimming, sunning – but prefers things on the quiet side. While the island is by no means undeveloped, none of the resorts are filled with the usual razzmatazz and clutter of 'organised fun'. Each has its beach, golden or pebbled, its fishing harbour, local market, restaurants, shops and a handful of discos. That's about it. The bonus is that all have a picturesque setting framed by mountains, and every kind of accommodation with the exception of cigarette-lighter hotel blocks. In Corsica, the homely two-star hotel is often good value. There are also some sybaritic top-class hotels and, at the other end of the scale, plenty of excellent camp sites.

Where to alight for a stay-put holiday? Calvi in the north is a long-established resort based around an old citadel where history slumbers. Smaller, but growing, are Ile-Rousse, St-Florenta and Algajola. In the west there is recently developed Porto. It's squeezed around a river estuary where a Genoese tower stands sentinel and country roads wind upwards into the mountains towards ancient hill villages that cling to the rock from which they're hewn.

Ajaccio is more sophisticated. Never will you forget it is Old Boney's birthplace, for a regiment of statues is scattered about town. Its casino, glossy shops and wide avenues remind you of the Côte d'Azur, but there are also the archetypal Corsican fishermen and some wonderful fish restaurants in the old port. Food in Corsica is a palatable mix of French and Italian. Eating out is fractionally pricier than in mainland France, but the superb local produce of fish, smoked hams, cheeses, fruit and wine is good value for self-caterers.

Other southern resorts are Propriano and Porto Vecchio. Both are fishing villages that have spread a little, but in a way that has not diluted their original flavour. If you don't mind a few hairpin bends or sheer drops, hire a small car and visit the hill town of Sartène, where old men sit black-hatted in the shade and a strange re-enactment of the crucifixion takes place at Eastertime, and you mustn't miss Bonifacio, an extraordinary stronghold teetering above limestone cliffs. First fortified by a Tuscan count sent by Charlemagne to fend off the Moors, Bonifacio's ramparts have never been breached.

From time to time, Corsica's home rule proponents make the news, but the island's political squabbles with France are its own affair and hardly ever affect tourists. The Corsicans have rather a soft spot for the British. If you can break through their innate reserve – which usually only takes a smile – they're likely to kill you with kindness.

THREE GREEK ISLANDS

Out of the shoals of Greek islands that bask in the waters of the Adriatic, the Ionian Sea and Homer's 'wine dark' Aegean, is it possible to pick out just three? Anyone who knows more than a scattering of them will doubtless quibble with my choice – lovers of Corfu, perhaps, which draws more British holiday-makers than all the rest put together. I have to admit that Corfu still has some beautiful corners, but Crete, Santorini and Lesbos are my special favourites. They each have something unique to offer and are also vastly different from one another.

Crete had a sophisticated civilisation 4000 years ago, before the ancient Greeks even had a word for anything. Its Minoan kingdom was unsurpassed for millennia in Europe. The Minoans' plumbing was as remarkable as their prowess in the arts, and evidence of it is clearly visible among the remains of the ancient city of Knossos.

Purists complain that the ruins of King Midas' great palace have been rather vulgarly restored, but the Knossos site, exposed amid a copse of tall dark cypresses near the port of Heraklion, is nevertheless riveting.

When an English archaeologist masterminded the excavation of the site in the early years of this century, the most valuable movable objects – statues, jewellery and so on – were swiftly taken into custody by various museums. But you can still wander around recumbent and re-erected columns, into palace rooms and mausoleums, and around fragments and frescoes and mosaics. The Cretan bull symbol is inescapable – a reminder that along with the Minoans' cultural sophistication went the singularly savage practice of pitting unarmed young athletes against vicious fighting bulls. It was their idea of entertainment. You have to make time for Knossos, wherever you're based on the island.

The busy main resorts are all on the north coast – Chania, Heraklion, Agios Nikolaos. But Crete is big. It's also long and skinny east to west, and therefore short north to south, so you can easily escape to the less developed beauty spots on its underside: places like Paleohora, Sougia, Pomeli, Loutro, Sfakla, Agalianos, Agia, Galini, Matala and Ierapetra. These are small picturesque bays where you'll find only a taverna or two and a plethora of Cretan smiles.

Chania is arguably the most interesting of the big ports. As the most southerly of the Greek islands, Crete historically has been at a crossroads of shipping lanes between Europe, Africa and Asia, so Chania has Venetian houses, Ottoman mosques and street markets like Arab souks. However, the lifestyle is unmistakably Greek. Old women cocooned in black peer from the windows of the narrow back alleyways where whitewashed houses close in upon one another and bougainvillea fills the gaps. In every canopied waterside restaurant the ubiquitous blue or turquoise wooden chairs are commandeered from dawn to dusk, either by the Cretans smoking strong tobacco and setting the world to rights over a glass of ouzo, or by tourists in search of inexpensive moussaka or a feast of shellfish.

When it comes to eating, nowhere does your pound go further than in Greece. On the other hand, the costume jewellery can easily charm you out of a sizeable chunk of your spending money, and car hire can clean you out. In order to

THE PERFECT HOLIDAY! - THE EXCITEMENT OF ATHENS AND THE ROMANCE OF A GREEK ISLAND.

ACROPOLIS

afford the luxury of having their own wheels for touring, many people prefer to live simply in Greek rooms. These are usually very clean and the loos work if you put the paper in the bin provided and don't try to flush it away. Modern Greek plumbing doesn't quite live up to the standards set by the ancient Minoans.

The rest of Crete is certainly worth seeing. Away from the wide coast roads that cut a swathe through hills covered in pink oleander beats the craggy heart of the island. There are wild mountains and deep gorges, valleys of plane and chestnut trees, orange and olive groves, vineyards and cherry orchards. Secretive villages often offer the surprise of a Byzantine church or a mysterious old monastery. There are also many archaeological sites that can only be second fiddle to Knossos but are never an anticlimax.

Crete is for you if you want to take your holiday early or late because its southerly position more or less guarantees a long hot summer season.

Santorini almost insists that you arrive by sea, although you can fly direct to its minuscule airport. You literally sail into the embrace of a volcano. A 1000-foot wall of lava-veined rock looms above, encrusted along the top with the gleaming white houses of Phira, the biggest town. How to get up to it? The faint-hearted take the funicular. The daring go by donkey, zigzagging at an angle of 45° and giggling nervously!

Tiny Santorini, a stunningly beautiful island in the southern Cyclades, is something of a phenomenon. A massive eruption and earthquake around 3500 years ago shook it to pieces, wiping out most of the population and, it's believed, the Minoan civilisation in Crete at the same time. Part of a buried settlement has been unearthed at Akrotiri and scholars have found clues to a life pattern similar to that of Knossos. This is well worth a visit.

The existence of the legendary lost city of Atlantis under the sea is also probable, if not proven. At Oia on the island's northern tip you won't be surprised to find a hotel named Atlantis Villas. Everything else about it is totally unexpected, for the villas are caves hewn out of the rock face, each charmingly furnished in rustic Greek style. No beach, since it's perched on the cliff top, but there's a seawater pool with a terrace which affords the nightly spectacle of a stunning sunset over the water.

There are other good small hotels and basic rooms around Oia. This is the prettiest of the island villages with its collection of little snow white houses and vividly blue-domed churches topped with triple bell towers – the essence of Greekness.

Phira is also a good base. It's more commercialised since cruisers dock here to let their passengers shop, but the souvenirs are classier than most and it's not too busy or noisy at night – except in the steamy little tavernas where tables are crammed together and the noise of animated chatter and laughter can be deafening!

On the flat side of the island, vineyards and vegetables stretch away towards amazing beaches of black sand at Kamari and Perissa. You can easily reach these by bus from Phira. Monolithos, which is badly served by buses and therefore quieter, is fine if you hire a car and enjoy getting away from the crowd.

For a stupendous view, make your way to Pyrgos in the centre of the island and its highest point. Because so few visitors bother to go there, the local people are agog with excitement when they see you, offer cigarettes and eagerly try to communicate in sign language if your Greek doesn't run to more than *Yasu*. Up among the daisy covered ruins of an old fortress, you can see the whole crescent of Santorini and the other scraps of islets that make up the rim of the once turbulent volcano. The present crater is in the middle of the sea, on the tiny island of Nea Kameni. You can get to it by boat and climb to the edge. Don't worry, it last spluttered in 1956 and seems pretty sleepy now.

Lesbos makes anyone who normally whinges about the monotony of Greek food eat their words. Never will you taste a moussaka with its egg custard topping so delicately flavoured with cinnamon, nor eat such crisply fried baby red mullet, such wonderfully stuffed aubergines or such tasty spiced sausages – and all for very few *drachmas*. Perhaps it has something to do with the fact that Lesbos lies a mere 12 miles (20 km) from mainland Turkey, and was under Turkish rule until 1912.

Lesbos is a pleasant medium-sized island of wooded herb-covered hills reminiscent of Provence – not remarkably beautiful but not unremarkable either. It is special, however, because it is really unspoiled and the people are kindness personified.

The spirit of the place makes fairly ordinary little resorts like Skala Kallonis seem like bliss if you like the quiet life. The living is very basic: there is only one small hotel – which possesses one of the half-dozen village phones – and a clutch of rooms in spotless purpose-built villa complexes that are cheek-by-jowl with local houses and gardens. This can mean a rooster waking you at five in the morning! But that's just a cue to stagger out and watch the fishing boats unload their catch of crayfish and sardines in the harbour.

On the pine fringed sands, there are no sun brollies or sun beds. There are no swimming pools. Anything approaching a disco is a mile out of town. But each evening when the lights come on, taverna tables overflow on to the village square and wonderful cooking smells lure you from whichever corner you happen to be lingering in with your chilled glass of retsina. Who could ask for more?

Skala Kallonis' sheltered position on an almost landlocked bay and its relaxed ambience make it ideal for families with young children. At least one tour company operates a club here for the little ones so their parents can freewheel.

There are other equally attractive small ports and resorts scattered about the coast, like picturesque Molyvos. From here you can take an excursion boat to picnic on Rabbit Island, where the bunnies may be a bit thin on the ground but the lamb kebabs barbecued on the beach by the boat's skipper and his wife will be both plentiful and delicious.

Mytilene, a sizeable port and kind of capital, looks across at Turkey. It's an odd mixture – an elegant muddle of Venetian, Byzantine, ancient and modern buildings with an atmospheric waterfront and a castle. There is also a statue of Sappho, the Greek writer whom lesbians revere as their prototype, though the evidence for believing she was other than heterosexual is pretty weak. She ran a finishing school for aristocratic young girls, encouraged them to be assertive and wrote erotic poetry. She also had a passionate love for the poet Alcaeus.

The only touristy event Lesbos offers – and it's fun at that – is an excursion into the hills for a typical Greek evening: complete with bouzouki music, waiters dancing à la Zorba and lifting tables with their teeth.

ENIGMATIC SICILY

When the ancient Greeks first landed in Sicily's Bay of Naxos, they knew they were on to a good thing. They hauled their boats ashore and stayed for a thousand years. No wonder, for the Mediterranean's biggest island has some marvellous spots around its rugged coastline, where the bonus for today's visitors is a relatively unpolluted sea.

In spite of being occupied by a string of conquerors, the last of whom were the Italians, Sicily has clung fiercely to its own identity, as if it were a country apart. You can't help being aware of this even in the popular tourist areas of Taormina.

Few resorts in the world can vie with Taormina for the sheer spectacle of its setting, the changes of mood it offers, the range of interests it caters for and the number of levels at which you can enjoy a holiday here. 'Levels' is the operative word, for the city teeters on a mountainous promontory, drops in layers around winding roads that descend to the coast, tucks itself into tiny coves and then sprawls left and right along the wide beaches of Spisone and Giardini-Naxos.

The antique town has been patronised by the British ever since Nelson's day – an expatriate Englishwoman even gave her garden to the townspeople and it is now the Giardini Publico. In Victorian times, the weak-chested came to winter here hoping the dry air would cure them. In fact, it is still pretty therapeutic because cars are banned in the centre of town and the only horsepower allowed is in the form of pony-drawn carriages decked with flowers. You can therefore wander in peace in the labyrinth of streets to find past treasures and present curiosities, like the fierce looking puppets which evoke the cruelty of medieval battles between Normans and Saracens, and the bizarre array of mafia dolls which poke fun at the island's sinister undertones. Don't worry, as an innocent tourist you're unlikely to bump into any of those menacing men in black, toting violin cases.

There are fifteenth-century palaces and baroque churches, but the city's great architectural stunner is the Greek Theatre whose proscenium arch – or what remains of it – frames the coast below and the smoking profile of Mount Etna.

Sicily's highest peak and Europe's largest active volcano is something the islanders have learned to live with and most tourists feel compelled to ascend – because it's there. A red minibus takes you up and up into a landscape that's like the way to hell. In mythology, that's exactly what it was supposed to be: Etna's crater was the entrance to the Underworld. It was also the forge of Vulcan, blacksmith of the gods.

Approaching it from the other side, the heart of the Nebrodian Mountains, gives you a very different slant on Sicily. This is wonderful touring territory, especially early in the year when each little mountain village is seen through a film of acacia blossom. Naso, Castel 'Umberto, Tortorici – each is more enchanting than the last. If you're lucky enough to strike a fiesta day, the cacophony of church bells, brass bands and transistor radios will be like nothing you've ever heard before. The locals will cajole you into buying anything from roasted chick peas to plastic spoons, and then draw you willy-nilly into the thick of the parades.

For more conventional holiday action, there is Cefalu on the north coast, the most attractive resort after Taormina. It's basically an overgrown fishing port with great restaurants and a lovely sandy beach. In the south there are Sciacca and Notto. But you cannot go to Sicily without exploring more of its remarkable ancient sites: the Valley of the Temples at Agrigento – the amazing relics of the city of Akragas, built 2500 years ago; or the Piazza Armerina, villa of one of the fat cats of Ancient Rome, with its extraordinary mosaic floors depicting hunting scenes and Roman women in bikinis (true!). Then there is Syracusa and its temple within a church, and Palermo with its palazzos, piazzas and ebullient street markets – though beware of getting lost in the sprawl of its suburban slums. The back streets of Catania aren't too salubrious either. If you pick up a hire car at the airport in Palermo or Catania, lock all doors and windows even while you're on the move against attack by gangs of small boys who'll pilfer anything they can grab easily. This is not as worrying as it sounds if you take adequate precautions. Then you can relax, for almost everywhere else the Sicilians will treat you like long-lost relatives.

The great thing about Sicily is that is has something for everyone – history buffs, young people on the lookout for life and style, families with children (who'll be spoiled rotten), and the adventurous who can wander in waders through the Alcantara Gorge, scale Etna on foot or take off for the Aeolian Islands. Here there are a few more volcanoes to explore, tourism with a capital T hasn't yet happened, and the largest Aeolian island, Lipari, boasts one of the best restaurants in Italy: Fillipino's.

BARBADOS, ANY TIME

Life on Barbados hits an up-beat note even when you can't hear a calypso – which isn't often. The Trade Winds temper the tropical heat and nowhere in the Caribbean is there an easier rapport between islanders and visitors, whatever the shade of either – and some of us, newly hatched from a flight from Britain, can be very pale!

A Caribbean suntan doesn't come cheap, but if you get your timing right it can be cheaper than you think. Barbados, like the other islands, has traditionally been somewhere to seek winter sun. Go in summer – *our* summer – and you can cut the price of your holiday by almost a third. Off-season – May to October – it might rain a bit more, but Caribbean showers are usually short and sweet. They keep the island looking lush and there's still plenty of sun.

There are two totally different sides to the island: the palm-fringed west coast where the towns, hotels and busiest beaches are, and the emptier, breezier, and beautiful east coast facing the Atlantic Ocean. It's emptier because there are strong currents, but surfers love the waves.

Hiring a moke isn't too expensive and finding your way about is no sweat. You drive on the left – a legacy of British rule – and although the road signs are somewhat sparse, the island's not big enough to get lost in. Non-drivers can go on taxi and coach tours.

If you only make it to the east side once, go for Sunday lunch, Bajan style, at the small Atlantis Hotel in Bathsheba. It's a big help-yourself spread of the island specialities. Most hotels and restaurants tend to please American palates, so the food is good but not particularly unusual – except at Bathsheba, where you get everything from sweet potato pie to plantain fritters, and there are always as many locals as tourists overeating at the long communal tables on the verandah.

The British connection is very noticeable in Barbados – the lilting almost Scots accent, the parish names of St James, St Andrew and St Michael (though no Marks & Spencer!), the old sugar planters' houses. At one of the latter, Nicholas Abbey, you can munch cucumber sandwiches on the lawn. In the capital of Bridgetown you can even gaze up at a statue of

Nelson – which actually preceded the one in London's Trafalgar Square.

Bridgetown, a free port, has a deep water harbour and an old careenage. One vessel that's always kept shipshape is the infamous *Jolly Roger*, the buccaneer boat. If you enjoy fun laced with rum, you can board it for a four-hour bash during which the crew dispense lunch and unlimited punch. Things get very relaxed and friendly, and you disembark with a definite list to port!

Hotel cabarets are the main source of amusement after dark: anything from fire-eating to the contortionist limbo. Troupes of performers drift from one place to another and there's nothing to stop you doing the same. The bill for your first drink usually includes the entrance fee.

Barbados remains one of the happiest islands in the sun, where the British are particularly welcome – and safe.

MAURITIUS – *SUGAR AND SPICE*

The great French writer Baudelaire thought Mauritius was special. He came when this Indian Ocean island was the Ile de France, and stayed on. He also fell in love with a Mauritian beauty, the dusky wife of a government official. But it was all above board and entirely proper – no trysts beneath the tropical moon, just a fervent admiration for the woman whom he immortalised in the poem *La Dame Créole*.

It's easy to see how he was smitten, for the Mauritians are among the most charming and good looking of any island people. Faces of Europe, Africa, Asia and mixtures in between smile at you the moment your feet hit the tarmac at Plaisance Airport. They haven't been changed by tourism – yet – nor do they seem resentful of visitors better heeled than they are. They're neither pushy nor shy. Wherever you meet them – in the hotels, the streets of Port Louis or the ramshackle villages – they seem helpful and happy to see you. If you hire a moke, you need never worry about getting lost – an octopus of human arms will soon wave you in the right direction.

A thousand miles east of Africa, under Capricorn, Mauritius

is special in other ways too. A sugar-and-spice island, where cane fields sway against a backdrop of strange saw-toothed peaks and Pierre Poivre gave his name to pepper, where the poor old dodo bird became extinct but the rare pink pigeon is now protected.

On shores free of sharks because of the coral reef, lush hotels cluster in ones and twos, offering water sports galore, pool games, casinos and cabarets. The jet set stays in the best of these – Princess Stephanie of Monaco, our own Duke and Duchess of York and the writer Frederick Forsyth. He likes to indulge in deep sea fishing and Mauritius is world-class for this as the waters are teeming with gigantic marlin and tuna.

But the island is by no means only for the rich. Inclusive holidays here are no more pricey than the Caribbean, and less so when it comes to extra spending. The food's also better than in most of the West Indies: remember the French influence. Although the British ruled Mauritius for the last 100 years before Independence in 1968, the French left a stronger imprint on the culture, the language and the cooking because they settled and intermarried. To Gallic flavours are added the spices of India and the seasonings of China. Restaurants specialise, but hotel food is a good mixture and always fresh and full of flair.

The only thing that's expensive in Mauritius is car hire, and you need wheels if you're not to languish in splendid isolation on your palm-fringed beach. The alternatives are to commandeer a taxi for a day or go by local bus – a hassle but not a hazard.

Don't miss Port Louis, the capital – a cacophony of concrete and clapboard with flame trees incongruously shading a statue of Queen Victoria in the centre and a market that's a must. Visit the *tisanier* who has herbal cures for everything from toothache to piles. Buy Chinese handicrafts and sari silks. Boggle at images of the Blessed Virgin jostling those of busty Indian goddesses.

Curepipe, the second town, is less interesting except for the workshop where they make exquisite models of the old wooden sailing ships.

Pamplemousses Gardens are worth seeing too. Like an overfertilised Kew with lily pads the size of dustbin lids and palms that reach for the sky, they're best seen sitting down – on a bicycle built for two with a fringe on top!

These are the sights of Mauritius. The sounds will linger in your ears long after you leave – the sound of the Port Louis market where the jabber of Bojpuri mixes with the Créole patois, the sound of tropical frogs in the night, the sound of the sega. Derived from slave song and dances, the sega is like audible sunshine.

SEYCHELLES

No collection of islands would be complete without the Seychelles, for they are probably the most gorgeous of all. Legend has it that they were the original Garden of Eden, and it's not hard to believe. Even the airport is beautiful. You touch down with the aquamarine sea on one side and a towering jungle of coconut palms on the other. These are massed on the foothills of the peaks of Mahé, the largest island. Largest? Well, you can drive around it in half a day.

Of the 100 or so islands sprinkled across 250 000 square miles (650 000 sq km) of Indian Ocean, only half a dozen can accommodate tourists. The rest are sanctuaries for rare birds and beasts or just deserted. Unlike Mauritius, the Seychelles have no industry except tourism. The local population have done rather well out of it, though. There is no poverty and no blots on the landscape – just pretty flower-filled villages hiding in the undergrowth, the odd old plantation house and the gracious capital of Victoria. This is full of craft shops, galleries, restaurants and a miniature replica of Big Ben! There are incredibly lovely, sloping beaches of silvery coral sand sheltered by tall takamaka trees – all like the advertising posters and often even better.

Anything of historical interest is scant. You go to the Seychelles to sunbathe, play in the sea and drink in their tropical beauty. The major fascination of these islands is their unique flora and fauna, developed because they are a thousand miles from anywhere else. The famous coco-de-mer, for instance, is a giant nut in the shape of a woman's pelvis – and it has inevitably had all kinds of highly coloured stories woven around it. You find this, along with the rare black parrot, on the island of Praslin, a 15-minute flight from Mahé. Then there is the pitcher plant with its lidded leaves and the vanilla orchid which gives vanilla essence. A trip to Bird Island is a magical experience for any birdwatcher, for it belongs to millions of sooty and noddy terns as well as flocks of mynah birds and little vermilion coloured cardinals, or bulbuls.

La Digue, with its 30 pairs of paradise flycatchers, is one of the most laid-back islands, though none of the Seychelles is particularly formal or grand looking. A bye-law forbids buildings to be higher than a palm tree, and though that leaves quite a lot of scope, the thatched cottage kind of development is most popular.

The Seychellois are mostly Créole – French mixed with African. They're slow to smile, but when they do, it's worth waiting for. The key to avoiding any frustration is to wind down to the islanders' unhurried pace. The French came upon the islands a couple of centuries ago, so the food has a French touch, but more often is a mix of European, Indian, Chinese and even Japanese.

New islands are opening up every year as the Seychelles spread tourism a little wider. Frégate is a gem. Its one hotel is the exclusive Plantation House – ten rooms and the attractions of 'scenic walks and giant tortoises'.

There is plenty of other accommodation down the scale in the Seychelles, including very simple small guesthouses. These are locally owned and serve up wonderful Créole food – often more fun than staying in a big de luxe hotel where cabarets soup up the local sega dance and the western disco beat seems so at odds with the islands' natural rhythms. But whatever your style, you'll find it catered for in the Seychelles.

CHAPTER FOUR

Self-catering Options

If there were a better term than self-catering to describe the fun of making yourself temporarily at home in another place, no doubt we'd have found it by now. But we haven't! So we're lumbered with this mundane name for an enormous range of promising holidays which essentially only have in common the fact that you make your own beds and meals. It covers everything from the most basic in a tent to the most luxurious in a villa or your own timeshared second home. You can self-cater down on the farm, afloat, on the road and in every kind of terrain from sand dunes to mountain slopes – and in almost any country.

Self-catering is the biggest boon for families with young children because it avoids the recurring ordeal of coping with toddlers at table in public dining rooms, which can sometimes ruin the entire holiday. It can also help cut down on your outlay when you have several mouths to feed, always providing you cook every meal yourself. Once you start going to restaurants every other evening, the final total may not be a great deal different from full board in a hotel. It may even be more. If you're going abroad, the key is to choose a country where the eating out is so cheap it's not worth eating in – Portugal or Greece, for example.

There's also the advantage of being able to bring with you from home any foods that your children are absolutely addicted to, such as baked beans or their favourite cereal. This is easier if you're driving rather than flying, but it's daft to cart too much with you. Unless you're heading for Outer Mongolia, you'll

find much the same items or their equivalents in almost any supermarket abroad, certainly throughout Europe and North America. To convince viewers of this we've whizzed our *Holiday* programme camera round grocery shelves from St Tropez to San Francisco. A curious exercise, this, as the smoothest way of filming is for our cameraman to sit in a shopping trolley. You can imagine the reaction of shoppers to the sight of a scrunched up body and a big camera being wheeled up and down the aisles!

It's true some things are more expensive abroad, like coffee and paper hankies. But all you're likely to save by bringing supplies with you is what you'll probably squander on a few extra drinks over dinner. In any case, there's a positive pleasure in shopping abroad, sampling the local brand of biscuits or fruit squash, going to street markets and trying out your French, Portuguese, Italian or whatever. It's all part of getting to know the place from the inside.

Having talked to lots of families who go self-catering year after year at home or abroad, I've found their prime motive is the freedom to do what they want to do when they want to do it. Most of all they like the freedom to be lazy on occasion and get up late – something you can't do in a hotel without missing breakfast.

It goes without saying that a perfect self-catering holiday depends on everybody mucking in and helping with the kitchen chores. If the one who normally slaves over a hot stove only gets a change of stove, there'll be more than a ripple of discontent. As a keen cook who doesn't often have the time to entertain at home, I personally revel in the chance to conjure up hearty meals for several people when on holiday, but I expect help with the washing up! Renting a gîte in France is a Gregg family favourite, sometimes involving three generations.

You can self-cater virtually anywhere, but I felt it worth pulling out a few facts about this kind of holiday: where to find the better camp sites; which countries have particularly good self-catering options and what's involved in home-swapping and timeshare. For what's actually available, every tourist office has a wealth of literature and information about travel companies who offer self-catering cottages, villas, apartments, houseboats – you name it – which they'll send you at the slightest nudge.

CIVILISED CAMPING

Campers fall into two distinct categories. There are those for whom living under canvas has a natural attraction, often triggered by early experiences in the Scouts or Guides, and those who aren't wild about the idea of roughing it but have surprised themselves by enjoying the freedom and informality of a camping holiday.

Life on a camp site is certainly relaxing and different. No schedules. No need to dress up. Few household chores and you're outdoors most of the time. The only potential spoiler is rain, which endears no one to tent life.

Being less expensive and considerably more flexible than a hotel, camping is definitely one of the most successful ways for a family to holiday abroad. Camp sites are sociable places buzzing with gentle activity, so there is always plenty of companionship for children of any age. Other forms of self-catering usually lack this.

Twenty years ago, the invention of camping packages offering pre-erected tents and including ferry crossings created a new breed of camper. Now, with everything from a corkscrew to a sprung double bed provided, the uninitiated can try out the idea without having to invest in equipment. The cost is similar to staying in a cottage, though prices drop significantly outside school holidays and children under 14 often go free. The tents are spacious, with separate sleeping compartments and comprehensive kitchen equipment often including a fridge and electric lighting. Many now also have their own 'loo' tents alongside.

The majority of sites used by British companies, most of whom now also offer mobile homes, are in the top three- or four-star category. This means they have tiled sanitary blocks with hot running water in washbasins, showers and sinks. Depending on the size of the site, there will be at least one shop, restaurant and bar. Leisure facilities range from children's playgrounds and swimming pools to sports and entertainment. Those with several hundred emplacements and internal roads feel almost like a village.

For young children, sites provide safe playing areas as well as a constant supply of playmates, with language invariably proving no barrier. Activities may even be organised for them, so parents often have great freedom except at mealtimes. For teenagers or younger parents, larger camp sites have evening discos, so are definitely not the place to go for a quiet time.

Site facilities in Britain generally tend to be less sophisticated than abroad, though the various tourist boards are now making a big effort to raise standards. You can expect to find far more caravans than tents – a reflection on the British climate. It's usually the other way round abroad. Some of the most scenic sites in Wales and Scotland are prettily set in the hills or beside lakes and rushing streams, for example those at Ogwen Bank in Snowdonia and beside the Tay at Birnam in Perthshire.

Across the Channel, Brittany has long been a favourite with British campers as getting to your destination involves only a short drive from the ports. Many of its sites are near attractive sandy coves and quaint villages. For more reliable weather, you need to go further south to the Vendée on the Atlantic coast. It is flatter, but has some of France's finest stretches of beach, often with sites close by.

To rely on finding the sun, you need to go beyond the 'gum boot line', halfway down France. Unfortunately the crowds are there as well as the sun in July and August. Inland sites in the hills of Provence or in the dramatic Cevennes are the quietest, often surrounded by wonderful scenery.

Compared with the Côte d'Azur, the flatter western end of the Mediterranean coast beyond the Camargue is much less hectic and crowded but well-endowed with sites. Argeles near the Spanish border boasts no less than 80. Further round the rugged coastline in Spain itself you will also find a good selection, backed dramatically by the Pyrenees.

Surprisingly, camping is the least expensive and certainly the most relaxing way to see Venice. Several large sites are spread along the sandy beaches of the Adriatic, only a 40-minute ferry ride away across the lagoon. Ideal for camping, too, are the green banks of Italy's Lake Garda with its clear warm water that's excellent for both swimming and water sports.

The many lakes in Switzerland and Germany also afford attractive settings for camping and often have beaches that rival seaside resorts. Lake Constance and Lower Bavaria are particularly favourites with the Germans themselves. There are also some excellent sites on the banks of the Rhine and Mosel. As you might expect of a nation which takes its camping very seriously, standards are high.

The same applies to Scandinavia which has some delightfully peaceful camping areas of immaculate quality. Sweden's two large lakes, Vänern and Vättern, are unbeatable for their setting and water sports. Sites are graded according to the facilities, which often include special loos for disabled campers, and on the degree of natural beauty and 'unspoiledness' of the surroundings.

When you have your own tent or caravan, you can book from among a selection of hand-picked sites throughout Europe, including France's top Castel chain, through the Select Site Reservations Agency (see address list in appendix). This service includes ferries and hotels en route.

The AA's *Camping and Caravanning in Europe* guide is

invaluable. It features 4000 recommended sites in 19 European countries with a short description and facilities list for each. The RAC/Camping and Caravan Club has a similar handbook.

Michelin's *Camping Caravanning France* covers 3506 of France's 11 000 sites. Each is inspected annually and graded for comfort, location and facilities. Over 600 are ranked as suitable for disabled people.

For Germany, the DCC national camping club publishes a graded guide and a leaflet on 400 of the best sites is available free from the German National Tourist Office (see address list in appendix).

The AA's *Camping and Caravanning in Britain* gives details of 1000 inspected sites, graded by one to five pennants. The English, Scottish and Wales Tourist Boards operate voluntary grading schemes for quality and the sites are listed in their respective guides, available at tourist information centres.

ON A SLOW BOAT TO SOMEWHERE

If we had been meant to live at the pace we do today, why weren't we fitted with wings and turbojet feet? There's a great antidote to rush-hour road jams and sardine-packed commuter trains, though – it's chugging along a canal at four miles per hour, going nowhere in particular!

You can set off from many places on Britain's canal network. There's a delightful voyage to be made from Whixhall Marina in Shropshire to Wales on the Llangollen Canal. The Caledonian Canal is another to try. You'll probably be required to get the boat back to the starting point by the end of your trip, so work out a looped route to save seeing the same scenery twice. Most companies provide suggested journeys plus bedding and kitchen equipment: everything you'd expect to find in a holiday villa, in fact.

You'll be shown how to operate the boat. This will take all of two minutes! Remember when you started learning to drive and kept oversteering? It's the same with canal boats – the lightest touch on the tiller changes your direction. You discover this the hard way. When your companions have pushed the boat off the hidden sludge beds near the banks a few times, you start getting it right.

There's a great feeling of camaraderie between the crews of hired narrowboats – you always exchange a cheery greeting as you pass. The same doesn't apply to some of the owner-occupiers who travel the canals in smaller boats. These experienced sailors consider themselves several cuts above the likes of you. Expect a frosty silence at best, and at worst remarks like, 'Do be careful – *our* boat isn't hired, you know!'

Locks are great fun and involve the whole crew. Someone delicately steers while the others frantically winch away, opening and shutting the gates to raise or lower the water level. It's confusing at first, but soon you'll be a well-drilled team.

There are often shops right on the tow path where you can stock up on food. Alternatively, tie up and stroll to the nearest village. After all, what's the rush? When everyone's tired of cooking, you can buy ready-made food from one of the farm kitchens which appear along the route. You'll often find true home-cooked grub at very reasonable prices. And if even

washing up becomes too much, eat at one of the many canal pubs. Have a cheap snack at lunchtime, chug on till evening, then splash out – but not that much – on a high-class pub restaurant meal.

Canal holidays are ideal for families with children (in life jackets) or for groups of friends, and if the British weather is at all kind for your trip, you'll find there's no place like a narrowboat roof for fast tanning. And when you see some of the beautiful and unique perspectives of British countryside from your canal angle, you'll realise what a pity it is that life can't always potter along at four miles per hour.

France is threaded with canals too and many British companies' brochures offer cruising holidays on the other side of the Channel.

A *GÎTE IS NEAT*

Renting a French gîte will give you one of the most inexpensive family holidays abroad. The word is untranslatable because there is no real English equivalent. Country cottages for hire are the nearest to it, but the gîte experience encompasses much more than a mere summer let. It has a hands-across-the-sea element which is designed to help you mix the *entente cordiale* a bit.

A gîte can be an apartment or maisonette attached to a farm, a converted barn or even a purpose-built cottage by the sea – but it is usually in a quiet rural area and always privately owned by French people who live locally and welcome you as guests. How much you see of them varies, but they will often invite you for a drink or a meal, offer to babysit and provide advice about where to go and what to see. If they're farmers, they may sell or even give you fresh produce. It depends on you as much as on them how the relationship develops. What is important to remember is that they are part of the gîte system because they like making friends with other nationalities – especially and perhaps surprisingly, the British – and for you to spurn their overtures would be rather ill-mannered. If you have prejudices about the French, prepare to shed them before you hire a gîte.

Always practical, the French have evolved a system which works well and makes everything clear cut for everyone concerned. Owners must agree to provide accommodation to a rigid set of standards and letting rules.

The reason the gîte is such good value is that you rent it by the week, not at a per-head price but at a fee based on its grade and the number it can accommodate. A gîte for seven or eight people can be rented for under £150 at the time of writing.

Obviously you have to get yourself there, and since part of the charm of the gîte is its rural setting, a car is more or less essential. Booking through one of the tour companies specialising in gîte holidays is well worth it because the Channel crossing will be included at a favourable rate, and you'll then pay so much per head for the package. If your family has one or more tiny tots, try to choose somewhere within a few hours' drive of the Channel ports. Because gîtes within easy striking distance are most in demand, booking early is vital – certainly before Christmas. Remember, you have the regions of Nord/Pas-de-Calais, Picardy and Champagne-Ardennes as well as the more obvious Normandy and Brittany to choose from.

If you want to go further south, consider putting the car on the train or going fly-drive. The holiday becomes pricier, but the convenience of getting there quickly might be worth paying for – and you save on motorway tolls, meals en route and overnight stops.

Self-catering in a gîte is hardly ever a chore with the well-equipped kitchen that's standard and a local market in some small town nearby. School-age kids get a great kick out of practising their French as they bring home the *baguette*, that wonderful, long, light-as-air bread roll. Food is a bit dearer than at home, particularly meat and fish, but the quality of the fruit and vegetables is superb and these won't break the budget.

A useful book is *Self-catering in France* by Arthur and Barbara Eperon (Christopher Helm). No doubt you'll also want to pop the *Guide Michelin* in the glove compartment to point you in the right direction for that delectable French meal on a special night out.

GREAT DANISH IDEAS

Pocket-sized, big-hearted Denmark is a delightful country. It is very rural, with rolling hills where farmhouses in shades of ochre and terracotta nestle in storybook settings. The villages are picturesque, the towns tidy, the cities well planned. The roads are rarely congested and, because the country is made up of the Jutland peninsula, the islands of Funen, Sealand and hundreds of smaller ones, there is an endless coastline often with wonderful beaches backed by sand dunes. Nowhere are you likely to find more opportunities for family fun or a better standard and variety of self-catering holidays.

It's simple. The Danes love children and make special efforts to please them, so the holiday business in Denmark makes family holidays a priority. In addition, a high proportion of Danes own second homes in the country or by the sea and rent these for part of the summer. This means a wide selection of extremely pleasant and comfortable holiday homes available to visitors. Since most owners spend quite a lot of money on furnishing their summerhouses, the accommodation is far from basic. It may be simple – Danish taste is usually less cluttered than ours – but you can be sure of comfort and a well-equipped kitchen and bathroom.

Summerhouses are categorised according to their quality and size, but range between £100 and £200 a week. Like most rented, privately owned accommodation, everything's provided except bed linen and towels. Be prepared for mattresses to be a little harder than you're used to.

Holiday centres are also popular. These offer self-catering flats or small houses within a central hotel complex so that you have a restaurant, shops, swimming pool, games room and other facilities on site. Prices are not too expensive considering that the standard of living in Scandinavia is higher than ours. The cost of food in shops is not so very different, but noticeably higher in hotels and restaurants. Even then, if you look out for the special Danmenu signs – signalling restaurants which have agreed with the tourist board to provide visitors with a reasonably priced meal – you can expect two courses for about £6 a head. The Danish Tourist Board in London provides a list of Danmenu restaurants for each region (see address list in appendix).

Another Danish self-catering option is a flat or house on a farm. Starting prices are around £120 per week. This is an extension of the Danish farmhouse holiday scheme whereby you're treated as a guest by your hosts, joining them for breakfast and evening meals. As self-caterers you'll be treated as insiders even if you don't eat with the family, and your children will be encouraged to get involved with the animals. If there are sheep, there's sure to be a lamb to cuddle, and when the cows come home, feeding time never fails to make small eyes widen with pleasure.

Wherever you're based, you'll never be far from the coast or from somewhere interesting to visit. Jutland, the nearest bit of Denmark to us, has more than its share of attractions. There's Legoland, a feat of Lego brickwork and electronic wizardry with canal locks and bridges operating perfectly in the miniature replicas of different countries. Cross the big bridge from Jutland to the island of Funen and you can visit Hans Christian Andersen's birthplace at Odense. His house is a museum and plays adapted from his fairy tales are performed at Funen Village, an open-air museum of bygone Denmark. Arhus has a wonderful 'old town' museum of bygone Denmark and a Tivoli-type amusement park, but the famous Tivoli Gardens are in Copenhagen on Sealand, the island nearest Sweden. Yet that's only four hours' drive from Esbjerg, the North Sea port where you dock en route from Britain.

Self-catering holidays in summerhouses, holiday centres and on farms can all be tied in with a sea crossing on DFDS Seaways cruisers (see chapter 8), so your car can easily go with you.

There's one other point that makes Denmark a particular joy: most Danes have some English, and they go out of their way to be helpful. Ask the origin of one dish on a menu and they'll translate the lot!

In fact, all things considered, this is a country where your chances of having a perfect holiday are very high indeed.

FACTS ABOUT TIMESHARE

Timeshare – or 'interval ownership' as the Americans call it – has got itself a bad reputation because of high-pressure selling, and anyone could be forgiven for running a mile at the mere mention. This is a pity because the idea has created a useful extension to the holiday scene and is certainly set to grow. There are now over 1.4 million timeshare owners worldwide, including 120 000 in Britain.

So how does the system work? For a one-off price you buy the same week or longer in a furnished apartment or house each year for perhaps 25 years. This could cost anything from £1000 to £15 000 per week, depending on size, standard of furnishings, location and the season you choose.

Most timeshare developments are purpose built, either completely new like most of those on the Costa del Sol and in the Algarve, or specially converted as is often the case in Britain. At the very least, there's likely to be a restaurant, shop and swimming pool, while some have impressive extras equal to those of a luxury hotel such as saunas, tennis and organised entertainments. American timeshare complexes can be especially luxurious, though several in England's Lake District and in Scotland are not far behind.

If you enjoy self-catering and actually look forward to going to the same place for your holiday each year, timesharing definitely has the advantage of being more personal than renting. Even though you may only own the place for a single week and haven't furnished it yourself, it will still have the feeling of familiarity that a second home has. There is also the likelihood of meeting up with the same neighbours – though you may or may not regard this as a bonus!

Timeshare should never be regarded as an investment because the re-sale market is such an unknown factor. However, compared with buying a property outright, there is none of the worry of it standing empty, open to neglect and vandalism. On-the-spot management should mean that it is kept secure and well maintained – but you have to pay for this. Annual maintenance charges can be anything from £50 to £250 for every week you own. The quality of management is therefore a point to check out thoroughly before buying.

When you feel like a change, there is always the possibility of exchanging your timeshare for a similar one elsewhere. There are now around 2100 timeshare 'resorts' worldwide, including 55 in Britain. Virtually all belong to one of the international exchange organisations, and the first annual subscription is often thrown in when you buy.

The largest agency is Resort Condominiums International (RCI), which covers 1460 resorts at the time of writing. It charges £38 annually – and £40 for each week exchanged. This has to be for the same number of bedrooms or fewer and for a similar time of year – no hope of swapping low season in the Lake District for high season in Florida!

Normally you have to specify four choices, and the longer in advance you do this, the better the chance of getting your first. Sometimes it is possible to 'bank' weeks and build up a reserve from year to year. There are also some excellent late deals if you are able to go at less than 45 days notice. These usually give you a better time and size of property than your own.

The leaflet *Your Place in the Sun*, free from the Department of Trade and Industry (see address list in appendix), has useful advice about buying timeshare. Above all, no holidaymaker should be persuaded to sign on the dotted line under the influence of the hot Mediterranean – or any other – sun.

HOME FROM HOME IN AMERICA

Bargain flights and the favourable exchange rate have made the USA almost as easy and as cheap to get to as Europe, but the cost of a family holiday there can still mount up, even taking into account some admittedly big advantages. These include double rooms in hotels with two double beds so you can sleep four for the price of two if your kids are under 20.

One method of keeping your budget within bounds is to hire a mobile home and go touring like a tortoise. Winnebago campers are great, sleep up to six and have a tiny streamlined kitchen with cooking facilities that could turn out a Thanksgiving dinner at a pinch. Wrestling with a Winnebago isn't that

easy, however. It's heavy to handle and tricky to manoeuvre, and driving in the USA can be daunting if you've never done it before. Not an ideal exercise if your children are very small.

Home-swapping is altogether less of a hassle. You link up with an American family who wants to come to Britain and exchange homes with them for the same period. The first step is to find an agency offering a directory of potential home-swappers. Your local travel agent should be able to locate one. If not, the best plan is to contact the United States Travel and Tourism Administration (see address list in appendix). You'll pay a small fee – something in the region of £25 – to be listed in the directory yourself. Then you contact likely candidates for swapping. Could be someone will get in touch with you first!

You do the spadework yourself. All that most agencies provide is names, addresses and some guidelines. It's up to you to make a thorough check on your swappee and ask all the right questions before you commit yourself. You also arrange your own travel.

There is one organisation which gives a more personal service by interviewing you, vetting your home, finding you a family to swap with, and fixing your flights. Naturally you pay more for this, which rather defeats the object of the exercise unless you decide it's worth the extra. By doing it yourself you should, in theory, have a holiday for the price of getting there.

Be prepared to swap cars as well – sometimes you need one just to get to the supermarket. Be considerate and leave plenty of local wisdom for your visitors, including who to contact if anything goes wrong. Be sure your kitchen is reasonably up-to-date – the most modest homes in America have stream-lined kitchens, and if yours is very down-at-heel it's not going to be a fair swap. If you send snapshots of your house's interior and exterior at the outset, everybody has a better idea of what they're getting.

Destinations like California and Florida are in big demand because everyone's seen them on television, because of their beaches, Disneyland, Disney World, and heaps of other leisure attractions. But don't blinker yourself to the potential of other parts of the wide and handsome USA – or Canada for that matter. You might prefer to discover Oregon (a real stunner) or Ontario, Colorado or British Columbia. Wherever you go, stepping into the shoes of a family with whom you have something in common – careers, tastes and so on – will certainly help you experience the American lifestyle at grass roots level.

CHAPTER FIVE

Off the Beaten Track

There's a risk in broadcasting information about secret holiday idylls. If everybody then flocks there, the idyll will be no more. At least, that's what writers say in the letters which hit the desks of the *Holiday* programme producers after we've filmed someone's favourite bolt hole in a particularly delightful corner of the world.

But since quieter places attract certain people, perhaps the idylls are not so liable to be overrun by unsympathetic marauders. After all, when more than a handful begins to look like a crowd, you can always get up and go somewhere else, because off-the-beaten-track territory is more or less unlimited. The major movers in the holiday business tend to concentrate their efforts in lumps around well-known coastlines, leaving plenty of scope for you independent travellers to find your own perfect holiday in all kinds of other less patronised places. About half of the millions who go on holiday at home and abroad each year make their own arrangements or get their travel agent to do so, without ever opening a brochure.

Having said that, do-it-yourself is by no means the only way to get off the beaten track. There are any number of excellent smaller tour companies who specialise in holidays that don't peddle the obvious, that give you a great deal of flexibility within the choices available and that offer you a holiday tailored to your taste and pocket – and they do it more economically than you could yourself.

This is particularly true when you take your car across the channel to France, Holland or Belgium, or brave the Bay of

Biscay to get to northern Spain. Whether you want to drive around when you get there and stay in small hotels or on camp sites, or settle in somewhere pleasant, it's a much better bet to find a company that includes the ferry crossing in the holiday price. You'll certainly get it cheaper.

You can also use inexpensive packages as a base from which to explore further afield. For instance, a winter bargain to one of the Spanish coasts can be a passport to discovering another face of Spain. While no one could call Torremolinos off the track, it's within striking distance of the peaceful hill country leading up into the Sierra Nevada, where sleepy villages hide and old monasteries perch. So hire a car and veer off at a tangent. Eventually you'll get to three of the country's most dramatic cities – Seville, Granada and Cordoba, delightful Andalusian centres of art treasures and vibrant street life.

Here at home there are many beautiful inland areas promising a special summer holiday for anyone not wedded to the idea of buckets and spades. Much of our old canal network is being revitalised to take narrowboats and cruisers, and quiet reaches of our rivers offer peace, perfect peace, as you glide through some heavenly countryside. By thinking laterally, you avoid the bottlenecks. While the Norfolk Broads are chock-a-block in full summer, the lovely Little Ouse that wends its way through Cambridgeshire all the way to north Norfolk is virtually empty. You'll hardly pass a dozen other craft yet there are plenty of pretty pubs and rural curiosities along the way. The main hiring companies cater for people who want to meander in all directions, and provide you with charts for unfamiliar waters.

Following the course of a river by car gives a touring holiday a sense of purpose, leading you through beguiling scenery to interesting towns and all manner of historical diversions. A ploy to use almost anywhere in Europe.

Places that don't figure too prominently in the brochures are also a good option for anyone who likes to tread where few tourists have gone before. Italy's Umbria, for example, the region of St Francis of Assisi, inland and north of Rome, has not yet been 'discovered' by too many.

Choosing countries with small populations guarantees that

almost everywhere will feel off the beaten track. The Scandinavian quartet – Norway, Sweden, Denmark and Iceland – are particularly endowed with wide open spaces and ribbons of empty roads. Notta lotta people live there and, in comparison with other European destinations, notta lotta people go there. The quality of any kind of holiday in Scandinavia is likely to be high. Yet the cost, surprisingly, is not always as high as you might imagine; camp and caravan sites and log cabin 'villages' are absolutely top class, superbly run and very reasonable.

While it may take a little more effort to plan a holiday along less-trodden paths, it's all the more rewarding. There's the fun of finding out before you go: getting gen from tourist offices, mapping out routes, reading books and guides. Once there, don't forget that local tourist information centres will help. If you're aiming for foreign parts, learn a bit of the language. It helps you make friends and get out of tricky situations. I manage just to get by in French, but it came in handy when I got lost filming in the hills of Provence, having driven out of two-way-radio range of the camera car. If I hadn't been able to glean shouted directions from passing drivers and local villagers, I might never have been seen again!

Getting lost is usually par for the course when you investigate strange terrain, but it's also part of the enjoyment. Bill Buckley's trip to Ireland for the *Holiday* programme was a case in point. He was to tour County Cork by bicycle and the starting point was the city of Cork itself. When Bill got on his bike, he suddenly realised the film crew had driven off in their van and he hadn't the faintest idea where they were going. He spent the next hour-and-a-half frantically pedalling around the county asking everyone if they'd seen a group of people with a big camera. Eventually he stumbled across them by chance, by now convinced it was all his fault; but as he pedalled furiously towards the director shouting his apologies, she came running towards him shouting hers!

A *NIBBLE AT NORTH YORKSHIRE*

There's no doubt that Hovis ads have done a lot for North Yorkshire with those tantalising glimpses of grey stone, red pantiled villages and roads plummeting from bleak moorland into deep wooded dales. But in this not-undiscovered big county, the crowds soon disperse. People who need people tend to go elsewhere, and one of the most gorgeous and unspoiled swathes of England is left for those who love peace and nature.

Whether you choose to wander the North York moors, delve into the great glaciated valleys of Wharfedale and Swaledale, or explore the spectacular waterfalls of the Three Peaks, you will be 'discomknockerated', as Ken Dodd says, by the beauty.

Even the edge of the dales has its highlights – the bit around Leeds, Harrogate and Ripon. For a start, there's the grandstand view from the summit of Otley Chevin, where an unusual Swedish-style luxury hotel, built entirely of wood, harbours actors on location for Yorkshire TV's successful soap, *Emmerdale Farm*. After a breath of appetite-giving air, head for Harry Ramsden's at Guiseley, arguably the best fish-and-chippery in the entire world. Harrogate, with its elegant stone houses and lovely gardens which have earned the town the tag 'Floral Resort of England', is a place to squander time. Don't miss the collection of Victoriana and costumes in the Pump Room, the country's first public baths, built in 1842. Ripon, too, is worth a halt. It's famous for its small but exquisite cathedral and for its 1000-year-old evening ritual of the Wake-man, or Hornblower, who, complete with tricorn hat, sounds his horn in the market square to let townsfolk know they can rest assured of an undisturbed night. As you can imagine, Americans in search of 'ye olde England' go bananas over this.

Out on the face of the windswept fells of Widdale and Ribbledale, visitors are fairly thin on the ground. This is great touring and walking country: a furrowed landscape where dry-stone walls divide the velvety sheep-cropped grass of the hill farms; where waterfalls like Harrow Force and Kisdon Force cascade over layers of slatted limestone; where, beneath the rugged flanks of the peaks, a honeycomb of caves and potholes invite spelunkers to burrow as deep as they dare.

Unpretentious market towns like Giggleswick – in whose sixteenth-century public school dear old Russell Harty once taught – and Settle, with its curious unfinished Folly Hall, are both focal points, so are Ingleton and Clapham, marvellous rambling and touring bases for the lovely Yorkshire Dales National Park.

The incredible contrasts of the North York moors and dales – wild, gale-torn highland dipping down into crevices of rural tranquillity – are often so stunning that all you want to do is stop, stare, and enjoy the therapy of feeling small. Among the most enchanting villages is Hutton-le-Hole where Hutton Beck bubbles through on its way to Westfield: a real little showplace, arrayed around mossy greens and impeccably kept. The Ryedale Folk Museum, in an ancient timbered dwelling, is worth a look. It boasts a host of early farm implements and an antique dairy. Levisham and Lockton, Stape and Rosedale, Wrelton and Goathland (where sheep, not goats, graze on the town's fringes) are all wonderful old Yorkshire settlements. Each has its own individual history and particular brand of charm – 'reet gradely', as the locals would put it. But then, there is little of North Yorkshire that isn't.

SCOTLAND'S GENTLE SOUTHWEST

The hills of Galloway are all too often ignored by those dashing north or south through them, but this mellow, fertile part of Scotland is a delightful potpourri of natural beauty, tidy towns and grand castles – some in ruins, others in excellent repair.

There's plenty to do – fish (sea and freshwater), pony trek, canoe, wander after a golf ball, or simply wander. You'll find some of the best walking country in the whole of Scotland here, especially in the gorgeous Galloway Forest Park. There are 160 000 acres of conifers and bracken, a haze of rust, gold and green, with beautiful Glen and Loch Trool in the centre. You get into the park by car or bike, then tramp along the marked footpaths, spread a picnic, look for wild flowers, or listen for the strange knocking sounds of the capercaillie, which bird-watchers will know is a very rare kind of big grouse. And even if you only climb halfway up 2764-foot-high Merrick, you'll be rewarded with a breathtaking panorama.

You can easily avoid Galloway's few trunk routes and enjoy ambling on a network of quiet roads, whether you tour its inner heart or follow the coastline's succession of wide bays, estuaries, sheltered coves and meandering inlets. It's 200 miles from the Solway sands with their fast-flowing tides to the rugged Mull of Galloway, and all of it is scenic. History doesn't force itself upon you, but there are some fascinating sites to seek out if you're interested: the splendidly reconstructed Roman-British villa in the Forest Park; the Twelve Apostles Stone Circle, assembled almost 2000 years ago near Dumfries; and the excavated site of Scotland's first Christian church at Whithorn.

If you have time for just two castles, make them Castle Kennedy near Stranraer because of its lovely gardens set between two lochs, and Caerlaverock on the Nith estuary because it is moated, medieval and marvellous – and you can squeeze in the romantic ruins of Sweetheart Abbey nearby.

Dumfries, the region's 'capital', is a pleasant market town on the salmon-bearing Nith – just the place to buy a length of tweed, some woolly mitts or a pot of heather honey to take home. Don't miss the house where the poet Robert Burns lived, loved, wrote and drank away the last years of his life.

Mary Queen of Scots spent her last night in her native land at Dundrennan Abbey, near Kirkcudbright, before fleeing to England where she was soon imprisoned and later beheaded. The atmospheric ruins of the abbey seem filled with foreboding, but you'll soon cheer up in Kirkcudbright itself (pronounced 'kir-coo-bray'), a 'wee' town near the mouth of the Dee which is effortlessly charming. Well-kept eighteenth- and nineteenth-century houses line the L-shaped high street, a castle ruin poses, and Broughton House offers a super art gallery.

Treasures also abound in the grandest lived-in castle in Galloway – Drumlanrig near Thornhill, one of the Duke of Buccleuch's homes. You can actually stay in other castles and great houses, for many of the top class hotels are converted from historic piles and the living is luxurious. If you've got to keep your costs down, however, there are plenty of good camp and caravan sites in idyllic settings, and the B&B circuit is the best value of all.

Curiosities? Convinced off-the-trackers might regard it as a bit touristy, but Gretna Green is unique. On the border with England, the Old Smithy where countless 'quick-fire' marriages were made still puts couples through the motions, although the ceremony is no longer legal.

FREEWHEELING AROUND CORK

Whatever else you pack when you visit southern Ireland, you won't need your passport. That, plus the nearness of the place, makes it a very tempting holiday destination. Suntans aren't guaranteed, as there's often rain and mist interspersed with the sunshine, but without these you wouldn't get that justly famous emerald greenness.

Space and seclusion are often expensive, but needn't be so in Ireland. The ferry is the cheapest way to get there, and biking the economical and leisurely way to explore. You could sail to Dublin, for example, take a train to Cork, hire a bike and discover County Cork.

Travelling light is essential: your saddle bag offers extremely limited luggage space and, in any case, the less you carry the less hard you have to pedal. Expect to wobble about a bit and suffer from aching calf muscles at first, but don't worry: even if you haven't cycled since childhood, you'll soon love being back in the saddle.

Staying at youth hostels is one way to punctuate the journey. There are 46 in Eire and they include castles, cottages, coast-guard stations, schoolhouses and military barracks. Despite the name, there's no age limit. Cost varies depending on location, season and age, but it's always amazingly cheap. You sleep in a dorm and do your own cooking, and you must bring your own eating utensils, tea towel, soap, towel and a sleeping bag or sheet bag (like a big pillowcase to cover the bedding).

Kinsale is one of the loveliest villages in the country. A visit there is incomplete without a drink at its famous Spaniard pub, named when the Spanish and Irish joined forces in the Battle of Kinsale in 1601. Kinsale is also one of Ireland's gourmet centres, particularly good on fish. So if you're budgeting for one posh meal during your stay, here's a good place for it.

At the nearby village of Ballinspittle, there's a statue of a madonna that became famous fairly recently when many people, some eminent, thought they saw it move. Rows of seats have now been erected and people stop to wait for the miracle in comfort.

Muckross House, outside Killarney, is a nineteenth-century manor, and a tour of the beautiful grounds in the horse and cart called a jaunting car is definitely recommended. Inside you can watch Kerry craftworkers demonstrating ancient skills still practised in the area. Sadly, there'll be no room in your pannier for a handthrown pot or wicker basket from the souvenir shop.

If your budget isn't quite so tight, stay at one of Ireland's many farmhouses or guesthouses. You'll get a warm, family welcome and good quality accommodation, particularly if you choose places approved by the Irish Tourist Board, labelled Failte Tuaghe. This means, roughly, Irish welcome. Look for the sign of the shamrock at farmhouses, guesthouses and B&Bs. At the thatched Salmon Leap Farm at Clonkeen, mum leads the Irish dancing while dad and son provide music on accordion and banjo. This is typical of the informality and friendliness you'll discover in Ireland.

COUNTY DOWN – AN UNEXPECTED PLEASURE

Amazing though it may seem in the face of its troubles, the province of Ulster offers holidaymakers many peaceful backwaters – and County Down has more than its share. The fact that so many of its inhabitants stay at home for their holidays speaks for itself, and when you meet travellers there from other parts of the UK and elsewhere in Europe, they are often third- or fourth-timers.

County Down is where the Mountains of Mourne, arranged in their gentle folds around the focal point of Slieve Donard, sweep down to the sea – Percy French country. The scenery is on a small scale, the fields are soft and hummocky and the hedges unruly, threaded with dog roses and hawthorn, sloe, elderberry and bramble. Here and there a whitewashed farm looks prosperous, or an old thatched cottage crumbles. As the contours rise, dry-stone walls take over the boundaries and yellow gorse – called 'whins' here – blooms. Up in this wilder and wider terrain, lakes suddenly shine amid the brown and green textures of the turf. There are small copses with picnic tables, Tullymore Forest Park – a swathe tamed by the National Trust – and magical Silent Valley nestling below the highest summits, where the reservoir which supplies Belfast's water is set in beautiful landscaped gardens.

A great way to enjoy all this – or any other part of Northern Ireland – is to tour at a snail's pace and stop at addresses approved by the NI Tourist Board from the *Farm & Country Holidays Association* booklet. At these you'll get bed, breakfast and an 'Ulster tea' if you want it, though you'll have to diet before you go to survive the potato cakes, soda farls and wheaten bannocks, not to mention the scones, fresh sponges and groaning fruit cakes!

Wanderers on foot can follow the Ulster Way, a network of signposted byroads which lead you into the prettiest corners, to an ancient dolmen, a historic village or a site where St Patrick is said to have set foot.

Newcastle, in the lee of the Mournes, is for old-fashioned seaside fun. It has a good beach, golf course and leisure centre.

The Slieve Donard is the up-market hotel but there are lots of small boarding houses and holiday homes.

Still within sight of the mountains is Strangford Lough, a thin finger of sea reaching in towards Newtownards and Comber. When the tide's out, a shrubbery of seaweed crackles on the muddy flats and motorists park to aim binoculars at the birds. The lough is more for sailing than swimming – though plenty do go for a dip when the tide's in, scrambling over stony foreshores. Sailing clubs thrive at Whiterock and Strangford. At the latter, you can take your car – or just yourself – on what must be one of the shortest ferry crossings in the world. It takes all of eight minutes to reach Portaferry on the other side, on the Ards Peninsula. For the best deep-fried prawns outside of Italy, head straight for the Portaferry Hotel, but get there early as it's become more popular since winning a Taste of Britain award.

Keen gardeners shouldn't miss Mountstewart, further up the coast, the stately pile of the Londonderrys. The grounds boast a superb collection of subtropical plants that do well in its especially mild microclimate, and children delight in the sculptured pairs of animals from Noah's ark.

Fifteen minutes' drive takes you across the peninsula. Here a string of small seaside towns, most of them fishing ports, link you all the way from Ballywiskin to Bangor. Each has a clean sandy beach or cove. At the weekend, if the weather's good, these get busier but hardly ever crowded.

Dave Allen used to quip that the reason Ireland was green was that half the Irish were in England walking on its grass. The truth is, there aren't that many Irish to start with, north or south – so you'll always find a bit more grass, sand or heather to wander on!

FOLLOW THE LOT

In France it is never difficult to get into what they call the *arrière pays*, the back country, because although there are as many French as British they have a country twice the size of ours in which to spread themselves.

The valleys of the rivers Loire and Dordogne, though not exactly overrun by British holidaymakers, are deservedly well-known. But there is another river, south of the Dordogne, on whose banks GB plates are rarely seen: the Lot, which rises in the Massif Central and flows through the old French provinces of Rouergue and Quercy.

The Lot is a lovely, lazy river, olive green and sinuous, at times bordered by fields of tobacco, maize and vines, at others by rocky spurs where ancient medieval villages cluster. There are tiny fortified towns to halt in – like Capdenac with its Roman beginnings, and Conques whose Romanesque church treasury houses the golden statue of little Sainte Foy, an early Christian martyr, and some exquisite bejewelled reliquaries.

The best way to go is via the delightfully named Bouzy, up to the unbelievably pretty St-Cirq-Lapopie, several times winner of the First Village of France award. Because of this accolade, it does get a few more visitors than other places in these parts, but either side of August it's never very busy.

The great plus of the River Lot, whether you tour by car, bike or Shanks's mare, is that it hardly ever lets you out of its sight. The roads follow the river line closely on either side. A series of wooded hills enclose the valley, giving it a secret feeling, yet you can always find good small hotels. Take the *Logis de France* guide with you (free except for postage from the French Government Tourist Office in London). Logis are small, reasonably priced, family-run hotels which often offer regional dishes on their menus.

Wherever you eat in the Lot area it's 'Hello, ducks!' They're the speciality of the region and are served up in a myriad guises. The rich and famous duck liver paste, *pâté de foie gras*, is something you may disapprove of because of the way the ducks are overfed to fatten their livers, but it is inescapable, potted and promoted in the windows of every specialist food shop. There is also *magret de canard*, slices of succulent duck breast (usually very pink); *confit de canard*, preserved duck that's delicious snipped over a salad; *cassoulet*, a duck casserole cooked with beans; plus other duck stews, soups and terrines. They haven't yet devised a duck dessert but they're probably working on it!

For those who prefer to come to a halt on holiday, somewhere near Cahors would be ideal, especially if you prefer to self-cater, for one of the joys of this gracious medieval stronghold is the daily market in the lee of the cathedral. The produce of Midi-Pyrénées, one of France's largest regions dipping towards the south, is a marvellously varied feast. Cahors' most photographed sight is the dramatically turreted Pont Valentré, spanning the Lot. Built in the fourteenth century, it's in splendid repair.

West of the city there are Lots more (sorry!) medieval towns to visit and wondrous châteaux – fairytale Bonaguil, Castelnaud, Puy l'Evêque. Or Mercuès which, if you're in the mood to push out the *bateau*, will put you up in truly grand style (it's a Relais & Châteaux hotel) and serve you some of its own château-bottled dark red Cahors wine for dinner.

OR FOLLOW THE DOURO

The most beautiful scenery in Portugal is a long way from the Algarve – not within range of a day's excursion from Albufeira. You have to make it the focus of your holiday. Not many people do, though it couldn't be easier to get to the valley of the Douro.

This majestic river flows westwards from Spain to make its exit into the Atlantic Ocean at Porto – a city whose name gives you the key to the kind of territory to expect in the Douro valley: wine country, where the crisp white Vinho Verde comes from as well as port itself. Vineyards green the craggy hills of the winding river's upper reaches, then steep gorges make its seaward path more and more spectacular.

There are two ways to enjoy the Douro: by train or by car. The train is terrific value with cheap fares and discounts (ask for 'kilometric' and special family tickets). A marvellous line follows the course of the river from Porto all the way to the Spanish frontier. You can pop on and off and change to little branch lines that filter you into delightful small hill villages like Amarante and Mondim de Basto. Or you can simply spend a day going and coming to enjoy the scenic splendour, having based yourself at some particularly charming town on the Costa Verde north of Porto. Vila do Conde, for example, is an unspoiled if not exactly undiscovered (by the Portuguese, at least) resort with a long, sandy beach, a flourishing fishing fleet and a pleasant setting dominated by the huge Convento de Santa Clara ensconced on a rocky rise above town.

Alternatively, a fly-drive package to Porto gives you the freedom of the Douro region – and the flexibility to spend time at either end of your trip in Porto itself, a very attractive city. By punctuating your meander up river with stays in *poussadas*, you can live the life of Riley. These state-backed, first class and luxury hotels are often converted from beautiful historic buildings. They are not overpriced by any means. A week's fly-drive with four sharing a small car could, at the time of writing, cost under £400 a head – including air fare, room and breakfast at the *poussadas*.

You would, however, want to tuck into at least one other meal per day at your *poussada* for they have a reputation for serving excellent traditional food and wine.

The Portuguese National Tourist Office in London is an approachable source for advice and information about visiting this lovely and little-known part of Europe (see address list in the appendix).

PS. Don't bank on the weather being as blistering here as in the Algarve. It can be fabulous but changeable – Costa Verde means Green Coast, and you know how things stay green.

TUNISIA – THE DEEP SOUTH

Imagine waking as dawn filters through the latticed shutters of your comfortable hotel room. You fling them wide to find a sea of sand – and a Bedouin's tent parked right outside. This is Tunisia's deep south.

Sand is not a commodity in short supply in Tunisia. From the long beige beaches that border the Mediterranean to the huge dunes of the Sahara, there's a lot of it about. But sand doesn't equal bland. The experience of travelling down to Tozeur on the edge of the largest desert on earth is a fascinating one, and a hundred times more interesting than merely playing at being a pool lizard in Hammamet, Sousse or the island of Djerba – though as an add-on later, one of these will make up a perfect combined package.

Anyone with an adventurous bent could hire their own transport. The track is, in fact, reasonably well beaten. The roads are tarmac most of the way, and Tunisia is quite safe. It's wise, however, to take a guide and hire something tough like a jeep, as rentals are not always well maintained here. By coach it's less hassle, and round trips are planned to offer as much variety as possible.

As you leave the coastal plain, the olive groves and hedges of prickly pear recede and camel herds begin to drift along the skyline. The vastness of Africa takes your breath away. You can stop at Matmata where a Berber community live in curious underground caves. It was here that much of the film *Star Wars* was shot. Cave rooms burrow into the sandstone from a central dug-out 20 odd feet deep – you can't help feeling that an invitation to drop in sometime might not be an entirely friendly gesture! Coach parties and independent travellers are welcome to view a show cave, incongruously fitted out in modern style as if by Times Furnishing.

Amazing in a different way are Tunisia's Roman sites. The country was the Roman Empire's first colony south of the Mediterranean, established after they conquered the Carthaginians. They called it Africa, and so named a continent. The colosseum at El Jem and the city of Sbeitla are among the most riveting ruins.

The natural spectacle of the Chott el Djerid makes the hairs on your neck rise. This is the vast salt desert you cross to get to the oases. The journey is a long one and the road straight as a die, but boredom is soon forgotten when you leap out to snap each other standing on the gleaming white floor of the chott. In fact, cameras keep clicking endlessly at the perspectives of strange cracked patterns stretching as far as the eye can see, and at the piles of desert 'roses' for sale on tiny isolated stalls. These crystalline 'flowers' are found several feet below the surface.

The sight of your first oasis is another stunner, especially if you reach it late in the day when the sun is dropping like a ball of fire into the desert. From a distance an oasis looks like a dark chasm. Nearer to, you can see it's a chasm stuffed with palm trees.

The main oases are at Gafsa, Nefta, Douz and Tozeur. The latter is the most luxuriant: a veritable market garden where dates and pomegranates, olives, onions, and even cabbages flourish. You can stay in a modest hotel or the luxury of the Sahara Palace. Both have pools, which is very pleasant, especially if you go in October when it's a nice dry 80°F (27°C). A camel ride through the oasis itself may be a touch touristy, but better than trudging on foot. If only they wouldn't deck you out in daft looking Lawrence of Arabia headgear! Take a sunhat if you cling to your dignity.

Entertainment in places like Tozeur is rustic and sheer delight as amateur musicians from the villages perform against desert backdrops.

If time allows on the return leg, a visit to Kairouan is fun for buying souvenirs. It has a wonderful seventeenth-century souk. But don't miss the mosques – the main one is 1000 years old and the exquisite little Mosque of the Barber has beautiful mosaics. Finally, don't forget Tunis itself, a tremendously sophisticated city with a French accent. The ruins of Carthage are nearby and so is picturesque Sidi bou Said, built by Andalusian Moors fleeing from the terrors of Catholic Spain.

THE WARMTH OF ICELAND

The Icelanders will tell you the only ice you're likely to find in Iceland in summer is at the bottom of a glass. Not strictly true – there are still a few glaciers about – but you would be surprised at how pleasantly warm it can be. In July, temperatures nudge 70°F (21°C) at sea level and, although the weather can be as changeable as any British summer, you can expect to see a lot more of the sun if the skies are clear – for Iceland almost touches the Arctic Circle. Nights are almost non-existent in midsummer, and if you don't actually catch a midnight sun, you can glimpse it as late as 11.45 pm. This is a marvellous bonus for anyone choosing an open air holiday: hiking or riding, camping in the hills, or hitting the schoolhouse trail – the Icelanders convert their schools to holiday accommodation in the summer and you can snuggle into comfortable, if basic, rooms at a very modest tariff.

Iceland is stunning. There's no other word for it. And the air is so unpolluted you can sometimes see for 80 miles or more. There is the strange beauty of wide glaciated plains enclosed by faraway peaks. There are spectacular waterfalls like Gülfoss and Goldenfoss; shooting geysers; fantastic sulphur fields and extinct craters; bubbling pools and thermal springs – the whole of Reykjavik, the capital, is centrally heated for free. You feel the power of the forces of nature as you marvel at a landscape which can be as stark as the moon or lush with a carpet of rare alpines and lichens basking in a breeze from the Gulf Stream. It's a David Bellamy wonderland.

Long before William of Normandy conquered England, Celts and Vikings settled in Iceland and formed the very first parliament in Europe, the Althing. It was an alfresco affair, and you can visit its site where a curving plateau falls away to form a sheltered enclosure.

The Irish/Norse cultural mix gave rise to legends of epic proportions – the Iceland sagas – which, by the way, are beautifully translated by Magnus Magnusson for the Penguin Classics series.

Icelanders are terrific leg pullers, but never in an unkind way. In fact, they are a tremendously hospitable people, never happier than when drawing strangers into their orbit to share their enthusiasm for Iceland. Amid awe inspiring natural beauty, they enjoy a finely tuned, very civilised lifestyle. Their towns and cities – never very large – are full of wooden 'doll's house' buildings brightly painted in primary colours. Everything is spic and span, the mod cons are ultra and, as you'd expect in a Scandinavian country, standards generally are extremely high.

Hotels range from international-posh-and-pricey to homely pensions which are plain but spotless. The food is first rate, too – marvellous fresh fish and shellfish, of course, but also tasty lamb dishes (plenty of sheep-grazing space) and the famous cold table buffets of delectable salads and open sandwiches.

Iceland is a country which keen off-the-trackers can enjoy on several levels and in an endless variety of ways. A flight-seeing package takes you on a round trip in comfort; you can tour by hire car or coach; trek on foot or horseback; go trout fishing or birdwatching or plant-spotting. But whatever you do, you can be sure there won't be too many other people doing it – just enough to provide good company.

WANDERING IN TUSCANY

As you stand amid the pointed hills of Chianti country, you can understand why so many of the great Italian painters were seduced by it. Leonardo da Vinci, Michelangelo and Botticelli were actually born here – and they portrayed its beauties in the rural backgrounds of their mellow canvases. Vine-clad slopes descend into deep gullies, slim cypresses stand like artists' brushes at-the-ready, tangled copses half hide weathered farmhouses whose eaves drip with wisteria.

The very essence of Italy, Tuscany is an enchanted landscape. And you can easily become a part of it, in *agriturismo* style – 'staying on a farm' – where a room with two or three sharing will cost no more than a single in a country hotel in Britain. The Italian Tourist Office in London will tell you where to write for this accommodation. You need to speaka Italiano a leetle if you're to make the most of being with your Italian hosts, though many like to practise their English. Alternatively you can try a Youth Hostel live-and-learn basic language course if you don't mind accommodation to match. Or you can move in to a small *albergo* in one of the country towns like Greve or Monteriggione. Beds will be clean and breakfast included for not much more than the YHA.

Since it is very much on the track of most visitors to the region, charming San Gimignano is more to look at than to stay in. It is about equidistant from Florence and Siena, a clutch of fourteenth-century towers rising above a walled enclosure of winding streets. Climb to the informal garden just below the battlements for a fabulous view of the surrounding countryside. On the way down, an outsize ice cream is obligatory!

Renaissance Florence is a special city which needs time to be savoured. Siena is special, too, but much smaller. One of the most painstakingly preserved medieval towns in Italy, it reflects the spirit of Tuscany, and its Campo is possibly the most spectacular square anywhere. More a lopsided oval, really, it dips towards the Museo Civico and is surrounded by pavement restaurants. This is the scene each summer of the Palio, an amazing horse race in which competitors from the 17 city districts wear medieval costume and the city seethes with exuberant crowds and waving banners.

Burnt Siena is, as any painter in oils will know, an artist's colour. This rich warm brown is the shade of Siena's bricks and tiles. The exception is the splendid Duomo which is striped in cream, old rose and sage green marble, and embellished with gilded murals. The richest (superlatives fall like overripe grapes in Tuscany) cathedral you'll ever see, it took 200 years to complete and is brimming over with elaborate decoration and magnificent sculpture. Even the marble floor is inlayed with illustrations from the gospels. The most riveting is Matteo di Giovanni's *Massacre of the Innocents*.

It is almost too much, and you think you've seen it all until you enter the Libreria Piccolomini. Here, so stunningly different from the sombre riches of the nave, is a series of brilliantly coloured frescoes by Pintoricchio. They seem as fresh as the long ago century they were painted – and they have never been restored.

The joy of Tuscany is really its combination of the sublime, the sophisticated and the supremely simple. When you're sated with culture and have worn out your soles window-gazing at elegant leather and gilded knick-knacks, the soft Tuscan hills are there, as timeless as they appear in the frescoes, to soothe and revive you. Then there is always a delicious meal of pasta to look forward to at some friendly *osteria*, perhaps with a tomato salad strewn with fresh basil and the green olive oil from the local groves. Plus a bottle of Chianti, naturally.

ISLAND HOPPING IN DALMATIA

Scattered like silver beads on the blue carpet of the Adriatic, the islands of Dalmatia will come as a surprise to any first-time visitor. It is not just that they are beautiful. It is not even that there are so many of them – over 1000 by the best estimate. Nor even that their inhabitants are friendly, for island people usually are. The real surprise is that they are so accessible, so historic, so unspoiled and unexplored: the perfect places for either staying put and relaxing or island hopping up and down the coast.

The main islands off the Dalmatian coast are Hvar, Brac, Korcula and Mljet and they lie just a few miles offshore. They are in fact the tops of mountain ridges, the valleys between now inundated by the sea. They lie between two marvellous historic cities: the old Roman seaport of Split in the north, and the ancient walled city of Dubrovnik in the south, where most tours of these islands begin. Ferries ply along this coast and between the islands, some of the large cross-Channel variety, others much smaller, flat-bottomed car ferries, push-me-pull-you little ships that run ashore in quiet little coves to pick up the locals and discharge a stream of tourists and travellers. The air is crystal clear and, unless chilled by the northern *bura*, that relentless Adriatic wind, the days are long and warm, especially on the island of Hvar which claims to be the sunniest spot in the Adriatic.

Your first glimpse of the offshore islands may well be from Dubrovnik on the one hour walk round the wall of the city. This is a dizzy stroll, only for those with a head for heights and feet encased in comfortable trainers. In fact, high heels and leather-soled shoes aren't suitable footwear anywhere in the islands of Dalmatia. Those who prefer to stay lower down can walk along the wide *Placa*, the central boulevard of Dubrovnik, shop for glassware or leather in the boutiques tucked into the narrow alleyways, dine in one of the historic bistros up the steep stairways, or have a drink or a coffee in the cafés which overlook the old galley port. Dubrovnik resembles a miniature Venice, a little world unto itself inside massive walls. Like Venice, too, it once was a maritime republic.

From Dubrovnik, a regular ferry boat serves the main offshore islands, stopping at major ports all the way north to Split or Rijeka. First island hop to Mljet, then to the 'black island' of Korcula.

Mljet is one of the loveliest islands of the Adriatic, a green jewel that's really a national park, famous for wild flowers and birdlife. Most islands are a little short of sandy beaches, but Mljet has a beautiful salt-water lagoon, where an islet supports a twelfth-century Benedictine monastery. This has been converted into a hotel and is the ideal stop for lunch. Then sail on to Korcula, which lies less than a mile off the mainland and can also be reached by the ferry from Orebic. This latter voyage gives you a marvellous view of the towers and ramparts of the walled Venetian city, which claims to be the birthplace of Marco Polo. The island itself, long and hilly and covered with vines, produces the strong Grk wine which is famous in Dalmatia.

The Venetians built the town and fortress of Korcula after they conquered the island from the Croats about 3000 years ago, and they held it until Napoleon overthrew the Venetian Republic. The town's architecture is sheer poetry, with a fine cathedral dedicated to St Mark and a marvellous fourteenth-century Abbot's Palace – a medieval gem just meant for strolling about in.

Sailing north from Korcula on one of the bigger ferries, you weave your way through scores of uninhabited islands to beautiful Hvar, a long sliver of wood-cloaked mountain, the coastline indented with deep fjord-like coves and sheltered beaches. Like Korcula, Hvar Town is Venetian and very beautiful with a deep piazza running into it from the old galley port, lined on either side with medieval or Renaissance build-ings. One of these is among the world's oldest theatres, built in 1612 and still the scene of live performances. Delightful as it is, Hvar Town is just one of several on the island and, since the local transport is both cheap and efficient, you can tour about by bus or taxi to see Starigrad and the fortified church at Vrboska.

Just across the water from Hvar lies yet another lovely island, Brac, the 'white' island. Galleys called at Brac long before the Christian era to haul away the local limestone which is still quarried. Some of it was used to build the White House in Washington, DC. Brac is full of pretty places, but the little port of Bol is perhaps the finest. It also has some good beaches and the great mountain of Vidora Gora hanging high above – the perfect vantage point, if you have the puff to climb up a little way, for a glorious view of these green islands of the Adriatic.

CHAPTER SIX

Don't Just Sit There

Not so very long ago, a change was considered as good as a rest and most people were content to spend their holidays on a beach with nothing more diverting than a little shrimping in a rockpool, nothing more energetic to break up the dozing than a wrestle with the deckchair twice a day. Things are different now.

A do-nothing holiday may still suit some, but many are ready for action. They look upon holidays as a chance to develop an interest, learn a skill, get fitter, or delve into another world or another culture. Hobby and activity holidays have become increasingly popular. So if you're bored with the traditional opt-out type, there are lots of alternatives to choose from.

Holidays with a purpose – mind-stretching or muscle-toning – now cover a vast variety of hobbies and activities. It is difficult to say at what point a hobby becomes an activity – or a sport, for that matter. However, all good hobby holidays have certain things in common. First, they should offer you the chance to pursue an interest in some depth and at a well-chosen location. Second, they must provide experienced, capable lecturers or instructors who know their subjects and can impart their knowledge with humour and enthusiasm. Third, there should be the opportunity to mix and mingle with like-minded people. Activity holidays are, in fact, a great way to make friends. People tend to go on the same one year after year, not only to continue their interests but to meet up with old mates.

Since such holidays are, by their very nature, specialised, they tend to cater for small groups. So they are generally the preserve of small, specialised tour companies – though, having said that, many of the larger operators and major hotel chains are jumping on the bandwagon and offering variations on the activity theme as part of their general programme or as a special package.

While holidays of the mind-stretching sort seem to attract slightly more mature travellers who have already tried the normal run of holidays and now prefer something a little more intellectually stimulating, the more active type of holiday still appeals to the young, fit and full-of-beans. In other words, to the Kathy Taylers of this world. *Holiday*'s action girl has tackled everything from pedalling to parascending, wall-building to walking backwards down a cliff. She's even got stuck in and worked on a kibbutz in Israel. Funnily enough, it's rarely the action bit that calls for courage on Kathy's part; as an ex-champion pentathlete she has the nerve for most of it. But one of the aspects of the kibbutz film she wasn't wildly enthusiastic about was getting covered from head to foot in grey slime. 'The Dead Sea is famous for its beautiful mud, but beautiful is hardly how I looked in front of the camera,' Kathy remembers. 'All you could see was the whites of my eyes!'

The English Tourist Board book, *Activity & Hobby Holidays*, published annually and available from Tourist Information Centres and good bookshops, is a mine of useful information and ideas. So are the national tourist offices of Scotland, Wales, Northern Ireland and countries abroad. All are keen as mustard to promote activity holidays and produce gen on almost any interest or sport. There are, of course, national differences. Wine tours happen in France, Italy and Germany; exotic wildlife safaris are the preserve of Africa, the Far East and South America. But there are plenty of fascinating choices nearer home.

Fortunately, almost every special interest or activity has a club or association and every club or association of any size has a magazine. From these, get-up-and-go holidaymakers can find out which companies cater for their particular pastime. Since many of these holidays are run by enthusiasts for enthusiasts, the standard is often exceptionally high.

Another useful publication is the *St James' Press Holiday*

Guide, which lists a huge range of special interest holidays. You don't need to buy this tome. Just pop into your local ABTA travel agent and ask to have a look at it.

The long-established Field Studies Council, which operates nine study centres in the UK and organises tours abroad, covers a wealth of subjects – brass rubbing, archaeology, photography, local history and painting, among others. National organisations which also give advice on hobby holidays and courses include The Royal Society for the Protection of Birds (RSPB) and the National Institute for Adults Continuing Education (NIACE). The NIACE issues a twice-yearly prospectus currently costing £1.15 (see address list in appendix).

If the trends of the last two decades are any yardstick, activity holidays haven't yet reached their peak. They certainly add an extra dimension to a week or fortnight's escape from the daily grind. The selection on the following pages may spur you to follow through on something you've been half thinking about – but remember, there are masses of other holidays-with-a-purpose on offer.

A *SPOT OF ART AND HISTORY*

People on both sides of the intellectual fence tend to go over the top about history. Some think, like Henry Ford, that it is bunk and see no point in exploring great acres of ancient debris. Others find their knees going weak at the sight of Syria's Krak des Chevaliers or Languedoc's Carcassonne. As with any specialised subject, it's as well to have a sense of proportion, so any good art and history holiday should balance the trudging around ancient sites and museums with free time. Most people, if the truth were told, have culture thresholds low enough to trip over. That said, there is one certain fact about history – after several thousand years, there is a lot of it about.

Most holiday operators offer optional excursions to local historical attractions – a coach tour round the ruins with some chat from the courier up front – but a proper art or history holiday will offer a carefully chosen itinerary, the guidance of knowledgeable and experienced guide/ lecturers, and best of all, the companionship of people who share your enthusiasm.

In Britain, we have the evidence of at least 2000 years of history in some delightful parts of the country. There are impressive castles in Wales and Scotland, marvellous cathedral cities like Canterbury, York and Durham, fine old towns like Rye, Winchelsea and Winchester. Many of these places are ideal for a weekend break. Many cities, like Oxford and Chester, for example, offer daily tours around the principal sights, led by a guide from the local tourist board. Many history societies and organisations like the Field Studies Council and the National Trust offer courses or guided tours of historic buildings. The National Trust now has well over a million members and the annual membership subscription (£14.50 in 1987/88) gives free admission to over 400 National Trust properties in England, Wales and Northern Ireland. Membership of the National Trust of Scotland covers you north of the border.

Of course, history doesn't stop at the Norman castle on the white cliffs of Dover. Every country has its own historic attractions which their national tourist boards are eager to promote, especially during the low season months when the crowds have gone.

France has 118 art galleries and museums in Paris, the châteaux of the Loire, walled towns like Josselin, great castles along the Dordogne. Italy is a treasure store: from Roman ruins in Rome and Pompeii, to the Renaissance city of Florence and medieval Siena, to the unique and glorious Serenissima – Venice – it is unmatched. Then there is Greece, a land full of awesome tumbled temples. Not everyone realises that some of the finest remains of Ancient Greece actually lie in Turkey – at Ephesus, Side and Aspendos. Move across the Mediterranean and history lovers can revel in the pyramids and temples of Egypt. Go east and there are the antiquities of India. Go west and there are the Aztec ruins of Mexico and the Inca cities of Peru.

There are many tour operators specialising in history-oriented tours to almost every corner of the world, some of the best being small companies affiliated directly or loosely to academic institutions. In fact, universities are often excellent sources of information about both commercial companies and non-profit-making group history-and-study tours.

Remember, even if you are more of an enthusiast than a fanatic, or merely fall into the I-don't-know-much-about-it-but-I-know-what-I-like category, you'll get more out of an art-and-history holiday if you dig into the background a bit before you set off. A guidebook with a good history content will do a lot to increase your enjoyment of the trip.

WATCHING THE BIRDS

As the Royal Society for the Protection of Birds (RSPB) has put it, conservation is about life. It's about the survival of our wildlife and the quality of our own lives. In short, it's important. Most people are concerned about the natural world, but many people wrongly believe that caring for nature, or working for conservation, is best left to the specialists and experts – which is not the case at all. Everyone can play a part. Put up a bird box in the apple tree or on a window ledge and you can provide shelter for nesting birds. Leave those nettles alone and you provide food for butterflies. Indeed, perhaps the first rule of conservation is to try to leave well alone, for nothing does as much harm to our wildlife as the relentless erosion and destruction of the habitat. Those who want to go further can join or support the RSPB, or the Worldwide Fund for Nature, or simply take an interest and go on a wildlife holiday.

Birdwatching forms part of any safari and is an immensely popular pastime with millions of devotees all over Britain. Membership of the RSPB is already well beyond a million, and growing. As a result of this enormous interest, an increasing number of large and small companies are offering wildlife and birdwatching holidays to the general public.

Birdwatching holidays, like the birds themselves, are available all over the world, but for some reason they seem to specialise in islands. In Britain, good birdwatching islands include Lundy, Shetland, Orkney, and a number of RSPB reserves off the Welsh coast. Abroad, the Seychelles, the Galapagos and Majorca are famous for their rare species.

As a hobby, or as part of a holiday, birdwatching calls for the right equipment. Good binoculars of 8×30 or 8×40 magnification are essential, as is a camera fitted with a long lens, say, 200 or 300mm, some fast film, and if possible a motor drive to catch birds in flight. A good field guide is the next essential. These can be purchased at most large bookshops.

Above all, probably the most vital requirement for successful birdwatching is a considerable amount of patience. Given this, the knowledge will come, and just learning about birds while seeing them in their natural habitat can become a really thrilling holiday.

You'll find the address of your local wildlife or birdwatching club at the nearest public reference library, or by contacting the two main organisations: The Royal Society for the Protection of Birds, and the World Wide Fund for Nature (see address list in appendix).

GOIN' FISHIN'

Fly fishing is much more than a hobby – it's an art. Like any kind of fishing, it requires skill, patience and local knowledge. Unlike many hobbies, it is one you must practise alone, getting the hang of dropping the fly oh-so, ever-so-gently, in exactly the right spot, where a brown or rainbow trout or even an elusive salmon may take the bait.

Until recently fly fishing was regarded as an elitist sport and, since nearly all British rivers are private water, simply finding a place to catch any kind of fish was neither cheap nor easy. Among Britain's four million or so committed fishing enthusiasts, fly fishing is usually regarded as the expensive end of the sport. Today, however, it has become much more widely available on lakes, reservoirs, sections of chalk rivers and trout streams rented by hotels for the use of angling guests.

If you once caught tiddlers and remember the joy of it, or if you simply want a little gentle practice with rod and line again, why not combine a few days' holiday with a fly fishing course? Some will give you the chance to try both wet-fly and dry-fly techniques. In wet-fly fishing, the fly just sinks beneath the water; in dry-fly, it sits gently on the surface. Either method requires a delicate, accurate cast to put the fly down quietly in just the right spot.

A typical fly fishing course of the kind offered by hotels in various parts of Britain lasts four days. It includes lessons on casting the fly, landing the fish, and the various knots needed to attach the fly – a small bunch of feathers woven carefully around a hook – to the line. The lessons will take up the time not spent on the river bank flailing away at the water. It may take days to land that first fish, but none of that seems to matter. Fly fishing is such an absorbing activity and requires such total concentration that time passes like a flash.

Fly fishing holidays are easily found in brochures from the main hotel chains or those in areas where the fishing is first class – Hampshire, Scotland, Ireland, northwestern Spain, Canada. The local tourist boards will have the brochures, and a phone call to the hotel you opt for will soon fill you in on when to come and how the fish are rising.

TAKING PICTURES

Nowadays a camera is part of almost everyone's holiday luggage, for no holiday is complete without its quota of snaps or slides to mull over and giggle at afterwards as you pass them around the family or bore your friends! Photography holidays, on the other hand, aim to produce a slightly higher standard of work.

The general rule for photography holidays is: shop around. Compare the facilities and, if in doubt, ask. The basic package will certainly include a competent instructor who will set projects, accentuate the positive *and* the negative, and help you develop your own individual style. It's usually very much a process of learning about the various kinds of photography: portrait, flash, landscape, wildlife, colour, black-and-white and so on, with darkroom work, lighting and film processing probably offered as extras. If the course covers tuition on the more arcane aspects of the craft, it is as well to check that the instructors are suitably qualified, the group not too large and the facilities adequate: a darkroom which is only available for one hour a week is not much use.

Usually you are expected to bring your own cameras and basic equipment, while the course provides lights and heavier professional gear, perhaps even tripods.

What do you want to photograph? The old cathedral cities of France and England are ideal for photographic holidays, providing unlimited subjects and a great variety of indoor and outdoor scenes. If you're keener on plants, wildlife and landscape, you have the whole world at your feet. Remember always to take an adequate supply of film, especially if you're heading for out-of-the-way places or the third world countries. The enthusiasm generated by exotic locations can gobble up roll after roll, and you don't want to run out where film supplies are poor.

You don't, of course, have to travel far or even keep on the move to enjoy your camera hobby and have a holiday at the same time. There are some very good courses in sybaritic places which combine photography with all the usual holiday pleasures of good eating, good company, sun and swimming.

The best places to look for photography holidays are the *St*

James' Press Holiday Guide (at any ABTA travel agent), and the photographic magazines, which often themselves run holiday courses. National tourist offices will also know of photography holidays available in their countries.

PAINTING PICTURES

A growing number of people choose a painting holiday to do something they have been intending to do since they left school: take up their sketchpad or paintbrush and easel and learn how to paint and draw. Everyone knows it's difficult. Everyone thinks – correctly – that it must be fun.

Many amateur artists begin to paint and draw on a summer course at home or abroad. The place matters a lot, so be careful to choose surroundings that appeal to you – scenery you really want to catch on canvas. Make certain, too, that the standard of tuition is high. Here again, the national or regional tourist offices can suggest suitable schools, courses or centres, and a good look at their facilities and the number of years they've been operating is a fair guide to their standard. Poor art schools don't last long.

The cost of equipment is quite small, even if you're starting from scratch, and any artist materials shop will be well-used to beginners and willing to supply good advice to go with all you need. This is, basically, three different sorts of brush, a putty rubber, pencils, paints, masking tape, a stool and an easel – all of which applies equally to watercolour and oils. Something less than £50 should be sufficient for these basics. The cost of the holiday will vary according to the location and accommodation. Some holiday painting courses go hand in hand with lush living, while others are more spartan. Some include art appreciation tuition and tours of local museums and galleries. All give you plenty of opportunity to offer and receive criticism when you assess each other's work.

Art defies frontiers, but the Greek islands have the light, Tuscany has the tradition and Provence the spirit of Van Gogh and Cézanne. Every area of Britain has at least one good painting holiday centre and one or more famous local artist –

you need look no further than Flatford Mill in Constable Country, now a field study centre, to realise that amateur artists aren't short of places to go.

COOKING FOR FUN

Enjoying good food is one of the main pleasures of any holiday. Perfecting your culinary expertise is also a pleasure if you're a really keen cook. A number of hotels in different parts of Europe deploy their chefs outside the confines of the kitchen and show guests how those delicious meals come about – at a price. Learning about good food and how to cook, serve and appreciate it adds another dimension to the trip. For after you've watched or helped the master chef prepare the food in the morning, you get to consume the results at lunch!

You should be aware of the fine difference between cookery courses and cookery holidays. Cookery courses, of which a number are run by long established cookery schools or modern restaurants here and abroad, are designed for chefs and people in the profession. Cookery holidays and gourmet weekends are rather more casual, although they also demand a love and appreciation of good food. Gourmet weekends of a high standard have flourished for over 20 years at Torquay's Imperial Hotel. Many other hotels around the country now offer short breaks where the chef presents some special dishes for the education as well as the enjoyment of the guests. Other residential cookery courses are more or less custom built as a holiday, like those at the Grange, Beckington, near Bath, where you can stay for four days to four weeks, and the only food you eat is the food you cook yourself.

France, that gastronomic paradise, naturally has a number of well-established holiday cookery courses. These at Montreuil-sur-Mer, Le Touquet, Dieppe and Paris, although the centres do tend to move about from year to year. The courses vary as to what dishes they prepare and how many participants they permit. The more people present, the less chance to actually cook; the fewer present, the higher the price. . . .

In France the chef generally prepares the meal, stopping at intervals to demonstrate technique and answer questions. The results are then whisked away for final preparation and presentation. One meal served at lunch or dinner is usually enough for any one day, so there is plenty of time to do other things – tour the countryside to see the sights, have a round of golf or visit a local cellar or *fromagerie*. The week – and a week is usually enough – almost inevitably ends with a banquet and an attack of indigestion! It's paradise for foodies, but can often be rather too much for anyone not used to rich eating. The benefits nevertheless can be far-reaching if your cooking improves at home as a result.

Information on cookery courses and gourmet weekends can be obtained from our own national tourist offices, regional tourist boards and the French Government Tourist Office in London for France. Classified ad sections in the glossy magazines are also a good source of up-market cookery breaks.

LEARNING ABOUT ANTIQUES

Holidays for lovers of antiques fall into two categories: the private ones where you hunt for that piece of glass or silver to complete your collection, and the appreciation ones where you join up with other enthusiasts to look at antiques and learn more about them. The antique-study jaunt follows the pattern of other thematic activity holidays and generally offers a guide/lecturer as course leader, with talks and visits to museums and country homes.

Most experts in antiques tend to specialise in some period or subject – eighteenth-century English painting, glass, pottery, arms and armour, furniture (the speciality of the late Arthur Negus, who almost single handedly created the present popular interest in antiques) – so at any one course, various guest speakers may pop in to cover their particular subject. The holidays therefore are usually based at a fixed centre where the experts can arrive to deliver a lecture or accompany an outside visit.

Antique holidays are often advertised in leading magazines

featuring antiques, and they tend to be set in very pleasant places – the Cotswolds, the hunting shires, the wilder parts of Kent or Sussex – places where there are plenty of historic homes and a good clutch of antique shops. The pleasures of the subject are not hard to define. Hearing experts who can transmit their delight in their chosen field and show exactly how this or that artefact came to be created is something most people can enjoy.

The great bonus is that these holidays are usually on offer during the autumn and winter – the perfect antidote to dreary days. They're held over weekends and organised by either the main hotel groups or some of the larger independent hotels. A good selection can be found in the ETB handbook, *Activity and Hobby Holidays*, available from Tourist Information Centres and good bookshops.

TRAILING AFTER VINES

Wine tasting holidays are off to a head start since they happen in some of the most attractive parts of the world: the regions of Burgundy, Aquitaine or Alsace in France, the Chianti country of Italy, California's Napa Valley, Australia's Murray River, the hills of Rioja or the plains of Valdepeñas in Spain. Wherever the grapevine grows, wine lovers follow. The best holidays are guided by someone who knows all about it, in the case of British companies usually a member of that prestigious group, the Masters of Wine – many of whom are women, incidentally. They can lead their clients unerringly to the finest vintages.

Then, since good wine is only at its best when accompanied by good food, you tend to stay in hotels with good restaurants and eat from menus designed to enhance and complement the qualities of the local vintages. In the course of visiting the various châteaux or wineries, you also learn a great deal and may spot a bargain in an inexpensive case or two to bring home.

The wine holiday companies are always run by wine lovers, and their tours are organised to show you the very best each country has to offer, which is not necessarily the most expensive. The world is now awash with wine, and following the grape can lead you into some rather unexpected places. For example, there are wine tours to Yugoslavia and Bulgaria – not countries that might immediately spring to mind when considering the pleasures of the vine, but many a high street vintner is now doing a brisk trade in the excellent state-subsidised labels from these countries. That said, the bulk of wine-tasting holidays take place in western Europe and are concentrated on the main wine regions.

There's nothing to stop you touring on a private basis – in your car on a break, or on a fly-drive holiday. All you need is one of the many good wine books currently available and a selection of leaflets from the relevant national tourist office which will be keen to promote visits to and sales from its national vineyards. Most château wine producers or local wholesalers are bottlers and keen to welcome visitors. They'll provide a guide for a tour of their cellars, which inevitably ends with a tasting back in the showroom and the expectation that you'll buy something.

In western Europe, all the wine regions now have well-marked wine trails round a selection of well-stocked cellars: Routes du Vin in France, for instance, where there are also wine-tasting stalls – *dégustations* – on many of the little winding roads that lead through the vineyards.

A comprehensive list of wine tours and courses can be obtained from The Wine Development Board (see address list in appendix). Good books for wine buffs include the *World Atlas of Wine* (Mitchell Beazley) which is particularly useful for travellers because it includes maps, and Tony Laithwaite's *Great Wine Trek* (Harrap) which suggests tours.

DIGGING INTO GARDENING

A glance around suburbia on any summer's evening will soon reveal one great truth about the British – we are a nation of gardeners. Tens of millions of us turn out every weekend to tend our plot of earth, so it is not too surprising that a number of companies, hotels, or a combination of the two, run gardening holidays.

A typical weekend might begin with an evening get-together in the garden of some pleasant hotel where guests meet a well-known gardener – often someone familiar from the gardening programmes on TV or radio. There are usually visits led by the gardener-guide to beautiful gardens, great and small, in the area, a lecture or two and question-and-answer sessions. The whole exercise is set off by good food and the chance to talk endlessly about gardening to other enthusiasts. Many of these weekends will have a theme or even several themes: herb gardens, Alpine flowers and shrubs, historic gardens, or the work of famous gardeners like Capability Brown or the great Le Nôtre in France.

Gardening holidays are most often brief and based at home – find them in the *St James' Press Holiday Guide*. You'll also get good information from the Royal Horticultural Society, the National Trust, and among the classified ads in the gardening magazines. Like many other hobby holidays, they are usually timed to fill hotels during the autumn and winter months.

ON YOUR BIKE

Anyone who enjoys touring anywhere knows the delights that await the traveller who avoids motorways in favour of byways. Exploring by bicycle can show you an even more remote part of the countryside – one you'd never find by car. The back country of France is a perfect example. It's covered in little lanes and farm tracks and you can wander from one sleepy village to another, taking all the time in the world.

Either choose an organised touring holiday, with overnight accommodation arranged for you, or take your own bike with you – it's cheap and easy. There is no charge for bicycles on the cross-Channel ferries and short journeys on French Railways are also free for your wheels, but it's worth paying the few pounds registration fee for journeys over 100 miles to take the train south to the vineyards of the Rhône Valley. Here you can combine your cycling with the culinary delights which are so much a part of a French holiday. The fresh air and exercise means your self-indulgence at dinnertime can be guilt-free. It's clearly safer not to be drunk in charge of a bicycle after drinking with your meal or wine-tasting, but there's plenty of time during the long evenings to appreciate the regional good things. Try a bottle of Hermitage, Crozes-Hermitage or Cornas.

Cycling can be pretty hot work in the sun, so it's a good idea to put most of the miles behind you by lunchtime. Then you might welcome a dip in one of the many streams and rivers which are safe for swimming. Many villages also have an outdoor pool in which to cool off. One of the villages on your itinerary could be St-Donat, where a Bach Festival is held each July. The music is played in the church – beautifully tranquil and cool after the heat of the open road.

The pretty village of Alixan has only about 100 houses but there is a family-run hotel. The countryside around produces cherries, peaches, sunflowers, melons and walnuts. Also look out for farms selling home-made goat cheese. Smelly but nice!

Montélimar is also worth a visit. A busy town with museums, a château and a twelfth-century fortress, it's most famous for its nougat.

If it's the quiet life you're after, pick your route carefully and the only traffic you'll meet will be tractors and combine harvesters. If you do meet French drivers, you'll find them surprisingly considerate towards cyclists.

A good set of panniers will carry as much as a medium sized suitcase, but travelling light makes the pedal pushing a little easier. Training shoes or strong sandals are essential for safe cycling, and it's best to avoid jeans because they can become uncomfortable and hot. An absolute must is a puncture repair kit. If you take an organised holiday, this will be provided along with a demonstration on how to use it.

For details about travelling with your bike in France, write to SNCF for the leaflet *Guide du Train et du Vélo* (see address list in appendix).

IN THE SADDLE

Horseriding and pony trekking holidays have long been a popular way to explore the British Isles. The landscape of Wales might well have been designed for trekkers and riders, and who could resist the exhilarating, windswept gallops across the wild moors and remote tracks of Scotland? The lush greenness of Ireland, too, is a perfect backdrop for a horseback holiday break. And England offers a wide variety of areas suitable for riding. Some are easily reached from London, ideal for city dwellers who want to feel the wind on their faces.

The word 'canter' owes its origin to the county of Kent – it's derived from the slower pace of gallop taken by pilgrims along their way across the North Downs to Canterbury. Today, you can still follow the hoofmarks of their horses, passing through some of the loveliest scenery of Surrey and Kent. The path stretches 140 miles between Farnham and Dover.

Hampshire contains one of the most popular riding forests – the New Forest. Originally enclosed by William the Conqueror as a royal hunting ground, it now encompasses thousands of acres of unspoiled woodland, soft, springy turf and heath. You can ride all day without crossing a road. The native ponies are a common sight, and early risers will often spot one of several species of deer. There are stables throughout the area, especially around Lyndhurst. You'll also find plenty of B & B accommodation, but it is in demand in the summer, so book in advance.

With the obvious risks on top of a horse, it's best to find a mount from a centre approved by the British Horse Society. A horse that's well cared for, proper supervision and a local guide are essential for a problem-free holiday. A book published in association with the BHS lists over 500 inspected and approved riding establishments throughout the British Isles, offering tuition, hacking and holidays. It's called *Where to Ride* and is obtainable from the British Horse Society (see address list in appendix). Check the current price with them.

WALKABOUT

If you think holidays of the energetic kind aren't your style, you might be surprised at how much fun a walking holiday can be. You don't have to be super fit and fearless to enjoy it, so why not have a go? You can set your own pace, get right into some magnificent scenery, and do yourself some good into the bargain. And it *is* a bargain – walking is free.

A slow ramble along country lanes and bridle paths might whet your appetite for something bigger. There are so many areas in Britain providing good walking country that, wherever you live, you won't need to travel far to find one. For easy walks, sturdy shoes or trainers are fine. If you want to tackle stiffer terrain, then a pair of supportive boots are a good idea.

Your aim should be to travel as light as possible, but never forget how fickle the British weather can be. Always carry a jersey and waterproofs if you're heading for the hills.

Many people slot a little gentle walking into their holiday (see *Tiptoe through the Tyrol* in Chapter 10), but more and more are fitting a holiday around their walking. Good networks of Youth Hostels, farmhouses and guesthouses provide accommodation in most walking areas. All you need in order to plan your own holiday is an Ordnance Survey map of your chosen part of the country, the YHA book (see address list in appendix) and/or an accommodation guide from the local Tourist Board. Don't overestimate how far you can walk.

Alternating days of walking with rest days usually works best.

If you prefer to have the organising done for you, many companies run walking holidays in areas such as the Lake District, the Pennines, the Cotswolds and the West Country. Details are in the *Activity and Hobby Holidays* book published by the English Tourist Board. Another good source of information is the Ramblers Association (see address list in appendix). Walking holidays abroad are legion.

ACTION UNLIMITED

Fancy walking backwards down a sheer 200-foot cliff with just a rope to cling to? Or maybe riding along the crest of a wave balancing precariously on your surfboard? If you're the kind of person who likes to have a go at almost anything, a multi-activity holiday centre could give unlimited thrills.

You've probably heard about the children's summer camps, which are perfect for getting your offspring healthily tired doing anything from abseiling to surfing. Well, many centres also cater for adults who hate standing on the sidelines.

You usually choose two activities a day, often from a selection of 20 or so. In some centres you concentrate on your chosen options. In others, you can choose afresh each day. Meals and accommodation are organised for you. The standard varies between companies, so check that you're likely to get what you want before you book.

Concern about safety is important when you or your children embark on new adventures such as canoeing, motor cycling or rock climbing. At present there is no government control, but the British Holiday Association was formed in 1986 in order to monitor and improve standards of safety and instruction. Check whether an activity holiday company is a member of the Association, and don't be afraid to ask questions before you book. Here are the questions you should ask to help you find the right place:

1 Will the holiday be run by the company named in the brochure? (If the holiday is subcontracted, speak directly with the subcontractors.)

2 How experienced are the staff? (They should have qualifications from the governing body of any adventure sport they teach.)

3 Will you or your child get the activities you ask for?

4 Are all activities at the centre?

5 What about safety precautions? (If the centre is recognised by the governing bodies of specialist sports, certain standards of teaching and equipment should have been met.)

6 What is included in the price?

7 What insurance cover is there? (This is especially important.)

If the centre is used by a local education authority to send school kids on courses, then it will conform to guidelines set out by the Department of Education and Science. These centres will have been inspected by the Local Education Authority, so you can always check with the LEA of that area.

CONTRIBUTING TO CONSERVATION

Heaving lumps of rock around might sound like taking the activity part of a holiday a little too far. But if you're interested in conservation, enjoy the outdoor life, and don't mind some hard work, one of the Natural Break working holidays of the British Trust for Conservation Volunteers (BTCV) might be just your style. As an added incentive, the total cost of board and lodging for a week is about £20.

The Trust organises about 400 holidays each year, ranging from weekends to ten-day breaks and based in many different parts of Britain. The theme of all these holidays is conservation and preserving the environment. One project is the maintenance of the Grosmont-to-Pickering steam railway line in the North York moors. It was one of the first to be built by the 'father of the railways', George Stephenson, and each year the BTCV run a holiday to repaint the stations, repair fencing and rebuild broken stretches of the wall lining the track. You are taught the traditional craft of dry-stone walling and have the satisfaction of saving the moorland sheep which wander through the gaps onto the track.

You sleep in old railway carriages at Goathland station and queue up for the outhouse shower. Toilets are outhouses, too, the women's at least nearer than the men's! Meals are served in an old first-class dining car. And as you do the cooking yourselves, buying the ingredients from your week's donations (about the cost of a parking ticket each!), the food is not exactly ambrosia and nectar – more like beans and bangers.

If all this sounds a bit primitive, it is meant to. The accommodation on these working holidays ranges from just comfortable to very basic, and wherever you go you'll need a sleeping bag. Most people find that, after a day's work in the fresh air, they feel so healthily tired they can sleep anywhere.

If the idea of building a wall doesn't excite you, how about hedge laying, planting trees, laying nature trails or footpaths, or even digging ponds for natterjack toads? Throughout the year and all over the country there is conservation work to be done.

All evenings and one day a week are free to explore and enjoy the area you're helping to conserve – or to try out the local hostelries with your new workmates. Anyone from 16 to 71 is welcome; also children from eight upwards with their parents, on the family weekends.

You wouldn't go on a break like this for the luxury of it or if you're fussed about getting bruised knees or broken fingernails. By the way, some sturdy shoes and working gloves make life easier. But 25 000 conservation volunteers carrying out 190 000 days of work each year can't be wrong – so for a cheap and highly satisfying activity holiday, contact the British Trust for Conservation Volunteers (see address list in appendix).

Similar working holidays, known as Acorn Camps, are run by the National Trust. Projects include haymaking in the Chilterns, restoring footpaths in a Victorian garden and improving the wildlife habitat on an island nature reserve. Details from Acorn Camp Holidays, The National Trust (see address list in appendix).

THE KIBBUTZ EXPERIENCE

If it's not so much a break from work you're after but more a working break, one way to earn your keep and a few extra pennies is to become a volunteer on a kibbutz in Israel. Since the start of the Kibbutz Movement, hundreds of thousands of people have visited and briefly become a part of these communal societies. There are 260 of them.

Kibbutz means a collection or community in Hebrew, and that's what it is – a collection of people living and working together. The volunteers live in their own area of the community but eat with the kibbutz members. They help out with every kind of job imaginable – in the kitchen, on the farms and in the factories. The work is hard, sometimes even boring; the pay is barely pocket money, about £10 a month, and the living accommodation can be very basic. But none of this seems to deter most volunteers, who often enjoy the experience so much they try to stay longer. Visits must be at least four weeks in length and can go up to three months.

The six-hour, six-day week often starts at dawn and ends

early so there's plenty of leisure time to visit biblical sites, Arab villages, Israeli towns, beaches and bazaars. Israel is a country of immense cultural and physical contrasts and an amazing variety of landscapes. There are mountains and deserts, fields and forests, valleys and lakes. Some of the land is achingly barren, some of it lushly cultivated, transformed by sophisticated irrigation schemes.

Most kibbutzim run excursions to local places of interest. Otherwise, borrow a bike or a horse, or use the excellent buses. After a month of work, you could use your extra two days off to travel further afield, perhaps to Jerusalem, the Dead Sea, Eilat or the Sea of Galilee.

As the supply of volunteers more than meets the demand, the Israeli Government Tourist Office warns travellers not to leave the UK without written assurance of a place on a kibbutz. You can obtain this by applying to Kibbutz Representatives who will allocate you to a kibbutz (see address list in appendix). Don't write directly to a kibbutz unless you are making a return visit.

A book called *Kibbutz Volunteer* by John Bedford, published by Vacation Work, is invaluable reading before you go (see address list in appendix). *Summer jobs in Britain* and *Summer Jobs Abroad*, edited by Susan Griffith for the same publisher, are useful for anyone interested in working holidays.

CHAPTER SEVEN

Spring, Autumn & Winter Breaks

When it comes to planning a holiday, never underestimate the benefits of the short as opposed to the long of it. Even doctors say several brief breaks are better for you than one annual crash-out, rather in the way a lot of light snacks are easier on the digestion than one heavy meal. Less of a shock to the system. How nice it would be if we could all afford several brief breaks, but there's no doubt a growing number of us manage to take at least one or two as well as our main holiday.

What's more, since the holiday industry is geared to operate in all seasons taking time off outside the bottle-neck months of July and August is both easy and makes good sense. The prospect of being stranded when the airports seize up with the sheer volume of peak-season traffic is one that swiftly knocks the pixie-dust off hopes for a perfect holiday. Families with school-age children often have little choice, but more and more are taking the option of going away in the Easter holidays.

If your off-season break is a second holiday, you probably want something different, something more stimulating than flopping down on the beach. Spring and autumn are the nicest times for touring by coach or car, especially in territory that might be too hot for comfort in the summer. Sometimes they are the *only* times to go for specific attractions – April for tulip fields in Holland, October for the *nouveau* cider in Normandy. And European cities can be wonderful in winter, when there are no leaves on the trees and you get a bare bones view of the architecture. In winter, tramping the streets is less enervating, museums are less draining, seats on public transport and tables in restaurants are more easily available and everyone from hotel receptionists to street vendors are more amenable. Add to these advantages the special winter pleasures of sniffing chestnuts roasting, admiring foggy sunsets as the city lights come up, snuggling into steamy bars to enjoy the local firewater, and who'd want to go city sightseeing any other time?

The *Holiday* programme has to, unfortunately. Filming cities is complex enough without the drawback of limited daylight, so we usually have to go with the crowds in late spring, summer and early autumn. That lands us with other problems: the heads of a hundred pedestrians in the way as the camera tries to focus on some intriguing detail; traffic snarling up and drowning the reporter's voice so we have to do the piece-to-camera again and again. I find this is sometimes hilarious when the camera is at a distance, out of the sight of passers-by, and I'm fitted with a hidden radio microphone. When people see me sitting down at a café table and spouting loudly into thin air, they think I'm round the twist! On one occasion a man at the next table told me to shut up!

In Britain, winter breaks can be bargain breaks. Most hotel chains, and some privately owned ones, offer splendid weekend

VISIT PARIS
IN SPRING!

SEE THE EIFFEL TOWER
~ IN FLOWER ~

packages. These not only include accommodation and meals but all kinds of additional incentives, like cut-rate ferry trips to France if you're staying near a Channel port, or a free 'do' at the hotel hairdresser. Competition is fierce, so shop around the brochures for extra value. At a Basingstoke hotel one November, we found they'd installed whirlpools in the bathrooms. Despite the picture of luxury that 'whirlpool' conjures up, the bathrooms were minute. We decided to film Kathy Tayler in hers. While she languished in the bubbles, the cameraman perched on top of the loo, the sound recordist sat in the basin and the director shouted 'Action' through the door. Talk about a tight spot! (In case you were wondering, Kathy was wearing her bikini.)

One way and another, it was a lot more comfortable than Bill Buckley's dip in a Swedish lake in September (when, by the way, you get great bargains on North Sea crossings to Scandinavia). The idea was that he should swim around the lake clad in a wet suit, pretending to be a cousin of the Loch Ness monster. The trouble was the loaned wet suit was a bit on the small side and we ended up with the representative of the Swedish Tourist Board and our film director – both women – rubbing moisturising cream all over his legs to try to force them into the suit!

Off-season breaks are often more fun than main holidays. There's so much less pressure involved in the booking, the paying, the getting there and back. The ideas in this chapter offer places you could go to at the drop of a hint – seaside, countryside and cities at home and abroad, as well as one or two winter sunshine destinations that aren't too expensive.

RAMBLING THROUGH RYE

There is something very English about Rye. It simply couldn't exist anywhere else but on the soft southern shore of England, an ancient little seaport left high and dry on the foreshore when the sea crept out beyond reach – historic, charming, and very beautiful.

Even from a distance Rye is a picture, standing on a small hill above the coastal plain. Once upon a time the Channel lapped at the very walls of this Cinque Port town. Then the waters retreated and left Rye well inland, though still linked to the sea by a tidal channel which today serves yachts and fishing boats. Close to, every inch of Rye is picturesque, with its red brick walls, leaning roofs and steep, narrow, often cobbled streets lined by medieval buildings draped in ivy, Virginia creeper or wisteria. Hardly surprising that the town has attracted painters and writers over the years, from Van Dyck to Henry James and, more recently, E.F. Benson. He re-created Rye as Tilling in his popular *Mapp and Lucia*, which shows where all the Benson characters lived and shopped and went about their business. Benson's ever-increasing admirers add their numbers to the tens of thousands of people who flock to Rye every year. There's no denying that today it caters mostly for tourists – every second shop is a café or restaurant and the one in between sells antiques or souvenirs – but happily nothing has quite managed to spoil the charm of this delightful little town or change its essential character.

Explore on foot – parking is anyway impossible – and begin, perhaps, with a look at the splendid relic of the old walls, the Ypres Tower, and Rye church. This Church of St Mary the Virgin is mainly Norman, badly damaged and much repaired after the French raided the town in 1377. It's full of stained glass and brasses and attractive memorials, and the clock in the tower which dates from the mid-sixteenth century is said to be the oldest working clock in the country. A few minutes' walk away in West Street is the supposedly haunted Lamb House. Henry James, who lived here from 1898 to 1916, claimed to have been visited on a number of occasions by the spectre of an old lady. Lamb House is now a museum of Henry James' work and the parlour displays examples of his writing and personal possessions.

For a little light relief, take a stroll down the High Street from the Landgate, in and out of the many antique shops, or visit the Mermaid Inn which dates from the Middle Ages and also boasts a ghost – some guests have seen it quite recently and recorded the fact in the hotel guest book!

Rye is worth a long weekend visit – or even several weekend visits, especially out of the main tourist season. When all the town's sights have been seen, there remains the lovely countryside round about. Rye is the perfect centre for exploring Romney Marsh, visiting the rival attractions of Bodiam Castle in the Rother Valley, or having a look round the seaside resort of Hastings. Needless to say, there are plenty of places to stay in town – and if a ghost should happen to drop into your room around midnight, it is sure to be perfectly friendly, like everyone else hereabouts.

THE ENGLISH RIVIERA

Elegant hotels in shades of clotted cream and immaculate gardens sprouting palm trees – the Torbay area of south Devon is justifiably named the English Riviera. At almost any time of year it has something to offer. There is the smart resort of Torquay, whose mild relaxing air has been rated highly by people in need of a pick-me-up since the middle of the last century. Like Rome, it is built on seven hills and has panoramic views across the wide sweep of the bay where, incidentally, Napoleon had his one and only close look at England. He described it as *très belle*.

The town and its surroundings are renowned for their gardens and lush, almost sub-tropical, shrubbery, while the double harbour, always busy with regattas and yacht races in summer, provides a nicely nautical outlook off season. A brisk walk along the seafront is usually accompanied by the soothing tinkle of rigging ruffled by the breeze. There are also lovely walks along four beaches and over the cliff tops to Babbacombe Bay with its unique landscaped miniature gardens.

Only a brief drive or bus ride from the town centre is Cockington, a tiny village which is almost too olde England to be true – a little huddle of thatched cottages, an old forge, a medieval church and sixteenth-century manor house. Outside of July and August, when it is impossibly clogged with cars, Cockington is unflustered and utterly charming.

Torquay's next-door neighbour is Paignton, an ideal family resort with superb sands, a pier and small harbour. There's plenty else of interest in the off season. Oldway Mansion, for instance, the palatial home built by the Singer of sewing machine fame, is now an excellent Civic Centre. There's one of the best zoos in the UK and, close by, the lovely Botanical Gardens. Paignton is also the starting point for the steam railway which runs down to Kingswear where you can ferry across to Dartmouth and visit the famous Naval College.

The third of Torbay's townships is Brixham where William and Mary landed in 1688 at the start of the Glorious Revolution we've recently been celebrating. Today it's a lively fishing port with houses rising in tiers from the harbour, and if you climb to the hilltop called the Battery, you'll get one of the best views of the whole of Torbay.

Also within easy reach by car or coach tour from any of the Torbay resorts is the wild beauty of Dartmoor National Park, one of the few remaining wide open spaces in southern England where hardy little Dartmoor ponies roam; there's Exeter, Devon's county town with its fine cathedral, excellent shopping and one of the UK's best maritime museums; or the historic port of Plymouth. Its old Barbican quarter is worth a visit and you shouldn't miss a walk on the Hoe where Sir Francis Drake spun out his game of bowls while the Armada advanced over the horizon.

ELEGANT EDINBURGH

If Scotland's wild side is the great escape from civilisation, it is perhaps all the more remarkable that its capital is one of the most civilised in Europe. Often dubbed the 'Athens of the north' for its culture and its own 'Parthenon' (the spectacular but unfinished memorial to soldiers killed in the Peninsular War), Edinburgh puts modern Athens in the shade. The grey granite city is a knockout even in the dead of winter – though a little sunshine always helps – and despite jokes about its 'refayned' inhabitants being ever so prim and proper, it can be frivolous, friendly and fun.

Edinburgh's profile alone gives it a head start, with that splendid eleventh-century castle towering on Castle Rock. It's here that the annual Military Tattoo takes place at Festival time. From the castle, once the seat of Scottish kings and queens, the

Royal Mile leads steeply downwards, and the narow closes of the old town cluster around it. The New Town, built at the turn of the eighteenth century, is a feast of Georgian terraces, and every now and then you glimpse Princess Street Gardens falling away in folds from the bustle of the busy main thoroughfares.

There are historical landmarks like Holyrood Palace, where poor old Rizzio, secretary to Mary Queen of Scots, was murdered before her eyes, and historical oddities like Lady Stair's house. It has a round tower, spiral staircase and reminders of literary luminaries Scott, Burns and Stevenson.

There are so many museums and galleries that you need a list of what to see in order to decide what to eliminate. You'll get cultural indigestion, never mind sore feet, if you try to cover the lot – but don't miss the enchanting Museum of Childhood, full of toys, doll's houses and old nursery paraphernalia.

The best plan is to let the city happen around you. Drop in to a bar and listen to the lilt and burr of local voices. Comb the alleyways around the Royal Mile for curiosities. One is the Scottish Celtic Armourers who make beautiful swords and daggers, some to Royal Warrant, as well as bagpipes. When the madding summer crowds have evaporated, the craftsmen will often invite you into their workshops. For the man or woman who has everything, you can order a skian dhu. Skian dhus are tiny daggers that the Scots traditionally used to tuck in their socks when otherwise disarmed on entering hostile territory. They are exquisite little weapons, their hilts embellished with ivory or topaz, and they make unusual if expensive paperweights. You can have them sent anywhere in the world.

You can also mail a haggis to a friend from Crombies, shop for tartans and Harris tweed titfers, and trace your Scottish ancestry – almost every name in the book, it seems, can be linked to a Scottish clan!

For a change of scene, catch one of Edinburgh's shining plum-coloured buses and make for Deans Village, an ancient milling community that is a delightful hotch-potch of converted mills and old bakeries by the Water of Leith on the city's northwestern fringes. Here you can picnic by the river, watch people fishing and hardly believe you're so close to the city's core.

NB. The Edinburgh International Festival begins in early August and runs to mid-September. While the city is marvellous to visit then, you need to book somewhere to stay *months* in advance.

LONDON TOWN

Dear old London. Yes, it's strewn with litter, parking's impossible and eating out sometimes calls for a second mortgage, but there's really nowhere else quite like it.

The shopping is still the best in Britain. Harrods is virtually a national monument. Even if you only window gaze or take away a souvenir mug, don't miss the food halls with their fabulous tiled ceilings. Oxford Street is less exciting; it may be world famous, but it's mainly just a row of chain stores selling the same items as their provincial branches – with the possible exception of Marks & Spencer, Marble Arch, which is their showcase shop and has many tempting specials. The pedestrianised Covent Garden area is fun, and it's amusing to go to Sloane Street or New Bond Street to gasp at the prices and the glitzier shoppers.

The speediest way to get around is by tube – the London Underground – although it can be a bit menacing at night. (Get an excursion rate for a bunch of tickets at any main station.) On Sunday, take the Northern Line to Camden Town and follow the throng to Camden Market. Here you'll find literally hundreds of stalls selling just about everything from third-hand tat to high-price art. Regular customers, as exotic as the goods, ooze street credibility.

If your London trip is a short one (most hotels do bargain break weekends) a good way to take in all the famous landmarks like Buckingham Palace, the Houses of Parliament and the Tower, is on a sightseeing bus. London Regional Transport and a host of private companies operate them.

In the theatre capital of the world, you'll almost certainly want to see a show. The choice is vast: comedies, thrillers, musicals, ballet, opera, serious drama – you name it! Queue at the ticket booth in Leicester Square for half price tickets on the day you want to go – no tickets in advance. But you don't have to stick to the West End. There are hundreds of fringe theatres lurking in the least likely places where actors, sometimes well-known ones, slog their guts out for 20 quid a week in front of a maximum audience of 30. In the fringe you take pot luck. You might sit shivering on a hard seat through a piece of incomprehensible experimental claptrap, or you might thrill to an innovative new work destined for mega-success. ('Oh, we saw that *ages* ago in the fringe,' you'll be able to crow later on!) Buy *Time Out* or *City Limits* magazines to track down these shows.

Eating out is rather a case of pot luck too. You can pay a lot for a little or enjoy a feast for a reasonable price. The London Tourist Board (under the eaves of Victoria Station) have booklets on where to eat cheaply, as well as stacks of other useful information. Overseas visitors must sometimes wonder why a capital bursting with Chinese, Japanese, Indian, Italian, French and American restaurants is so short of British ones. You do have to hunt around a bit for indigenous cuisine, but try Porters at Covent Garden for traditional British pies (such as good old steak and kidney), Geales Fish Restaurant in Farmer Street, Notting Hill Gate, for the best fish and chips, and the Hungry Horse in Fulham Road for upmarket English grub.

London seethes, especially in summer, and you may want to escape its crowded centre. Take a Thames pleasure boat to the Royal Botanic Gardens at Kew, where you can admire more than 25 000 species of plants gathered from all around the world. At Hampton Court Palace, built in 1514 and once owned by Henry VIII, the gardens are also beautiful and the famous maze is not as baffling as you might think. You *won't* be lost in there for ever!

Or boat down to nautical Greenwich which has the National Maritime Museum and the Royal Naval College. You can see round the tea clipper *Cutty Sark* or *Gipsy Moth IV*, in which Sir Francis Chichester sailed single handed round the world in 1966.

Everyone knows about Madame Tussaud's waxworks, but try also the London Dungeon just by London Bridge with its life-size tableaux showing the appalling torture, death and disease of medieval Britain. Very scary – and unsuitable for under-10s! One other thing you must do. It only takes a moment, it's free and it will give you one of the biggest laughs of your stay. Find an estate agent's window and look at the property prices!

TULIPS AND AMSTERDAM

In the seventeenth century, a peripatetic Dutchman brought home the bulb of a vivid flower with waxen petals which he'd admired in Persia. He tried growing it in his back garden and it thrived. That was how the tulip came to Europe, the Dutch came to start what was eventually to develop into a billion-guilder industry, and why nowadays thousands converge on the Netherlands each spring to gaze at the spectacle of massed blooms in the tulip fields.

You can get there quite cheaply by boat and train or coach, but it's almost worth the extra to fly in order to see the bulbfields from the air as you approach – a giant's paint box with great blocks of red, yellow, white and shades of pink.

Holland is very flat, like Norfolk, and very moist. Ideal conditions for spring flowers. While you don't get to tiptoe through the tulips – that part of the scene is viewed from the windows of a coach – you *are* able to wander with the crowds through the amazing gardens of Keukenhof. As well as tulips, there are drifts of narcissi, crocuses, polyanthus and hyacinths beside the lake and beneath the trees. The sheer abundance of colour against April-green lawns puts a smile on everyone's face.

On most Dutch tulip tours a trip to a flower auction is also thrown in – surprisingly high tech with computers, other automated hardware and vast crates of culled blooms visible only through glass from the visitors' gallery.

For gardeners and garden lovers, all this adds up to the perfect spring break – a Dutch treat, in fact, since most organised trips include a full programme of excursions to other bits of Holland that are too good to miss. Vollendam, for instance, an old fishing village right on the polder lands, where the legendary boy stuck his finger in the dyke. If you keep eyes peeled you may catch sight of some of the older fishing folk who still wear national dress. They're shy of being stared at, so it's only polite to ask before you point a camera in their direction.

Cheese farms and clogmakers feature strongly on tulip itineraries and there's usually also a visit to Delft – an unbearable temptation for anyone collecting blue-and-white china. Delft is a delightful town, built on a web of canals like Amsterdam only smaller, more peaceful and provincial.

Amsterdam is a marvellous city, and a good base for touring. The centre has changed little since the 1600s. It was then that the ships of the Dutch East Indies Company sailed the seven seas to fill their hulls with cargoes of spices, sugar, tea and tobacco – and curly gabled mansions built on the proceeds of their trade still stand admiring their reflections in the waterways. The great Dutch canvases were painted in this Golden Age, too, by artists who couldn't turn out enough to meet the demand. Now they hang in the Rijksmuseum – the great Rembrandts, de Hoochs, Vermeers and Van Dycks.

Today's Amsterdam is fun. There are canal boat voyages and lively pedestrianised shopping streets, a flower market and a flea market, chiming church bells and beautiful barrel organs. Don't be surprised if you hear them wheezing out *Tulips from Amsterdam*. They usually do!

NORMANDY CALLING

A hop across the Channel is bound to be among the first thoughts that pop into anyone's head when you mention short breaks. The briefest crossing is, of course, Dover to Calais or Boulogne. But the rewards of sailing from Portsmouth to Caen for a taste of Normandy arguably have the edge, despite the longer time at sea – about five-and-three-quarter hours.

For a start, the voyage on Brittany Ferries is part of the holiday itself, since you're on a French ship with French food and wine and therefore feel 'abroad' the second you step aboard.

Then, the port of Ouistreham, where you dock, is particularly pleasant – a tiny resort really, with a line of bleached wooden bathing huts along the sand, and fish and *frites* suppers to be had in little restaurants with sea views. And if you want to be out of it in a trice, you can be, with a score of interesting places within half-an-hour's drive. Bayeux, for instance, and the remarkable 230-foot-long tapestry that tells the story of events leading to the Battle of Hastings. It's extraordinary in more ways than one. An embroidery worked in eight mellow medieval colours, it shows in graphic detail what a soldier's life was like at the time – his suit of chain mail was carried on hangers; he had to picnic on his shield while the dukes dined at table off roast chicken and kebabs.

You could easily while away a weekend in Bayeux. It has a delightful layout of sixteenth-century timbered houses and eighteenth-century mansions and one of the finest Gothic cathedrals in France, with stonework as delicate as Bayeux lace. Miraculously, the town wasn't bombed in the D-Day invasion of the Second World War, although only eight miles from the landing beaches.

Any military enthusiast would have a field day here. The Allied armada began to sweep ashore at Ouistreham – on Sword beach – then all along the coast, and there are many moving reminders. At Arromanches, chunks of the specially constructed floating harbours remain in the bay and a fascinating museum brings to life the strategy and tactics of 'Operation Overload' with working models and life-size effigies of Monty, Eisenhower and other great personalities of the battle.

Sensualists may veer in other directions: to the smart resorts of Deauville and Trouville perhaps, to feast on *moules à la crème*, mussels the way the Normans cook them; or Honfleur, the picturesque fishing port where the Impressionists came to paint; or perhaps along the Cider Route in the heart of the Pays d'Auge, where contented cows munch lush grass in apple orchards, and in autumn many of the pink timber-framed farmhouses will show off their ancient presses and offer samples. Careful. Drivers should go easy, for although Normandy cider is lighter and finer than ours, it is just as lethal.

The Cheese Route criss-crosses the Cider Route, taking you through Vimoutiers where Marie Harel invented camembert, and to Livarot and Pont l'Evêque – all delicious cheese names.

The Normans are big on 'routes'. There is one for William the Conqueror, too. In a few days you might not want to trace his every footstep, but it is worth making a trip to the walled city of Falaise, his birthplace. Built on a rocky spur overlooking the River Ante, it's quite a spectacle. Stop where the Porte des Cordeliers, the best preserved of the town's gates, looks down on a limpid fishing pool, and imagine William standing on the ramparts, as he did in later years, calling his men to arms prior to the conquest of England.

You can ramble through the ruined twelfth-century castle next to the formidable earlier keep which is all that remains of William's actual birthplace. There's a scary dungeon to prowl around, too, and in the garrison chapel, you can check the names of the 300 or so men with whom he set sail for Hastings.

Normandy has so much more – the wonderful cities of Rouen and Caen, the rolling Suisse Normande countryside to the south, Monet's garden at Giverny, and fabulous cooking – with lashings of butter, cream and calvados, the local apple brandy. Perhaps a few days is all your waistline will take!

THE RAIL THING – IN SWEDEN

Mention you're off to Sweden and some people assume you're made of money. Sweden can be expensive, but it doesn't have to be prohibitively so.

For example, if you're going for a short break of a week, say, a cheap way to travel around and get the feel of the place is on the Inlandsbanan. The word means 'inland route' and is the name of a train line running up and down the middle of the country. You get on and off wherever you like, all for one modest price. It's an ordinary commuter-type train, pleasant if not plush, but it has a great holiday atmosphere. Sometimes it's held up by deer on the line, many so tame they take ages to move out of the way – and if a mother is feeding her baby on the tracks, you simply have to wait until she's finished! Often, local folk musicians get on and give impromptu concerts. Your views through the train windows are everything you'd expect – endless glorious mountains, forests and lakes.

You could leave the train at Mora, a town of 20 000 people with plenty of attractions. There's a large hotel and camping complex which attracts many families with small children, and a beautiful lake (of course) which is warm enough for swimming in summer. There's also a youth hostel with snug insulated wooden huts which sleep two on bunks and are amazingly cheap.

Strolling around Mora is a real pleasure for, like most Swedish towns, it is spotlessly clean and uncrowded. Sweden is twice the size of Britain but its population is only roughly that of Wales.

There's a bear park at nearby Gronklitt – again it's cheap and you get an excellent, and safe, view of those deceptively cuddly beasts.

When you stop for coffee, you can sniff the clean air at mountain villages like Fricksauce. Then, if your youngsters are getting bored, visit Mora's famous wooden horse factory, a great favourite with children. Millions of the brightly painted, intricately decorated toys have been turned out since people made them at home in the seventeenth century to pass the dark winter months.

The train heads north to Östersund where there's a lake (surprise! surprise!) which is said to be home to the Loch Ness monster's cousin. If it exists, living underwater is a blessed relief against the mosquitoes, which plague human visitors unless they protect themselves with repellent.

Further north is Lapland, where you can visit a typical Lapp village and meet these independent people whose way of life still depends on following the reindeer.

Even further north, you cross the Arctic Circle – hard to imagine you're doing so if you go in late spring or early autumn when it's gentle and warm. The line of the circle is marked in white stones. The train obligingly stops and everyone leaps off to take a pretty special picture.

Finally, while you're up near the top of Sweden, there's one other sight you must stay up for – the amazing midnight sun. Pray for a cloudless night, though. It's quite a long way to go to be disappointed!

A *QUIXOTIC JOURNEY*

Anyone who has ever heard of Don Quixote must also know of his homeland, La Mancha, a place of sun, wine and windmills, well imagined as archetypal Spain. Cervantes wrote his classic tale of the mad knight errant, *Don Quixote de La Mancha*, in the late sixteenth century solely to make money, and were he still around to collect the royalties, he would be a wealthy man. The book has been translated into over 30 languages, is never out of print, has become a ballet, a musical and, with a few changes, a wildly successful film. La Mancha, on the other hand, has hardly changed at all. It remains much as it was in Cervantes' time – wild, sun-smitten, very beautiful, and something of a surprise. Lovely for an early or late holiday.

La Mancha is very flat. It begins about 50 miles (80 km) south of Madrid, where the road to Andalucia winds up past the little town of Arunjuez and delivers you onto a seemingly endless plain, a vast sweep of land and sky. In fact, about half of Spain is occupied by plain – the *meseta* – and the southern half of it is the province of Castilla La Nueva, of which La Mancha is a region. Those windmills which Don Quixote once rode against, scorning the advice of his sensible squire, Sancho Panza, are still there – though you do have to look for them. Here and there, they stand in little clumps of five or six, spread out along a low ridge, faces turned into the relentless, tugging Castilian wind. Only a few have sails but all are desperately picturesque, standing out stark and white against an eggshell blue Castilian sky.

Climbing up to the line of windmills at Consuegra, all La Mancha lies below, running away across that smooth plain to the far horizon. Seen from up here by the castle of Consuegra, what the scenery lacks in contours it more than makes up for in colour, especially early in the year: red earth, green vines, white and pink blossom in the orchards, golden stone towns and villages. Each has its church and crumbling castle, all clear and vivid in the translucent light, the sky above picked out with fluffy sheep-shaped clouds, the air warmed by the southern sun. La Mancha fairly glows with colour and the views across the empty plain are utterly breathtaking.

This is a far cry indeed from the Spain of the popular costas, for apart from the creaking sail on the occasional windmill, La Mancha seems empty of people. It is wine country, the vines running off everywhere in their precisely aligned files, turning the red earth into one immense pomander like an orange studded with cloves. It is also the land of the knights, for during the long-ago days of the Reconquista, when Christian Spain fought to recover the land from the Moors, the king ceded much of La Mancha to the Order of Calatrava. They set up their headquarters a little to the south of Consuegra in the town of Almagro. Here, their old fortress is now one of those wonderful Spanish hotels, a *parador*, state-owned and offering considerable comfort for a reasonable price. Almagro also has a beautiful central square, or *plaza mayor*, surrounded by colonnades and containing a statue of Pedro Almagro, the conqueror of Chile.

Only a few days in La Mancha give you the real feel of it. A fly-drive package via Madrid has you there in no time. Spring and autumn are the best times to travel as the plain gets oppressively hot in summer, and touring by car is decidedly uncomfortable. There's a lot to see: great castles like the ones at Calatrava or Belmonte, old towns like Alarcon and Cuenca and, of course, the village of El Toboso where Don Quixote met his lady love, the divine Dulcinea. In the narrow unpaved streets you'll find a statue of Don Quixote and Dulcinea's Inn, and in the town hall there's a collection of Cervantes' works in every conceivable language. Though Don Quixote never actually existed, he seems very much alive in El Toboso even today.

Contact the Spanish National Tourist Office for details about fly-drives and *paradors* (see address list in appendix).

THE RHYTHM OF VIENNA

If violins aren't actually lilting in the background as you walk around the streets of Vienna, you imagine they are.

At the eastern edge of western Europe, the former headquarters of the Hapsburg Empire in many ways lives up to its publicity. It's what you expect it to be: ornate, graceful, gilded – decorated to the nth degree. Rather unkindly, the Russian writer Solzhenitsyn compared it to a collection of old stage scenery. But its baroque splendours and nineteenth-century pomp are in reality too substantial for that.

Vienna oozes old-fashioned charm, as irresistible today as when the great composers were drawn here in centuries past – Brahms, Mozart, Beethoven, Haydn and, of course, Strauss. This family of musicians started a dance craze and their waltzes became almost synonymous with the name of the city. Johann the younger wrote 400 waltzes in his time, the most famous about the river that flows by the city – *The Blue Danube*.

The easy way to get your bearings is to see the sights – the Hofburg, the Belvedere, the Karlskirche – from a fiaker, a two-horse carriage. Then you must do as the Viennese do: find a space on the terrace of a coffee house, perhaps in the Kärntnerstrasse, and indulge in the national pastime of people-watching. The tradition of the coffee house dates back to the 1600s when, it's said, a Hungarian captured a few sackfuls of coffee beans from a Turk and opened the first café in Vienna. Nobody minds how long you linger over a cuppa, for the coffee house is a kind of bolt hole to escape to from the daily grind.

The Spanish Riding School is one of the unmissable sights of Vienna. During the Second World War, when the going got rough, General Patton spirited the forebears of its beautiful white Lippizaner horses to a safe place. Had it not been for this evasive action on the part of the American army, Vienna would have lost a magnificent spectacle. Watching a morning rehearsal for a dressage show is almost as much of a thrill as the real thing – and a fraction of the price. The combination of chandeliers, sawdust and horsey smells is a curiosity, but the voluptuous little dancing stallions are sheer magic. Centuries ago they were bred from Spanish stock to entertain Vienna's Imperial Court. Today they tour the world.

The joy of shopping in Vienna is that there's a marvellous network of pedestrian-only streets. People look glossy and well-heeled, but on the whole it is no more expensive than London. However, it's something of a trial for the sweet-toothed as confectioners and cake shops full of waist-thickening pastries tempt you at every turn. At every turn too, there's music. An oom-pah-pah band, or a student practising and passing round his hat. Young musicians are never ignored in a city where the successful have the star status of screen idols.

Even if you can't tell a crotchet from a semiquaver, try to catch a performance at the State Opera, home of one of the world's great orchestras, the Vienna Philharmonic. You can book tickets two weeks in advance from Britain – and don't forget to pack your best bib and tucker.

For more informal evenings, veer out of town. Strung around the city are a collection of village suburbs like Grinsing which have a lovely country feel to them. They're a bit too Hansel-and-Gretel-like not to be touristy, but the fact that the Viennese themselves go there makes them more than a cliché, and gargantuan meals of wiener schnitzel with wine aren't over-priced. Grinsing is well-endowed with wine gardens where, on summer nights under the stars, people crowd together at scrubbed pine tables to eat, drink and enjoy a little *gemütlich-keit* – that cosy pleasure this untranslatable word conveys.

ROME SPRINGS ETERNAL

Pick almost any adjective you like and it applies to Rome, the Eternal City: noisy, serene, holy, worldly, relaxed, stylish, exasperating, expensive, cheap. Well, Rome is all of them and more.

Its antiquity knocks you sideways. There are endless palaces, churches, museums and fountains, some ruined, some perfectly preserved. Even if time is tight, there are 'musts' to be seen. You simply couldn't miss Vatican City. You're not a Catholic? Not even religious? Don't let that put you off for a moment. The Vatican is, in fact, a city within a city, a tiny sovereign state complete with its own postage stamps. About 1000 people live there, 13 500 more commute each day to work, and there are goodness knows how many thousands of visitors.

St Peter's Square is an immense masterpiece dating from the seventeenth century with a quadruple colonnade of nearly 300 columns and 140 statues. At 11 a.m. every Wednesday morning, the place teems with tourists and pilgrims awaiting the Pope's weekly audience. Anyone can watch and it's free. He's driven through the crowds in an open jeep, then gives his address in Italian, French, English, German, Spanish, Portuguese and his native Polish. If there's a group of pilgrims who don't speak any of those languages, he'll do it in theirs as well! It's possible, by prior arrangement, to get your marriage blessed, and you can bring a gift which is put on display – the inhabitants of a tiny, poor, Italian village might turn up with a crate of homegrown tomatoes.

St Peter's Basilica is the largest Catholic church ever built. Its array of gold, mosaic, marble and gilded stucco is genuinely breathtaking and you need at least half a day to see its treasures. So many pilgrims have kissed or touched the foot of the medieval statue of St Peter that it's worn completely smooth. If you're feeling energetic, walk up the 537 steps to the top of Michelangelo's St Peter's Dome for an unparalleled view of Rome. And you don't need reminding to see the Sistine Chapel, do you?

From the cool peacefulness of St Peter's back to the sweat, noise, bustle and buzz of Rome proper. Walk round the Colosseum, the best preserved ancient amphitheatre in the world. Imagine the bloodthirsty crowds, and trace the route the terrified slaves took from the underground 'dressing rooms' to the arena for their final, fatal appointment with a waiting lion.

Throw a coin in the Trevi Fountain. This is said to guarantee your return to Rome. The fountain is somehow smaller than you might expect, but very lovely, especially at night when it's floodlit. Every day, 20 million gallons of water flood through it, travelling 19 miles (30 km) over a 2000-year-old aqueduct to get there. In fact, Rome has fountains the way other cities have lampposts, they're an intrinsic part of the city's character.

The Spanish Steps are also unmissable. They rise in three sections to Rome's main French church, the Trinità dei Monti. In spring they're covered with azaleas – and most of the year they're covered with tourists, teenagers and souvenir sellers. At the bottom of the steps is the Via Condotti where the beautiful people buy their beautiful clothes at beautiful prices. You could easily pay several hundred pounds for a simple jumper or pair of boots, so if you can't afford to lash out go to window shop and watch the most stylish residents of a uniformly stylish city making their purchases. Then make yours elsewhere. Silk, knitwear and leather are all good buys in Rome.

The city is fabulous at night. The weather remains warm and pleasant after dark for much of the year, so eating outdoors is the number one evening pastime. Even the humblest café squeezes a couple of tables on to the pavement, and if you go to the Piazza di Santa Maria in the Trastevere district, you can choose from a wide range of alfresco eateries whose prices won't cane your pocket. If you just fancy a snack, that's fine; no one will pressure you.

During the day, take coffee or a drink in the Piazza Navona, one of the most beautiful squares in the world, full of fashionable Romans busy being Roman – strolling along with their arms round their lovers, sketching, arguing good-humouredly with dramatic gestures, languidly smoking cigarettes, looking cool behind dark glasses. What more can one say – except, when in Rome . . .

LA SERENISSIMA

Neither canvases by Canaletto nor cans of celluloid can prepare you for the thrill of your first entrance into Venice by water bus, swishing along the Grand Canal. That's how most visitors arrive, surprised that it is the only way to get to their hotel.

Suddenly you're confronted by a dreamlike reality: the weary beauty of its waterside palaces colourwashed in terracotta and ochre, the magnificence of its bone grey stonework and greened-copper domes, the charm of little side canals passing in a flash of festooned washing and disappearing gondoliers. It is just like sailing into a painting.

Except that – and this is the second surprise – the Grand Canal is unbelievably noisy. Remember, it's the main city thoroughfare, full of the daily traffic of *vaporetti* (the water buses), *traghetti* (cross canal barges), and delivery boats with cargoes of furniture, laundry, the post and the rubbish (where, you wonder uneasily, is it going?).

Then, as you approach the Piazza San Marco, the scene widens into cinemascope with that incredible skyline of the Doges' Palace, the Campanile and the island church of San Giorgio Maggiore, all afloat in a green sea. If you have goosepimples, prepare to raise them now.

Venice is a city that surpasses its own publicity – and don't the Venetians know it. They are adept at relieving you of your lira, but somehow they do it so charmingly you rarely resent the loss. An hour's gondola ride for two at £50 is extortionate, but where else can you savour such a sybaritic experience – even if the strains of *Just one Cornetto* keep welling up inside! If you want to dine at All'Angelo's or people-watch at Harry's Bar you'll pay for the privilege. And if £4 for a pot of tea for one on the sidelines of San Marco seems a bit steep, remember it will cover the cost of the palm court musicians serenading you with tunes from *My Fair Lady*!

Since Venice itself is a work of art, and fortunately not in such dire peril of disintegration as it used to be, you feel you get your money's worth without ever crossing a threshold – just by gazing at the amazing St Mark's Basilica, sighing at the Bridge of Sighs and wandering around the Rialto, where the city began as a powerful marine republic. Today shopping, not shipping, is the preoccupation. The Rialto bridge is crammed with boutiques selling leatherwork, masks and golden trinkets. It's also crammed with people. A wander through the fruit and vegetable market beyond is actually more fun.

You must choose your own priorities among the major sights, but try to fit in I Frari, where Titian's *Assumption* hangs over the altar and Donatello's beautiful wooden statue of *John the Baptist* stands in a niche; and Santa Maria dei Miracoli, the small Renaissance church built by the Lombards which the Venetians call their 'golden jewel box' and often choose to marry in.

There are two points to remember if you want to enjoy a brief break in Venice. One: avoid summer at all costs. The canals are smelly and it is humid and overcrowded – even as early as April and May the school parties trample you underfoot on the *vaporetti* and clog museum queues. Winter is the time to go. Then it's more La Serenissima (the most serene) and mists and moody skies seem to suit it. But take wellies to wade through San Marco at high tide. In February you'll catch the Carnival when masked revellers haunt the streets, lending a surreal touch to the already unreal.

The second point: more than in any other city, veering off the main tourist track will reward you. Forget the yellow signs and lose yourself in narrow lanes that open out onto quiet little piazzas. Here you'll find bars where the camparis are cheaper, and homely trats where the tagliatelli is just as good as All'Angelo's for half the price. Above all, take time to observe the fine details: a crow-black priest stooping to give a prayer card to a wide-eyed child; scrawny cats being fed spaghetti scraps on balconies; the glint of heavy glass doors revealing luxurious foyers with chandeliers and plump pastel sofas; the smell of coffee beans roasting and the rattle of mussel shells hitting the plates of hungry diners. Couples of any age hold hands and sop up the antique magic of a city made for lovers.

Everyone falls in love in or with Venice. The royal, the rich, the famous, the poor and the packaged. It cannot disappoint you.

A *BITE OF THE BIG APPLE*

When the songwriters wrote that New York is a wonderful town, they were being both entirely correct and economical with the truth. New York *is* a wonderful town. It's also dirty, noisy and crammed with people who are notoriously impolite. But putting those few drawbacks aside, New York possesses that essential ingredient which makes it one of the world's most exciting cities. It is unique. Travel where you will, there is no New York clone. You may not like it, but you won't be able to forget it.

As to what element puts that zing in the air and gives New York its electric heartbeat, it has to be a combination of the setting, the pace and the people. New York may be many things but restful it isn't. Mind you, half of that fast pace visitors ascribe to the city is self-generated by their own need to rush about and see and do everything, grabbing a swift bite of the Big Apple.

For most people, New York means Manhattan, the heart of the city, the part with the skyscrapers and the fashionable shops and most of the glitz. Here are the canyon streets of Fifth Avenue, Madison Avenue, the Avenue of the Americas – better known as Sixth – and Broadway, which runs down from Central Park across Times Square and through the hub of theatreland. This is as good a place as any to start a visit to the city, although many people choose to begin at the top – by getting an overview from the dizzy heights of the Empire State building. At 1472 feet, the Empire State is no longer the tallest building in the world, or even New York – the World Trade Center is higher. But it is still undeniably impressive, and you do get a terrific city panorama as you look down on some of the world's most expensive real estate. Yet in 1626 a Dutchman, Peter Minuit, bought the entire island of Manhattan from the Algonquin Indians for just $24 worth of beads, one of history's better bargains or an outstanding piece of sharp practice, depending on your point of view!

Back on the street, a visit to Macy's, the mega-store, is a real eye-popper, especially so at Christmas when a large sign advertises its traditional attraction in typical New York style: 'Visit Santa's Grotto – 34 Santas – No Waiting'. New York signs are a permanent source of amusement. Who can resist a delicatessen which offers a 'six-foot Italian Hero', even if he – or it – turns out to be a sandwich.

After Macy's comes Madison Square Garden on 31st Street, a centre for sporting spectacles and shows. Heading up Seventh Avenue from here, sightseers on foot eventually arrive in Theatreland around Times Square, where all the big shows are put on – the lucky ones may even survive opening night! Along and around 42nd Street from Times Square lies the city's sleaze centre, but from Sixth Avenue it's not far to the Rockefeller Plaza, an open air ice rink and pedestrian resting spot right in the buzz of the city. Nearby is Radio City Music Hall, still the world's largest cinema boasting 6000 seats, and once the home of the famous Rockettes. There are special tours of the building laid on.

Getting about in New York requires concentration. The subway underground train system is complicated and big. In the summer the weather is usually hot and humid and in the winter, frequently freezing. It can be a pleasure to walk about in spring and autumn – and it's safer than you think, especially if you're with someone. It's also quite easy to find your way about in the grid arrangement of streets. If you don't want to walk, there's a good bus system, the subway is less dangerous than stories suggest, and no visit to New York is complete without at least one encounter with a yellow cab driver.

There are city tours and visits to the main sights, with tour buses picking up at all the main hotels, and every porter is full of information – often highly personal – on what you should go for and even eat. There are great restaurants and every kind of cuisine. You're simply stunned by the choice. Then there is the theatre and the opera, the ballet and dance of all kinds, and great art galleries and museums like the Museum of Modern Art and the Guggenheim. There is the United Nations building and Central Park, Harlem and Chinatown, Little Italy and the artists' and writers' area of Greenwich Village. New York is nothing if not cosmopolitan, but getting a handle on the city is not easy in the course of one visit. There is so much going on that the city can quickly exhaust you, so take time to stop and stare. You'll notice that New York can also be very beautiful.

One of the most lasting impressions will be the shape of this electric city. Take a trip across the harbour on the Staten Island Ferry. Halfway out from Manhattan, look back across the water from somewhere near the Statue of Liberty, that symbol of America you simply mustn't miss, and there, rearing up into the sky, are the towers and pinnacles of fabulous unforgettable New York.

SPANISH WINTER SUNSHINE

From November to March, the Costa del Sol isn't exactly sweltering but temperatures can get well into the 70s F (20s C), and jogging along the beach is a lot more appealing than running up heating bills back home.

It's a favourite destination for older people with time on their hands who are able to take advantage of the bargain long-stay holidays that last from four weeks to six months. But there's nothing to stop anyone at all slipping away for an inexpensive break. Families with children under school age can have a holiday at this time of year for virtually half the cost of a summer one.

Resorts like Fuengirola, noisy and crowded in July and August, take on a totally different character in wintertime. Around the core of an old fishing village has sprouted a modern town with a dozen or so big hotels. Big on the outside, but rooms are usually fairly small. If you are staying for a while, choose travelling companions whose hobbies don't involve cumbersome paraphernalia! If you want to be alone, comb the brochures carefully; there's usually a limited period when you can have a single without a supplement.

For the gregarious, there's an endless social round of keep-fit classes, whist drives and tea dances. Independents can simply use the hotel as a base and cut loose – amble into the local bars or take a bus ride into the hills to visit picturesque towns like Mijas or Benalmadena.

The Andalusian countryside around here is peppered with old whitewashed villages that reveal a very different face of the Costa del Sol – a more picturesque Spain, well-kept and prosperous because of the *pesetas* that pour in during the

summer. In winter, you can wander around the streets in peace. Yet all the shops are open, the hot-sugared-almond seller is busy at the brazier and the donkey taxis are lined up for business.

In the foothills of the Sierra, it's cooler and you can sniff the fresher scents of mountain air. You can go further if you like – Torremolinos is only a 45-minute train ride away, and there are excursions to Marbella and Puerto Banus where glossy girls with sinister-looking boyfriends park on café terraces, and money drips like honey from the sleek yachts in the marinas. It doesn't cost you anything to look, though!

There need never be a dull moment here, even if the skies do turn grey now and then. It rains a bit in winter, but you'd be very unlucky to see a week go by without some of that Spanish sunshine.

MADEIRA, M'DEAR

The climate of Madeira, like its wine, is mild and sweet. Only a few degrees separate the average winter and summer temperatures. Summer is like an ideal English summer (70°–74°F or 21°–23°C) and winter like our late spring (61°–63°F or 16°–17°C). This, together with a rich volcanic soil, makes this beautiful Portuguese island a great place to grow things. Basking in the eastern Atlantic, on a level with Casablanca, it is virtually a mega-market garden, producing an abundance of fruit, veg and flowers for export all over Europe. Every inch of the terraced hillsides seems to be cultivated, and a visit to the covered market in the old port of Funchal is a tonic in itself when you've escaped from the drabness of frosty Britain.

Madeira, whether the drink or the place, has always been regarded as a pick-me-up. Army personnel returning from the heat and dust of India were sent here for a spot of R-and-R before facing up to the rigours of damp Victorian parlours. Winston Churchill came to paint. And countless ordinary packaged travellers now enjoy the respite of a winter warmer here.

Be prepared, however, to notice evidence of the building bonanza that's taken place over the past several years. The whirr of cement mixers is not unfamiliar. What's more, hotels sited along the coastal trunk roads leading into Funchal are constantly buzzed by heavy traffic. Make sure you choose somewhere off the main road, well out of town (public transport is frequent, efficient and cheap) or insulated by a big garden. A pool is essential (most hotels have them) because there are virtually no beaches; the coastline is spectacularly rugged with minuscule and usually inaccessible bays of black sand. But the large and attractive lido on the fringes of town is a real pleasure.

So too is walking up into the hills through banana palms and fields of gladdies – the tourist office offers a little book of rambles. And if you're game for a laugh, you can toboggan downwards in one of the wicker baskets which were used in olden times to drag groceries up the steep paths from town to the grand mansions.

Driving further into the mountainous centre of the island takes you into very different terrain and climate. The mossy pine-clad slopes are reminiscent of Scotland, and in the northern hills you come upon strange grass-roofed, half-buried cottages.

There's lots to see and to do, the food is exceptionally tasty and inexpensive, and even if you've never touched a drop of Madeira before, ten to one you'll be persuaded to haul home at least a pack of three bottles at the end of your obligatory visit to a wine lodge.

FLY AWAY TO FLORIDA

Winter is high season in Florida. The 'Sunshine State' swelters in the 90s F (30s C) during the summer and native holiday-makers stay away. But in winter, when New Yorkers are struggling through snowdrifts, Florida enjoys temperatures in the pleasant 70s F (20s C) and America flocks there.

Florida is not short of water. It has a fabulous coastline stretching from the Atlantic Ocean on the east to the Gulf of Mexico on the west. There are miles of inland waterways, and plenty of paradise islands surrounded by warm waves.

If you fancy a change from sun worshipping, take a river boat trip. The *Jungle Queen IV* in Fort Lauderdale, north of Miami, takes you along the New River, named by Spanish explorers when they first saw it about 100 years ago. Your ticket includes a commentary which dwells mainly on the enormous and surprisingly stylish houses you pass. You'd need several million dollars to buy one, yet almost all are second homes, occupied for only a couple of months a year when the owners take their holiday – or, as they say in the States, their vacation.

Or try a fast whizz round the Everglades, that vast expanse of reed-covered swamp, in an airboat, which is a sort of combination of a speed boat and a huge electric fan. Often the reeds are so high you can't see where you're going, so it's an unnerving if exhilarating experience. You may even spot an alligator or two – unless it spots you first.

The last thing a place blessed with so much water needs is an artificial water theme park, but this is America, so they've got plenty of them. There are heart-stopping water slides which fall almost vertically, some as high as an eight-storey building, artificial waves in the gigantic pools, and displays of aquatic acrobatics. If it rains for more than an hour, you can come again another day for free (your ticket is your 'raincheck'). Who would dare make an offer like that in Britain?

Just because the wealthy like Florida doesn't necessarily mean it's an expensive place to stay in. You'll find good modern hotels where many rooms have two double beds. Yet you invariably pay for the room, not the number of people in it, so a mum and dad with two kids, or two friendly couples, could live very economically. In summer – out of season, remember – it's cheaper still.

If you want a quieter more exclusive holiday and have a little more cash to spend, head for one of the many tiny islands to the south of the peninsula, called 'keys'. They have fabulous self-catering apartments. Hire a boat, head off to some tiny uninhabited key, and you could be all alone on a perfect sandy beach with a crystal clear sea to cool off in.

All this *and* Disney World, Epcot, the Seaquarium and so much more makes Florida too good to miss. Whether you want to be cooked on the beach all day or explore in an air-conditioned hire car, you'll have a tremendous time.

CHAPTER EIGHT

Cruise Views

Once cruising was for the elite – those who not only had the wherewithal to fork out for wining and dining aboard in style but who also had the time to move from here to there at a leisurely pace. Nowadays cruising has become more affordable to a much wider spectrum of passengers, a less protracted experience and, on the whole, a good deal less stylish – many of the big cruisers plying routes in the Mediterranean and Caribbean are more like up-market floating holiday camps. But the romance lingers on, as do the rituals of the captain's cocktail party, the nightly cabaret and ship-to-shore manoeuvres.

Cruising is ideal for people who prefer to travel than to arrive, because the lion's share of the holiday is usually spent on the water. Ports of call that loom enticingly in the brochures may, in reality, be seen in a bit of a rush and from the windows of a coach. You don't always get to taste, touch and smell the place. Of course, you might just prefer that. The prospect of returning to predictably hygienic mod cons aboard each night does have its appeal.

Generally speaking, cruising is a middle-aged scene – the vast majority on any passenger list are in the 40 to 70 age group. This is not to say younger holidaymakers don't also cruise – the non-stop entertainment programmes devised by the major cruise lines have mainly the lithe and energetic in mind, with each day's timetable packed with every kind of action from hula hoop competitions to pool volleyball. You might also learn a language, Greek cooking, or macramé. Whatever, the image of people sitting about on deck with rugs round their knees or taking off for a constitutional fore to aft is as dated as a scene from Somerset Maugham. You have to be keen to join in the fun, though, because it's more or less inescapable.

You also have to be a reasonably able-bodied seaperson. When the big liners have to anchor offshore, the only means of transfer to an excursion boat can be via a precariously slung ladder on to a floating jetty. Willing hands reach out to guide your progress, but it's not for you if you're prone to a twinge of vertigo or unsure of your footing. What's more, you have to be patient, especially when the ship is full. Clearing customs can be interminable.

There are also hidden extras on a cruise which bump up the final bill. One is tipping – on many though not all shipping lines this is not built in to the inclusive price (read the small print). So it can come as a nasty shock on the last evening aboard to find little envelopes left lying around pointedly marked 'Thank you from your steward/barman/etc'. You could easily get through a further £50 even tipping on the mean side.

The other not-so-hidden extra is that you may have to pay to get to the point of departure and home from the last port of call. Sometimes a package price will include this but not always. However, you can usually get a reduced air fare if you book through the company you are cruising with. Or there's the possibility that the cost of a city break to journey's start and end might be cheaper than the full air fare.

These are all things to be aware of before you consider booking a cruise, but there are plenty of positive reasons to look forward to a floating holiday. It's a tremendous escape from loneliness or a socially uneventful life. You can't help making friends. In fact, you can't help relaxing because the shipboard atmosphere on a good ship with a pleasant crew and company can give you a real lift: your every whim is catered for, you get live entertainment every night (and the standard of cabaret on ships is usually high), you have plenty of good food and companionship. You don't have to tax your brain about anything – just breathe in lungfuls of invigorating sea air and, if the ship is sailing in southern waters, enjoy the sunshine. When Bill Buckley reported on one Mediterranean cruise for the *Holiday* programme, he became friendly with two cruise addicts. 'What I liked about them,' says Bill, 'was that they both lived in tiny council flats on a state pension, and scrimped and saved like mad so they could go on a cruise every year. What a refreshing sense of priorities!'

Not all cruises need be on the Mediterranean or Caribbean. My own favourite, the Norwegian Coastal Voyage, is vastly different from these archetypal sailings: you journey beyond the Arctic Circle to the land of the midnight sun. The only problem is that you stay up later and later each daylit night to see the stunning scenery and end up with Arctic circles under your eyes!

Far from the briny, you can cruise on the world's great rivers too – the Nile, the Rhine and the Danube. River cruising is quite another experience. Or you can take a mini-cruise across the North Sea. Or think still smaller – join a handful of shipmates aboard a *gulet* breezing along the coast of Turkey. Take your pick. This chapter briefs you on some of the most seaworthy – and riverworthy – cruises on offer. While precise routes and programmes may vary from season to season, the basics remain the same.

CARIBBEAN COMBO

Mixing a short spell at sea in the Gulf of Mexico with a few days fore and aft in Florida is a good idea for anyone who doesn't want to cruise for too long. Putting your feet up by the pool at a nice hotel in a leafy suburb of Miami helps you shake off the jet lag after a transatlantic flight. Then it's all aboard the Chandris ship RHMS *Britannis* to set sail for America's 'last resort' – Key West. On the most southerly point of Florida, Key West is unbelievably photogenic, full of pretty clapboard houses garnished with tropical greenery. Artists, writers and a US president or two used to hole up here for the summer. A cute little tram whizzes you past the former homes of Harry Truman, Tennessee Williams and Ernest Hemingway – as well as Hemingway's favourite bar, Sloppy Joe's.

The humidity creeps up, a hot breeze wafts across your bow and the flat-as-a-pancake outline of Mexico stretches on the horizon. You anchor at the custom-built resort of Cancun with its Persil-white beaches and improbably turquoise sea, and lunch on tortillas and tacos. Just a downbeat note or two: the nearby flea market is tacky and local lifestyles seem a sad contrast to the brave new tourist developments.

Next port of call, Cozumel island. This also lacks contours but is delightfully laid back and lush around the beaches. While these lure the sunbathers, the ancient Mayan ruins claim the attention of the curious. As ancient columns stand crumbling in a forest clearing, the buzz of cicadas lends an eerie accompaniment to the guide's tales of human sacrifice.

The *Britannis* is the oldest cruise liner in existence – power points for shavers only in cabins mean you have to visit the hairdressers or ironing rooms to keep looking smooth – but what the ship lacks in streamlining is more than made up for in other ways: decks are bordered by old-fashioned rails of polished teak and there are a real ship's wheel and brass fittings on the bridge. You feel you're on a proper liner and not just a floating hotel. A multinational ship's company and Greek crew make for a sunny atmosphere even if skies are grey (not very likely). The food is known to be consistently good and entertainment first class. There's also an unusually high proportion of younger passengers which keeps the ambience lively.

After returning to Miami, there are three days in Orlando with visits to Disney World and Epcot.

MOROCCO BOUND

Cruising on a budget might seem a contradiction in terms, but if you're prepared to cut down on glamour and luxury, the Italian ship *Eugenio Costa* (Costa Lines) is the perfect answer. It's typical of many moderate cruise liners offering a holiday afloat that's jolly good fun, lets you unwind and throws in a bit of sightseeing. Most of the passengers are Italian and the age range is huge: honeymoon couples, families with young children and the older set.

While age is more or less immaterial, personality is important. Loners loving solitude and open spaces shouldn't cruise anyway, but least of all on this ship. It's like a small densely populated town. Dinner tables are packed in a huge dining room, decks are crammed with rows of sunbathers, team games are noisy and no one misses the cabaret – a style of cruising that's definitely for joiners. In fact, it's the ideal ship if you're longing for a bit of life, laughter and friendship – which is why it particularly appeals to older people who need to be taken out of themselves.

Lunches and dinners consist of nine or ten courses, though you aren't expected to eat your way through them all. You could have soup, meat and salad, for example, or pasta, fish and pudding. Food varies from absolutely mouthwatering to instantly forgettable. Service is usually excellent.

The ship departs from Genoa and a package includes getting there by a flight to Nice and a coach from there. It stops at Barcelona in Spain before crossing to North Africa. There's great excitement when Casablanca is reached on the coast of Morocco. You can book places on excursions in advance. One goes to Marrakesh, a long journey with more time spent travelling than sightseeing. A better bet is a morning in Casablanca itself followed by an afternoon in Rabat. The old and the new don't just meet in Casablanca – they collide head on. Clothing and transport are a jumble of ancient local and modern western, and the casbah traders take credit cards. In haggling, never agree to the first price stallholders quote – they simply don't expect to get it.

Cocktails in Rick's Bar is obligatory. No, it's not the original as immortalised in the famous film starring Bogart and Bergman – that Rick's Bar is long since demolished. This reincarnation in the Hyatt Regency Hotel is ritzy – certainly no gin joint, but there are lots of Bogey pictures around to make sure you get the connection.

Rabat, though smaller, is Morocco's capital. It has the royal palace and mosque to visit, and the mausoleum where Mohammed V, who led the country to independence, lies. The decoration of its interior is so stunning that your shutter fingers itch, but cameras are absolutely not allowed.

Next stop, Tenerife, where you can go and see the exquisite seventeenth-century House of Balconies at La Oratava and admire beautiful but expensive lacework. Then on to Funchal, Madeira (see chapter 7), and Malaga on the Costa del Sol before returning to Genoa. If you can take the crowded atmosphere, and the long queues for things like excursion tickets, the *Eugenio Costa* is terrific value for money.

ADRIATIC/AEGEAN ROUND TRIP

The bonus of cruising in the seas that swirl off the eastern Mediterranean is that there's something to look at most of the time you're sailing. The coastlines of Italy, Yugoslavia, Albania, Greece or Turkey are never far away.

British Ferries offers a cruise that is just about all things to all people. It's on the Orient Express – not the super train but a liner-like car ferry – and it starts and ends at Venice. There are several variations on the cruise theme. For an inclusive price, you can board with your car at Venice, drive off at any of the ports of call and pick up the ship a week or two later. Or you can simply settle for the one week round trip, making your way to and from Venice by whatever means you choose.

Highlights include squeezing through the amazing steep-sided Corinth Canal with only inches to spare – a manoeuvre no one wants to miss, so people stagger out of their berths in the small hours to witness it. On the itinerary are Athens and the Parthenon; Istanbul with its mosques and bizarre covered bazaar; the Roman site of Ephesus where St Paul was heckled as he tried to preach the gospel; and the ruined stadium near

Katakolon where the Ancient Greeks lit the first Olympic torch.

Amusements on board the Orient Express ferry are legion. There's a casino, cinema, indoor and outdoor pools, shops, sauna, live entertainment at night. Four restaurants and a coffee shop dispense food that's worth waiting for. (Hint – sometimes you have to wait.)

FOR LOVERS OF ANCIENT GREECE

Not everyone's glass of ouzo but perfect for Grecophiles are Swan Hellenic cruises in the Greek islands, with accompanying guides and lecturers as you drift in and out of places that figure in myth and history.

Life aboard is informal – although men are expected to wear jackets and ties for dinner – and there isn't any noisy programme of non-stop fun and games. Just the occasional brain-teasing quiz.

It's not all swot, however. You get time to sunbathe, take a dip in the tiny ship's pool, enjoy a little Greek night music and dancing, and sometimes stop at pretty islands like Mykonos or Delos simply to shop as a change from treading the path of the ancients.

VOYAGE TO THE MIDNIGHT SUN

When the Norwegian sea is calm and the air like crystal, the razor-edged peaks of the Lofoten Wall are among the most stunning sights you'll ever see.

Awe inspiring scenery is what lures people aboard the Norwegian Coastal Service, and there's rarely any sense of anticlimax. It is, after all, one of the great journeys of the world, sailing from Bergen to the land of the midnight sun and back again.

Although the price of a 12-day trip runs well into four figures for inclusive holidays from the UK, these are usually booked up 18 months ahead. Yet it may come as a bit of a surprise to find that the ships aren't luxury cruisers. They're regular working boats delivering passengers, cargo and the post, and they do it year round – so you could, as an independent traveller, get aboard at any port of call, maybe for a night or two.

Cabins are clean and comfortable but compact – no frills. Some have showers and loos, many don't. It's a quick nip along the corridor to the nearest bathroom – and on the older ships, that's the only place you'll find a power point for things like a hairdryer. If you aren't an easy sleeper, an inside cabin is a positive advantage as it's shut away from the endless daylight.

Once you're beyond the Arctic Circle, night never comes and you can go on seeing the sights for as long as you can keep your eyes open! Exploring quiet northerly fjords around the witching hour is a magical experience. Because the Fjord of the Trolls is so sheltered, an extraordinary forest of miniature trees thrives on the rugged surface of its rocks despite the northerly latitude. You can see exactly why it has given rise to tales of the supernatural. In Scandinavian folklore the trolls were a bit of a pest, so when hot 'troll' soup is ladled out for supper aboard, everyone downs it with gusto and a deal of speculation about what the main ingredient – chopped up frankfurters – is supposed to represent. Troll fingers, presumably.

To assuage the kind of appetites sea air creates, food is plentiful, tasty and not too exotic. The lunchtime cold table offers the best nosh of the day, with excellent fresh salmon, fat Norwegian prawns, and traditional fishy salads. There's a noticeable dearth of anything other than bottled water on dining tables. Both wine and beer are expensive even for the Norwegians, though it's there if you want to pay for it.

Evenings on the Coastal Service ships are very informal – absolutely no dressing up. Apart from a little leaping about to canned music on deck, the only organised amusement is the visit of one of King Neptune's henchmen for the ritual of dropping ice cubes down the necks of anyone crossing the Arctic Circle for the first time.

Trips ashore are often necessarily brief in order to keep to the Coastal Service timetable which is not primarily planned for tourists. Ports of call, 35 in all, include small fishing villages like Bodo and Svolvaer, where you can have a pleasant wander for an hour or two, and cities like Tromso, birthplace of Amundsen, the explorer who pipped Scott to the South Pole. Here a coach takes you touring to see the shining white modern cathedral of the Arctic, standing like some incredible block of ice high above town. A cable car ride gives you an overall view while a party of hang gliders takes off, right on cue, like supermen and wonderwomen soaring above the scenery.

The overland trip to the North Cape marks the halfway stage of the Coastal cruise. An empty landscape, lunar almost, can be hot or cool in summer depending on cloud cover – from 77°F (25°C) to 56°F (13°C). The engaging Lapps, original inhabitants of north Norway, appear from small encampments wearing wide grins and colourful clothes, to do a little trading in reindeer skins. Then, a huge sphere atop stark cliffs marks the spot of the most northerly point in Europe and cameras click. From Honningsvag, the ship sails on to Kerkenes near the Russian border before returning to Bergen, stopping at the ports you docked at in the night on the way north.

Given even reasonably good weather, it is a truly fantastic voyage – one you'll never forget.

DOWN THE DANUBE

There's something especially soothing about river cruising. Very little heave-ho disturbs your balance and you get a continuous close-up of lapping water through your porthole – on most river cruisers 90 per cent of cabins have an outside view. Many river boats are as stylish and spacious as oceangoing cruise ships. Bunks convert to seating, and there are sometimes video films to watch on your own TV screen if you get bored.

Not that there's much chance of being bored drifting down the grand old Danube, the longest river in Europe. It may not be terribly blue, but it certainly is some river, flowing through or bordering eight countries. Four of these are in the eastern bloc, and it gives you a strange feeling to cruise in comparative western luxury through a chink in the Iron Curtain.

A voyage on the *Danube Princess*, a very classy German purpose-built river boat, begins and ends in Munich, but you travel as far as Budapest, the Hungarian capital. This is the highlight of the trip for most people. Your entrance into the heart of the city by river is the first thrill, sailing towards the eight mighty bridges that link the older city of Buda with nineteenth-century Pest.

Visas all present and correct, there are usually no hiccups for passengers disembarking, but official eyes miss nothing. A local guide can be arrested for putting a foot on the gangplank. Medieval Buda, though much restored, is delightful, the turrets and towers of its Fisherman's Bastion providing a wonderful foreground for city panorama snapshots. Pest's massive monuments and political parade grounds make heavy sightseeing, but the statues of the Magyar warrior kings are magnificent and there's a vitality about its street life, its cafés and leafy boulevards that's reminiscent of Paris. After the city tour you're free to wander at will.

The joy of this sort of cruising is that you're able to cover a good deal of ground without the hassle of packing and re-packing your suitcase, and you get the opportunity to spend a considerable amount of time on land. For a whole day you depart from the ship and travel by coach through the Hungarian countryside, visiting the whitewashed village of Szentendre with its gypsy air and peasant embroidery, and Eztergom, Hungary's Vatican, where the great Byzantine cathedral is a storehouse of priceless ecclesiastical treasures.

On the return leg, you visit the university city of Bratislava in Czechoslovakia. Here there's no freewheeling. You follow your guide in crocodile fashion while a plainclothes officer lurks at a distance. The city itself has an up-beat atmosphere, and you usually end up mid morning having a lively brunch at a beer palace. This doesn't stop the big eaters from tucking in to the usual seven course lunch when they get back on board! Food is top-notch on these ships, and you drink the best wines of the areas you sail through.

Vienna, at the eastern edge of western Europe, is an incredible contrast after the communist countries – all of which were once part of the empire under the Hapsburgs. There's plenty of time to enjoy this ornate, gilded and graceful city of grand opera and lilting waltzes, of coffee houses and trotting carriages (more in chapter 7). During the cruise you also visit romantic Durnstein, where the minstrel Blondel serenaded and saved King Richard the Lionheart, and Melk with its baroque monastery.

The whole exercise is fascinating, very up-market and slightly middle-aged. An absolute treat for a quiet couple whose kids have grown up. But children would be bored out of their socks since there's little to do aboard except eat and sit out on deck when the sun shines.

A Danube cruise like this can be pricey, though it does offer value for money when you consider what living at this level of luxury would cost in a hotel, never mind seeing the sights on one of the world's most celebrated rivers.

ALONG THE NILE

The massive scale of the temples and tombs of ancient Egypt has you bending over backwards. It is a staggering array, set along the banks of the wide and timeless Nile, where fiery sunsets turn the evenings into pictures straight off the top of a date box.

'The Nile is Egypt and Egypt is the Nile' – how true. This great waterway, Africa's longest at 3500 miles, is liquid history, nowhere more so than in the land of the Pharaohs. In Upper Egypt there is the High Dam at Aswan, holding back the waters of artificial Lake Nasser on whose banks is the stunning reconstruction of Abu Simbel.

Down river from Aswan is a succession of splendid temples, each more impressive than the last. Grandest of all is the complex of Luxor and Karnak, once the ancient city of Thebes and already 1500 years old when the voluptuous Cleopatra ruled. On the west bank of the river lies the Valley of the Kings with the famous tomb of Tutankhamen and, close by, the Valley of the Queens. Painstakingly uncovered from the desert sands, these tombs are monuments to the past glories of this fascinating land.

There is no better way to appreciate these wonders than on a cruise along the Nile. For from three to ten days, you travel in considerable style with air-conditioning, cabins with private facilities and picture windows, dining saloon, lounge, lots of deck space and even swimming pools on larger vessels.

But a word of caution. Due to the drought in the upper reaches of the Nile, its water level is well below normal. Cruise itineraries can be altered at short notice and you might well have to do part of the journey by coach. However, that's a small inconvenience for such an odyssey.

Osiris and *Isis*, two boats operated by Hilton, are better equipped than most to cope with low water as they have the shallowest draught. They ply upstream or down between Luxor and Aswan, offering a relaxing five-day trip as well as gentle education. Even if you aren't a fervent Egyptologist, a little knowledge is a welcome thing as you wander like a Lilliputian along the avenue of ram-headed sphinxes towards the Temple of Amon, or gaze up at the giant profile of Rameses II. He was the master builder of the Pharaohs, who were both rulers and gods.

There are times when past and present seem to fuse – when you board a felucca with its one sail, for instance, for the design of these working boats of the Nile hasn't changed since Tutankhamen was a toddler.

A cruise is by far the best way to see the riches of Upper Egypt, not only because the river itself is fundamental to the area's history, but because after a day of exploring the temples it is sheer heaven to return to your floating home and sip your favourite aperitif under a galaxy of stars.

GOING BY GULET

With a coastline that fronts on to the Aegean, the Mediterranean, the Sea of Marmara and, beyond the Bosphorus, the Black Sea itself, Turkey is perfect for a cruising holiday. Every coast is punctuated with places well worth anchoring at, places ancient and modern, small and large. You can cruise in a wide variety of ships, but the most fun is the traditional Turkish cruising craft, the gulet.

Gulets are built of pinewood and are decked, schooner rigged, twin-masted craft 56 feet long. They were originally for fishing and trading along the Turkish shore or among the islands, but today more and more are being converted into or built as cruising yachts. Most new gulets take shape in or around the Crusader port of Bodrum, where there is a long tradition of boat building. While they are still constructed with all the old care and skill, they're also fitted out with essential creature comforts like loos, showers and separate cabins for the passengers, plus quarters for the captain and the crew of two.

The crew work the ship, cook the meals and sail the gulet gently to the less-frequented beaches and the smaller ports. Nowadays, though, the sails of these schooners are more for display than for use; most of the voyaging is done by engine power. You can sunbathe on deck, doze in the shelter of the canvas awnings, or simply prop yourself up on one elbow to watch the beautiful Turkish coast slip by. Although the captain is responsible for the craft, the passengers can decide where to stop, how long to stay, when to sail on and, within the time available, where to go. The choice is almost limitless and most gulet cruises allow plenty of time to slip ashore to see the historic sights of Turkey, which often lie close to the coast and are within easy reach on foot or by taxi.

The most popular route is the Blue Voyage along the Mediterranean shore from Bodrum to Antalya, past Marmaris and Fethiye. It's the perfect two-week cruise, but many gulet cruises form part of a split holiday package with one week ashore. They begin at the port of Marmaris, and then sail east to Dalyan, where they anchor in Ekincik Bay. Motorboats take you on up the channel to the Dalyan delta and the site of

Caunos, a great antique city. East lies the town of Fethiye and the popular beach resort of Olu Deniz, which has one of the best fine pebble beaches on the Mediterranean coast. It's a good place to stop and swim before sailing on to the resort of Kalkan. Gulets can moor alongside the marina and stock up with essentials like cheap and excellent Turkish wine or the powerful raki – a bit like Greek ouzo.

Kas, half a day's sail east of Kalkan, is another classic little resort. Once a quiet fishing port, it's now a centre for the cruising yachts and a great place to step ashore for some sightseeing: Demre, for instance, where they say Father Christmas was born about 2300 years ago – the statue outside the church looks just like him! A couple of hours further out is the island of Kekova, where the ruined city of Aperlae can be clearly seen beneath the clear waters – snorkellers can take a closer look before sailing on to Kale on the mainland for a visit to the castle on the cliffs. Before returning to bustling Antalya where the Blue Voyage ends, you have a chance to see the historic sites of Phaseles near Kemer, Side and Aspendos.

Gulets can be hired privately or through many UK based tour operators. Once aboard, your extras are few and formality is non-existent. Meals and evening drinks are taken round a table on the upper deck beneath the shady awning, and you can wear bikinis and swimsuits from dawn to dusk. Skippers are

always cheery and unhurried, making no great effort to cover long distances in one day. It's a lazy, graceful, restful sort of holiday, cruising along wherever the fancy takes you and stopping at little ports for the evening, or a deserted cove for a little swimming or a run ashore.

NORTH SEA CAPER

A couple of nights sailing to and fro on the North Sea in winter might not immediately strike you as the stuff of which cruises are made, but you'd be surprised. The Danish DFDS Seaways' mini-cruises are every bit as sybaritic as any in warmer waters – and a great deal more than some.

The ships are no mere car ferries but car/passenger cruise-liners, fitted out in the kind of style Scandinavians demand – which is high. Cabins are neat, well-planned and always spruce. There are carpets underfoot almost everywhere, acres of space, plenty of comfortable seating and plush cocktail bars.

If the weather's choppy, you won't feel rough – unless you're a very poor sailor – because the ships are so well stabilised.

The nice thing is you're abroad the minute you step aboard. You change your money and eat Danish food. The restaurant lays on a groaning traditional cold table complete with smoked salmon and caviar (well, lumpfish roe) and offers a fixed-price menu as well as *à la carte*. Snacks and more familiar nosh can be had in the coffee shop.

Sailings are from Newcastle, Felixstowe and Harwich to Esbjerg in Denmark, Gothenburg in Sweden and Hamburg in Germany, all attractive ports to wander and shop in during your few hours ashore. The length of the voyage varies according to which port you're heading for, but most people find it's not long enough anyway. There are duty-free shops, a sauna, heated indoor pool, cinema and even a children's playroom. After dinner you can try your luck at the casino or dance to live, usually Abba-like, music.

For anyone suffering from midwinter blues, these mini-cruises are a real cheer-up, especially as the bill – roughly half the cost of staying in a first-class hotel – won't cause your bank balance to blush.

REALLY PUSHING THE BOAT OUT...

Wing your way across the Atlantic faster than a bullet from a rifle. Live it up for a few days in exciting Orlando, gateway to Walt Disney World. Then luxuriate homeward-bound for five nights on one of the world's most magnificent liners. If you prefer, do it the other way around. Either way a holiday on Cunard's Queen Elizabeth 2 and British Airways' Concorde is tops. The QE2, the last great liner to ply the Atlantic on a regular basis between the old and the new worlds, links many of the gracious styles of bygone traditonal voyages with every contemporary amenity. It even has a computer centre where you can catch up with the latest technology.

Built in Clyde in the late 1960s, the QE2 recently had a £110 million refit and complete refurbishment, ready to sail into the twenty-first century. With over 900 suites and staterooms, four restaurants, elegant lounges, a 25-unit shopping complex, 450-seat theatre/cinema, casino, nightclubs and disco, ten-channel TV in every cabin, nine bars, top-class entertainment galore, four swimming pools, gymnasium and health club and heaven knows how many acres of deck space, the ship is a floating resort, never mind a floating hotel.

The cuisine is in keeping with the ship's other facilities and the service is friendly, efficient and discreet. Slimming it is not, with three full meals a day plus late night buffets, afternoon teas and morning snacks!

You're in a very different world when you step on board Concorde, the most beautiful of all flying machines. The takeoff is dramatic, but when you go through the speed of sound and well beyond you hardly feel a thing. Look out of the little windows at 60 000 feet or so up and you really can see that the earth is round – and jumbo jets far below appear to be going backwards. You have six-channel audio entertainment, *haute cuisine*, fine wine and superb service. The three-and-a-half hours, London to New York, go by all too quickly.

These holidays, which operate from May to November, are steep to start with and prices rise according to choice of cabin, length of stay and hotel. But life's luxuries never come cheap.

CHAPTER NINE

Snow Scenes

The perfect way to break up the long grey months of a British winter is to take off for some sunny Alpine slope and ski to your heart's content. The air crackles with vitality, the views are fantastic, the sensations exhilarating. There is no other holiday quite like it, and ski holidays are getting better all the time. So it's not surprising that every winter sees more and more British skiers in day-glo anoraks assembling at UK airports, headed for the snowfields of Europe – and beyond. Well over half a million of us count no winter complete without a week or two hurtling down some dazzling piste, or getting away from the crowds by skiing the untracked powder of the high mountains or, at the other extreme, using skis for their original purpose and following long, quiet, cross-country trails on slide-and-glide cross-country skis.

We're getting better on the snow, too. Gone are the days when taking out a party of British skiers was regarded by the average Alpine instructor as a kind of penance. We now rank with the best in the world, while we can be proud that our skiing athletes regularly win medals in the Lowland Championships and are challenging strongly in World Cup Races. How long before the miracle happens and a British skier brings home a medal from the Olympics?

History is on our side, for the British are rightly credited with the invention of Alpine skiing. Modern skiing began barely 100 years ago, when a group of hardy Britons at Murren in the Swiss Alps spent their winters climbing up the snow-clad local slopes all morning for the brief thrill of sliding back down to the village in the late afternoon. Today, that sort of skiing, on empty mountain slopes, seems like a glimpse of another, gentler world.

Skiing today is one of the holiday industry's best organised activities. Go to any country and any mountain endowed with a regular supply of snow is festooned with chairlifts and tows. The local village will have its ski school, staffed with carefully trained instructors, and the hotels, pensions, chalets and bars stand ready.

As skiing has expanded, it has also changed, offering greater challenges and variety. Since the last war, skiing has broken free of its Alpine roots. Today there is good skiing all over the world in both hemispheres, summer and winter. All you need is a glacier. There are ski tours; ski safaris; powder skiing on off-piste, untracked snow; great lift and run ski circuses. Whatever you want, the ski world has it – though, of course, the facilities vary. If you're keen to break new ground, you can ski in Canada and the USA every winter – Kathy Tayler brought back the first USA ski report from Breckenridge in *Holiday 88*. Then there's Turkey, Greece, southern Spain, New Zealand, Australia, Chile, and even the High Atlas of North Africa, high above the desert sand. One of the bonuses of America, Kathy found, is that there's no language problem – until they start saying things like, 'We favour the humanistic approach'. Unscrambled, that means, 'We'll help you learn what you want to learn!'

However, the pick of the world's skiing still lies in western Europe, in the Alps, the Dolomites and the Pyrenees. Here the facilities are top notch, the après-ski glittering, the lift and run networks at their most extensive, the instruction at its most professional. Nowhere in the world can match the 400 miles of run and the 176-lift network of the Portes-du-Soleil, which straddles the Franco-Swiss frontier by Avoriaz; or the 300 miles of run and 180 lifts available from Méribel, Courchevel or Val Thorens, across the Trois Vallées; or the marvellous network of lifts and runs and shuttle buses that make up the Italian network of the Superski Dolomiti around Cortina and San Cassiano.

European resorts not only have the finest skiing but also offer the richest mix of lifestyles and atmosphere on and off the slopes. Here is skiing for every kind of skier, from the all-out, off-piste, gung-ho expert to the timid beginner or the holiday intermediate, from those who want to ski and ski to those who rate the sunshine, the scenery, the food and the nightlife every bit as important as the depth of the powder or the steepness of the pistes. Like me. The first ski location I reported for *Holiday* was Zermatt, and I did it as a non-skier. This was perfectly valid because a great many people go there simply to enjoy the glorious clear air, the ambience of this Christmas-card resort and walks in the valleys. Since then I have learned to ski – luckily not on film since I spent most of the time horizontal! This was in the French Pyrenees, a great area for anyone who wants thrills without frills. You don't have to keep up with the smart set, which is non-existent, and everything is reasonably priced. There is also plenty to occupy non-skiers or off-duty skiers. Late in the season, when there's still snow on the glaciers, the resorts are dry, full of spring flowers and the sound of rushing streams. Then you can swim in outdoor pools and play tennis.

The ski scenes outlined in this chapter give you an idea not only of the kinds of skiing available in half a dozen different countries, but also of the kinds of different attractions and people you're likely to meet. Skiing isn't just for the jet set or the posers in their chinchilla trimmed anoraks, any more than it is purely for crack skiers. It's for freewheelers and families, young enthusiasts and old hands. So there really isn't a 'best' ski resort. There is only the best for you. In this short list, there should be something for everyone.

THIS RESORT'S CERTAINLY GOT STYLE

ST JOHANN-IM-TYROL

For many British skiers, especially those who cling to the traditional idea of what a skiing holiday should be like, there is really only one country – Austria. This is the country with the small, friendly, exquisitely kept hotels, the gnarled instructors, the Tyrolean evenings with the thigh slapping and the *lederhosen*, the *glühwein* and the *schnapps* – all those little touches that add up to the *gemütlichkeit* (the untranslatable term for cosiness and bonhomie) which makes the perfect ski holiday.

Although most of the resorts in Austria offer the same appealing mix of atmosphere and facilities, there are distinct differences. Those who want to mix and mingle with the jet setters will choose Lech; those who like a challenge will opt for the steep slopes of St Anton; those who like it quaint choose Alpbach. Those who want a typical resort which is ideal for first-time skiers, keen intermediates and family parties, will choose St Johann-im-Tyrol.

St Johann lies on the far side of the Kitzbuhler Horn peak, an old and very pretty Tyrolean village. It is full of hotels which lean over the narrow streets and offer all the elements of traditional Tyrolean hospitality: hot spicy wine, fattening cakes and strudel, frothing steins of beer, hot chocolate – and big smiles.

The skiing is fairly limited with only 16 lifts giving access to just 20 miles (32 km) of piste, plus a small amount of off-piste; but this is excellent, on wide, well-tended and delightfully bumpy slopes, just perfect for carving a turn or cutting a dash. Like many Austrian resorts, St Johann is perfect for absolute beginners. They find the slopes fairly merciful and the instructors patient. The resort also suits mixed-ability groups of friends or family, for everyone stays on the same mountain and there are plenty of places on the slopes where you can rendezvous and meet up for lunch or mid-morning coffee. The best word to sum up the skiing in St Johann is 'flattering' – for however good or bad you are, St Johann's slopes will make you look better!

Above all, St Johann is the perfect setting in which to enjoy to the full those well-tried daily routines. First of all there is the skiing and the long lunch in the sunshine. Then, after the skiing, it's the après-ski bar for wine or hot chocolate and dancing to the local oom-pah-pah band. Some of the players, on closer inspection, may turn out to be the ski instructors who were busy on the slopes less than an hour before. Then comes dinner at the hotel, where clear soups and various kinds of veal are the menu staples, and then out to a bar for more dancing and, for the younger ones at least, on to a disco. In Austrian discos, modern rock is interrupted from time to time by the strains of a Viennese waltz, which everyone seems to enjoy. Finally, there is the folklore evening, when the dancers – who, strangely, may also turn out to be the ski instructors – appear in leather shorts to demonstrate the iron workers' or the woodchoppers' *tanz*, plus sing songs with a great deal of yodelling. The noise is tremendous and the kids love it!

Yes, St Johann has successfully kept all the traditional elements while adding on, as most resorts must, the newer attractions of a swimming pool, indoor tennis courts, ice rink, and so on. There are also excursions to Salzburg and Innsbruck. It really does offer everything you could possibly want on a winter holiday.

BRAVE NEW LA PLAGNE

France is said to be the country for the serious, competitive holiday skier, and this view is almost certainly correct, for France has all the essential ingredients. It has the great ski lift circuses, the steepest slopes, the most impatient instructors. It has resorts where skiers can ski to their own front door and it has fast and furious lift systems.

France also has La Plagne. Now La Plagne can be confusing. The resort consists of a number of custom-built residential complexes, currently six, littered across the mountains of Savoy high above the old village of Aime. Each complex comes complete with shopping mall, disco, restaurants, ski shops – indeed, all the comforts of away-from-home; but since all the complexes look rather alike, visitors can spend a lot of time trying to work out which is which, especially at the end of a long day.

This confusion is not helped by the similarity of names: La Plagne and Plagne Bellecôte and Plagne Village and Plagne 1800, for example. All are linked by a lift and run system that accurately claims to be the largest single resort ski system in the world. This is, in fact, the secret and the great compensation of La Plagne – the skiing and the skiing facilities are simply superb.

To begin with, the resort is only three hours by coach from Geneva airport. Then, the nearby Bellecôte glacier is not only open for summer skiing but also guarantees skiing when there is little snow elsewhere. This is an advantage for early or late season skiers. The skiing here falls into two main categories: excellent on-piste for the intermediates and a great amount of off-piste for the experts. Much of it is on slopes around the resort complexes, with the possibility of long full-day tours to Les Arcs and Courchevel – although to do that you must hop on a bus here and there and leave the resort very early the next morning. Beginners are catered for with plenty of nursery slopes and a high standard of instruction that aims to have complete beginners doing parallel turns by the end of the first week!

La Plagne is largely an apartment/self-catering resort and the first rule is to book an apartment one size larger than you think you need. Most self-catering apartments seem to be designed for midgets, so four will be much more comfortable in an apartment advertised for six – unless they are all very small, very friendly, and don't mind keeping ski boots in the bath! Sensible people use their apartments merely for sleeping, changing and eating breakfast, spending as much time as possible on the slopes or the après-ski circuit.

There's a good selection of mountain restaurants and perfect cafés for pit-stops, though for a really good lunch you need to return to base, whizz down the mountain to Montchavin, where Le Sauget or La Ferme are always popular, or try for a table on the sunny terrace at La Tormente of Montalbert. Mega lunches are normally taken at Chez Thérèse in Champagny, where you get five or six courses plus all the wine you can drink at very bearable prices. Few skiers can resist this lure, and since many of the people who go to La Plagne go in groups, the lunch parties at Chez Therèse sometimes last all afternoon.

The wide spread of the resort tends to complicate nightlife in La Plagne: that dishy fellow or gorgeous girl is always staying at one of the other complexes, which are not very accessible after dark. Fortunately each centre has its own share of après-ski, the Pescalune being everybody's favourite for a *vin chaud* or hot chocolate. There are several good restaurants, like the Refuge Savoyade in La Plagne, where the locals go, and Le Matafan at Belle Plagne, which is always good and sometimes excellent. Although discos abound, there isn't a great deal of ritzy nightlife.

La Plagne is a resort for families of mixed ability, for groups of friends who all ski quite well, and for couples who like to ski a little and eat out rather a lot. Given the enormous variety of slopes, the amount of skiing in one tight local area, and the masses of other British visitors, the enduring popularity of La Plagne is easy to understand.

TWO SWISS WINNERS: VERBIER AND ZERMATT

Switzerland has so many top class resorts, it's quite hard to choose just one, so here are two! In any selection of the best, few would deny Verbier and Zermatt places in the top six. But they couldn't be more different.

Verbier is the younger, in more ways than one. It dates from the immediate post-war period and attracts the younger set. In fact, not to put too fine a point on things, it tends to be Sloane Square on the Slopes, the Alpine rendezvous for Hooray-Henrys and Fionas. Having said that, Verbier would not have earned and kept its position in the top rank of Swiss ski resorts if the facilities weren't excellent and the skiing first class. It's also a great centre for that uniquely British institution, the chalet holiday, and that indispensable attraction, the chalet girl. Verbier is full of chalets, large and small, all offering big breakfasts, cake at teatime and a chance to put the world right over dinner to an audience of like-minded Britons. These holidays resemble house parties, so it helps to take a friend if you're not instantly gregarious. But chalet holidays can be the perfect answer if you're on your own, since you have the chance to make friends on the very first evening and will probably find someone of similar ability to go skiing with during the day.

Verbier's skiing can cater for every level of skill, but Swiss price levels dictate that to get real value for money from Verbier's slopes you need to be able to ski. Much of the piste and all of the off-piste skiing is suitable only for experts, and some of the local black runs can be very black indeed. Verbier is really a resort for those who ski well and like to ski all day and every day throughout their holiday.

After testing skiing and a tasty large chalet dinner, many people are more than ready for bed, but those who step out for fresh air usually end up in one of the local night spots, perhaps among the chalet girls at the Milk Bar or in the Farm Club or Tara's with the expatriate Sloane Rangers. Like everything else, the nightlife in Verbier isn't cheap, but it's varied and great fun for those with the collateral and the stamina to enjoy it.

Zermatt is another story. One of the oldest ski centres in Europe, it is different both from Verbier and from practically everywhere else in the Alps. It is different because it has class, old money, and above all, the Matterhorn, that beautiful knife-blade of a mountain which looms over the town, following you everywhere like the eyes of the Mona Lisa.

Zermatt goes back to Roman times, and from the Middle Ages until quite recently the village, with its cuckoo-clock houses, and the surrounding countryside, including the Matterhorn, were the exclusive possession of three Swiss families. It actually took a High Court action by the Swiss government in the 1970s to persuade the burghers of Zermatt that the entire nation owned the Matterhorn!

The charm of the town itself owes much to the fact that cars are not allowed. Everyone makes the last ten minutes of the journey from nearby Tasch by train and then by horse-drawn carriages. Exceptions are made for some business deliveries and taxis, but even these vehicles have to conform to a kind of electric milk-float design which, oddly enough, evolved from an actual British milk van someone sent there over 20 years ago. The lack of traffic helps preserve the Christmas-card feel of the place.

Zermatt has chalets, too, but is really more of a hotel resort, and since no country in the world possesses such excellent hoteliers as Switzerland, the standards are naturally first class. The duvets are like cumulus clouds, the rooms spotless, the central heating efficient and the service beyond criticism. The food is always delicious, even halfway up the slopes in the mountain eateries. The resourceful Swiss seem to have devised more permutations of potatoes, onions, ham, eggs and cheese than any other nation. Nothing comes cheap, but you certainly get your money's worth.

Apart from old world charm, the great attraction of Zermatt is the high quality of the skiing which, like the resort itself, can be summed up in one word: excellent. There are three main skiing areas – Sunnega at 7000 feet, Gornergrat-Stockhorn at around 10 000, and Klein Matterhorn at 12 500. These offer over 100 miles of exciting, varied piste, plus the possibilities of skiing round the Matterhorn and down to Cervinia in Italy or, for off-piste experts, a section of the famous Haute Route.

Compared with custom-built resorts with ski lifts on their doorsteps, Zermatt is less convenient. You have to tot up the cost of getting yourself and your clobber to the ski lifts every day, and that can mount up. The lift system used to be frightful, but is now vastly improved with 35 lifts of different kinds.

Another point to remember is that, unlike many of the French resorts, there aren't unlimited nursery slopes: Zermatt isn't a haven for beginners or children, though there are the usual high standards of tuition and good ski schools should you want to learn. It is, however, a marvellous resort to take a non-skiing partner. Quite a few people come just to walk – even in winter – on the miles of waymarked trails through the valleys and the lower slopes, enjoying the sun and mountain air without living too dangerously.

LITTLE ANDORRA

Lying in the centre of the Pyrenees, Andorra is in a category by itself. A rocky little condominium ruled jointly by France and Spain, its official language is Catalan – the dialect spoken in Roussillon and Barcelona – not, as you'd imagine, French or Spanish. It's very small and all the resorts are within easy reach of each other. It's very cheap – therefore popular with young, first-time skiers on a budget. And since the whole of Andorra is entirely duty-free, it's a mecca for compulsive shoppers.

Andorra has only developed as a ski destination in the last ten years, but has spurted ahead with lots of new accommodation in hotels or self-catering apartments. Today there are five well-equipped ski resorts, all offering perfectly adequate skiing up to the intermediate level. The skiing is boosted by a great deal of inexpensive nightlife and, of course, by all that duty-free shopping.

Several British companies use Andorra as a centre for specially organised beginner's courses and 'Start-to-Ski' weeks. The resorts selected are not too testing and the package includes everything from skis to lift pass, lots of instruction, and the company of people in the same boat, to mix a metaphor. A big plus is that the local ski schools are staffed by competent instructors, many of them English speaking. Indeed, many of them are British or Australian or from New Zealand, graduates of that excellent institution the British Association of Ski Instructors (BASI), which has done so much to raise the standard of British skiing. BASI instructors can now be found all over the Alps, but mostly in Andorra.

Of the five ski resorts, Arinsal and Soldeu are the favourites. Arinsal is a traditional mountain resort built round an old village, where skiers of every level have a place. There is the usual excellent ski school and a good selection of challenging red runs from the 2572-foot Pic Nègre mountain, which should keep even a competent intermediate happy for a few days. Real experts are served by two hard off-piste black runs from the top of La Capa. One little novelty at Arinsal is the pre-set slalom slope, where would-be ace skiers can pit themselves against the clock through a series of gates. This really gets the competitive urges going, and also sharpens up those parallel turns rather quickly.

Though small, Arinsal has a lively bit of après-ski – several good piano bars and one popular disco, L'Oliba. Food tends to be local and tasty rather than refined and expensive – there are lots of soups and stews on the hotel menus – but there are several fine restaurants like the Borda del Avi just two miles down the road, halfway towards the resort of La Massana. Transport between resorts is no problem.

Soldeu is a busy town and very popular with the young, economy-minded jet set. The skiing here might have been designed for beginners, or those ubiquitous ever-improving intermediates, for all the slopes fall within the intermediate range. Soldeu is the largest of the Andorran resorts – Canillo, Andorra-la-Bella, La Massana, La Mollera and Arinsal are the others. If forced to choose, it's worth remembering that Soldeu has a very good sunshine record: even in February skiers can acquire a most impressive tan on the wide, open, sunny slopes spread out above the town. For Andorra, where the resort runs tend to be limited, there is a surprising amount of skiing here, with no less than 32 miles (52 km) of waymarked piste plus a certain amount of off-piste. As everywhere else, the après-ski is both cheap and cheerful with a very wide range of bars and discos. If you want something more sophisticated – even a little up-market – there is excellent French cuisine available at the Hôtel Bruxelles.

All in all, Andorra is the perfect choice for energetic, outgoing beginners, or small mixed groups of friends who like to ski a little and dance a lot. Over the years, it has introduced tens of thousands to the basic joys of skiing. Since skiing never lacks for fresh contenders, it's likely to go on doing so.

ITALIAN STYLE IN CORTINA D'AMPEZZO

Italian skiing is colourful and lively – the Italians see to that. Listed in the top three 'best' countries by British skiers, Italy offers a wide choice of resorts: beautiful Courmayeur at the foot of Mont Blanc – or should that be Monte Bianco – with varied intermediate runs and lots of good nightlife; the 'motorway' pistes of Cervinia, with reliable snow and a pass to Zermatt; challenging Bormio; ever-popular Sauze d'Oulx, especially with younger Brits; fashionable Sestriere, which the Italians prefer to most other places; charming little Santa Caterina . . .where do you stop?

Most of these are Alpine resorts. Italy has a great many mountain ranges and one well-kept secret, an area still little visited by British skiers – the Dolomites. Yet the sheer-sided Dolomites must rank among the world's most beautiful mountains, and in their heart nestles one of the world's most attractive ski resorts, Cortina d'Ampezzo.

Many Dolomite resorts have a distinctly Tyrolean feel, but Cortina has always been an Italian town, so the atmosphere on and off the slopes reflects that laid-back lifestyle and lazy charm that makes any holiday in Italy doubly relaxing.

Committed skiers who've travelled a lot rate Italian skiing high and discount those well-worn stories of amorous instructors and fifth-hand lift systems. The truth is that Italian skiing is amazingly well organised, great fun and greatly

underrated. In fact, nowhere in the Alps are the skiing and the
lift systems better than in Cortina d'Ampezzo. Around it you
have the great ski circuit of the Superski Dolomiti, which can
offer hundreds of lifts and hundreds of miles of run. Depending
on the route chosen, these are suitable for every skier of
intermediate ability or better.

Cortina sits in a snow bowl, an old town full of hotels and
attractive chalets. It's a winter centre for the Italian glitterati,
who gather every evening to stroll up and down the Corso
Italia. This main thoroughfare is lined with jewellers, boutiques
and ski-wear shops selling the absolute latest in slope-side
fashion. Mind you, whether you can actually ski in some of
their streamlined suits is open to question. Even the crowds are
worth looking at on the Corso Italia: a heady collection, all in
dark glasses, dripping with jewellery and snow-sweeping fur
coats – and that's only the men! A fur coat is a unisex garment
in Cortina, but rumour has it that many of them never actually
leave the resort – they're simply passed from one group of
friends to another somewhere behind the railway station!

By day, the smart set shifts to the surrounding slopes where,
since Cortina has hosted the Olympic Games and World Cup
events, the skiing is superb. There are four main ski areas: the

Faloria; the San Forca-Cristallo; the Tofana, which is served by the marvellously named cablecar *Freccia nel Cielo* – Arrow in the Sky; and the Sella Ronda circuit. Cortina actually lies a little off the Sella Ronda, but it is on the Superski Dolomiti ski pass and has easy access to both circuits. The start of the Sella Ronda tour, and access to the other local areas covered by the Superski pass, is within easy reach of Cortina by shuttle bus and the interlinked lift system.

Most visitors begin their skiing in Cortina with a trip up to the Faloria, where there are good open slopes with wide, bouncy pistes running through the trees, and a good end-of-the-day run down to the restaurant at the Rio Gere. All the Cortina slopes are well supplied with terraced bars and restaurants where you can while away a rather long lunch hour or stop for a capuccino. Serious skiers will find the Tofana slopes more challenging than the Faloria, and everyone from the intermediate stage up will want to spend at least one day on the Sella Ronda, swooping and soaring through that fabulous Dolomite scenery round a circuit of attractive resorts which includes Corvara and the beautiful village of San Cassiano.

There's no doubt about it, Cortina has a fantastic atmosphere. The very air pulses with pzazz. You can breathe it in on every sunlit terrace and in every bar and restaurant after dark, which is when the town comes alive. The après-ski scene here is very much part of the holiday, and the evening will probably begin in one of those little piano bars off the Corso Italia, followed by a visit to one of the town's top discos, like the Lub Dlub. Here the tiered seating gives older hands a chance to watch the *jeunesse dorée* gyrate on the floor – and the restaurant stays open until dawn. Or there's the Orange, which is great fun for the young, or the Ippopotimus, which tends to attract wilder spirits in even wilder clothes.

A final plus: Cortina is only a couple of hours by train from Venice, that achingly beautiful Italian city which no romantic should resist (see chapter 7). So with terrific skiing, style, splendid nightlife and great excursions, Cortina really has a superabundance of assets.

BRECKENRIDGE, COLORADO, USA

Skiing in Europe has the tradition; skiing in the States has the dash, the spice and the space. It has all the expected elements of efficiency, friendliness, excitement, noise – in other words, the vitality of America – plus lots of snow and vast amounts of stunning scenery.

In many ways the skiing is very different, in spite of the superficial similarities of snow, sun and high mountains. In fact, the whole ambience is different. In America the scale of the mountains tends to be bigger while the resorts, on the whole, tend to be smaller. Most Europeans find this surprising and many Americans greet it with disbelief (it is, after all, a well-known fact that everything in America is bigger). Many of the resorts have plenty of skiing and some resorts are linked, but American resorts still cannot match the great European ski areas of, say, the Trois Vallées, the Portes-du-Soleil or Italy's Superski Dolomiti for runs, lifts and the sheer amount of skiing available.

On the other hand, small is friendly. The great attraction of skiing in the USA for many European visitors is the welcome you get from American skiers, and the general air of politeness and consideration. In America there is none of that queue-barging and rudeness you find in all too many European centres. In fact, there are very few queues. Most American ski resorts operate double or triple chairlifts and all these operate on an informal 'singles' queue system. This means that any lone skier arriving at the lift line yells out, 'single!' Other single skiers in the line, or couples looking for a third for the ride, reply by yelling back 'single!' Then they team up. Reserved British skiers sometimes find this familiarity with total strangers somewhat alarming, but since the result is that all chairs travel full and the lift lines shrink dramatically, most soon adopt the system.

There are many fine ski resorts in the States, but Colorado has most of the best known: Aspen, Snowmass, Copper Mountain, Buttermilk, Vail, and Breckenridge – the one where good skiing is combined with a distinctly American, indeed western, atmosphere. Eighty miles west of Denver, Breckenridge is the only resort in the world, according to local enthusiasts, where you can enjoy some of the finest skiing plus the unique ambience of a mining town that is *all of 130 years old*. In America, that's historic.

At 12 000 feet Breckenridge has loads of snow, and the low humidity makes it dry and generally easier to ski. There is skiing on three mountains which, somewhat unromantically, bear the practical titles of Peaks 8, 9 and 10. Together these offer over 100 varied pistes, or trails as they are called in America, plus large amounts of off-piste and that powder snow skiing which attracts skiers from all over the world to the slopes of the Rocky Mountains. The resort caters for all levels of ability and offers every type of skiing, from gentle cruising on open slopes to steep, bumpy 'moguls' and ski touring above the timberline. If this seems too serious, there are scores of restaurants and over 70 bars, many of them housed in '100-year-old authentic Victorian buildings'. As is usual in the USA, the accommodation tends to be in ski lodges or apartments in sprawling condominiums. From these the skiers set out for the slopes in shuttle buses or explore the town by night, taking in all there is of that friendly, open-hearted, American hospitality – and there's a great deal. However, it would be fair to say that the après-ski scene, though lively, is not terribly sophisticated.

As a little bonus, American skiing is fairly cheap – at least once you get to the slopes and as long as the pound stays strong against the dollar. What wouldn't be cheap is a hospital bill if you came a cropper – remember medical care is very expensive in the States. So if you plan to ski there, be sure you take out the best possible comprehensive ski insurance, just in case.

America is not for beginners. Colorado is a long way to go if you can't ski well enough to enjoy those long runs and all that Rocky Mountain powder, so you've got to be keen – and good at it. Wise holidaymakers will go for at least two or three weeks, hire a car and go touring as well as skiing.

CHAPTER TEN

The Perfect Place for a Honeymoon

Shirley Conran once remarked that Paris was wasted on lovers since the ceilings there were the same as anywhere else. While that may be so, there's a fine difference when it comes to honeymooners – especially these days when newlyweds are rarely preoccupied with bed. Spending a honeymoon where there is plenty of interest is therefore quite important. Apart from other considerations, two people suddenly given an undiluted dose of each other's company after the delirium of wedding fever need an antidote. So Paris is very much on the books.

There are other utterly beautiful and distracting places for your honeymoon where the backdrops are stunning, the foreground romantic and well seasoned by lovers past and present. Hence the inclusion here of two locations in Italy with no apologies. Kathy Tayler spent part of her honeymoon at Lake Maggiore – needless to say, without the rest of the *Holiday* team in tow! When I went filming there, we couldn't aim our camera anywhere without catching loving couples draped around each other on walls, terraces and in the back row of the lake launches, totally oblivious to a BBC crew observing their clinches.

Almost every place in this chapter has lured one or more of us back with our nearest and dearest or a very good friend. Bill Buckley went back to Ravello, Gillian Reynolds to Austria. That's as good a recommendation as any.

It may seem a basic point, but if you want to nurture romance it's not a bad idea to choose a place where the standards of plumbing are circumspect. This minimises the risk of spending a gastric time in bed. It also helps if the standard of service is high. Haranguing waiters is not the stuff of which happy times are made.

What all this adds up to might be a mite too civilised for some. If so, they will find alternative and more adventurous options in other chapters. These honeymoon suggestions will appeal to anyone who wants to play out sentimental scenes in a truly romantic atmosphere. That goes not only for newlyweds but also just-good-friends, husbands and wives reviving flagging marriages, and Darby-and-Joan contestants celebrating golden weddings.

BESIDE THE LAKE, BENEATH THE TREES

An inspired location for a spring honeymoon or end-of-winter fillip is the Lake District. Among the top half dozen most popular holiday destinations in Britain, it is inevitably busy in summer, but when Wordsworth's daffodils are in bloom, it can be idyllic.

Mind you, it is perhaps stretching things a bit to hope to find the daffs where the great poet actually saw them 'tossing their heads in sprightly dance'. They have sadly all but petered out in the woodland at Gowbarrow on the shores of Ullswater where William wandered not 'lonely as a cloud' but with his sister Dorothy. It was she, in fact, who first wrote about the daffodils in her diary, providing her brother with some of his choicest phrases for the famous poem.

But Ullswater is still heavenly, and you won't have to go far to discover a host of narcissi – for instance, next to the church below Rydal Mount. Wordsworth actually planted them in this patch, known as Dora's Field. A visit to pretty Dove Cottage with its slate roof and lattice windows is an obligatory pilgrimage for seekers after Wordsworthiana. Here in Grasmere William began his married life with Mary Hutchinson, and Dorothy stayed on, Mary being a childhood friend of both. As you tour the tiny rooms you can imagine how the ergonomics of living *à trois* might at times have tested their affections for one another.

There are several points at which you can trace the Wordsworth story: at the Rydal Mount house, to which they eventually moved and which is full of touching personal reminders, even down to family picnic boxes; in the woodland around it; and at the Wordsworth House in Cockermouth, the lovely Georgian mansion overlooking the River Derwent, where the poet was born.

Cockermouth is a wonderful old market town on the fringe of this National Park area of Cumbria. There are magnificent mountain walks and endlessly photogenic flashes of incandescent water reflecting wooded shores.

Where to stay? There is the pleasant three-star Broughton Craggs Hotel just outside Cockermouth or the four-star Wordsworth (there had to be one) in Grasmere. But perhaps the best plan would be to retreat to a distance after sightseeing and treat yourselves to a stay at one of England's gastronomic landmarks, the Miller Howe Hotel and Restaurant at Windermere. John Tovey, the celebrated chef and proprietor, describes Windermere as 'the gateway to heaven'. The view from the terrace at Miller Howe on a good day certainly renders guests speechless: the gardens, then the green and gold fields falling gently away to the lake with the great peaks of Scafell, Crinkle Craggs, Pike O'Bisco and Wetherham piercing the distant skyline. The food at Miller Howe will also render you speechless – with pleasure, of course.

HIGHLAND FLING

Scotland is so full of beauty spots with honeymoon potential that it's almost impossible to pinpoint one. But Oban, on the edge of the Western Highlands, gives an infinitely varied range of options for having a lovely time in a lovely setting.

The trouble with Highland scenery is that it has a habit of hiding behind a veil of mist or rain. May and September visitors have the best chance of clear skies.

It's worth taking the train to Oban via Glasgow, for the approach through the mountains is one of the country's most scenic routes. Alternatively, go the other way on a day trip *from* Oban to see the renaissance of Glasgow and the magnificent Burrell Collection of art. Total perfection would be to arrive in Oban by sea, for you get the best view of it sailing into its sheltered harbour, the backdrop of rugged mountains and rolling green hills a foil for its solid red stone and whitewashed buildings. Crowning the town is what appears to be a half-scale reproduction of Rome's Colosseum. Known as McCaig's Folly, this interesting structure was built by a local businessman in the final years of Queen Victoria's reign, partly to satisfy his own vanity and partly to give work to the unemployed. It was never finished – but it certainly adds distinction to the skyline.

For well over a century Oban has been an attractive resort, a leading yachting centre, fishing port and market town. It's a bright and cheerful place without the razzmatazz of bigger centres, just right for a couple who don't want too many noises-off to spoil their own dialogue.

Boat trips to those romantic islands, the Hebrides, are pure pleasure if the weather is kind. You can hop on a ferry and sail across to Mull, grandest of the Inner Hebrides. In the main summer months non-stop cruises go round Mull, showing you Staffa with famous Fingal's Cave and dear little Iona, birthplace of Christianity in Scotland.

On the mainland, drive north along the spectacular coastline to Ballachulish, then inland and up the dramatic Vale of Glencoe. Return via Loch Awe, arguably the most beautiful of Scotland's inland lochs. Loch Fyne, Loch Eyck and even Loch Lomond are within striking distance. Southwards you can follow another pretty route and reach the small fertile island of Seil by 'crossing the Atlantic by bridge'. It's not a local leg pull – the elegant stone bridge that links the mainland with the island has always been known as the Atlantic Bridge. And, of course, it is.

Anyone planning to have a really grand home in the future can perhaps pick up some tips on a visit to Inveraray Castle, a delightful 40-mile (65-km) drive from Oban. This splendid mid-eighteenth-century pile is more a palace than a castle, and the traditional home of the Dukes of Argyll. It is one of Scotland's most magnificent great houses.

The Oban Tourist Office will send you as many details about where to stay and what to see hereabouts as you need (see address list in appendix).

THE CITY OF LIGHT

A 'honeymoon in Paris' may seem a cliché, but there's no denying the French capital is still as alluring as ever to people in love, whatever age they may be. From Eloise and Abelard to Edward VIII and Wallis Simpson to Charlotte Rampling and Jean-Michel Jarre, the City of Light has drawn couples to its flame. Even if you sometimes have to run the gamut of bloody-minded taxi drivers, snooty waiters and arrogant salespeople, its magic somehow remains undiluted.

From the second you arrive in some delicious hotel room – perhaps at the famous L'Hôtel in the rue des Beaux Arts, or at the exquisite Lancaster in the rue de Berri, or somewhere more modest covered in a riot of flowered wallpaper – you feel excited, stimulated, ready for *je ne sais quoi*.

A candlelit dinner aboard a *bateau mouche* drifting along the Seine is a good start, followed by a stroll on the Left Bank, down the Boul' Mich and along St Germain, stopping at the

Café de Flore or the Deux Magots for a cognac and to evoke the spirit of the existentialists in the days when every Parisienne who hung out around here wore a Juliette Greco bob. Then a walk around the lovely church of St Germain-des-Prés and into the intriguing little rue St-André-des-Arts, full of bookshops and the boutiques of small avant-garde designers, of late-late cafés and *crêperies* with their syrup jars set up to glow in the light. Back to the river and Notre Dame until the floodlights go down at midnight, leaving the cathedral's glorious pinnacles and flying buttresses paling in the shadows.

Paris is small enough to see almost entirely on foot, provided you section it off in malleable chunks. The odd Métro ride helps and is an enjoyable experience anyway. Montmartre, forever touristy but never trite, has its artistic ghosts – Utrillo, Van Gogh, Renoir. Look out for the Moulin de la Galette of their paintings, now restored and presiding over a development of chic apartments. Today's painters in the Place du Tertre may know more about street theatre than about art but they don't spoil the scenery. Then there's Montparnasse, where Hemingway lingered to scribble at the Closerie des Lilas and Gauguin flaunted his Javanese mistress at La Coupole – a great place to eat among the latest literary and media luminaries.

Central Paris is the Louvre and the Tuileries, the Champs Elysées and the Faubourg St Honoré. Window gaze unless you feel like squandering a few months' mortgage money, then buy a picnic at Fauchon (designer deli) and retire with a bottle of Veuve Clicquot to the delightful little Jardin du Palais-Royal. Colette's old flat looked down upon this quiet rectangle where strangely few people go.

Another unmissable square is the fourteenth-century Place des Vosges in the Marais, where the elite used to go to flaunt their finery after Louis XIII's wedding festivities made it an in place. And don't forget that charming lesser island in the Seine, Ile St Louis, across the bridge from Notre Dame's Ile de la Cité. Here, in one of the most elegant quarters of Paris, the Aga Khan and other jet setters keep expensive *pieds à terre*.

But Paris is also about the new. The essence of its appeal is that it has always been a creative hotbed. There are some very exciting new areas like that around the Centre Pompidou art centre, nicknamed 'the oil refinery', and the Forum des Halles shopping and culture complex. The latter is a more acceptable architectural innovation, all conservatorial glass corridors and open spaces – and the easiest place to shop for clothes since all the designer labels are under one roof. The surrounding streets are great fun after dark, throbbing with life and more lively restaurants than ever there were when this was the old Les Halles food market pitch.

Whatever nightlife you fancy, don't ditch the obvious without investigation. The Moulin Rouge may not be all it's cracked up to be but the Lido show is superb, and great value if you go in after dinner and stand at the bar to watch the spectacle. A couple of double-measure drinks pays for everything. The Crazy Horse night club is very expensive, but there are lots of other smaller places listed in papers like *La Semaine de Paris*. These are not only cheaper, but younger and more typically Parisian. If you're on a tight budget, a stroll around Pigalle is often entertainment enough, though nowadays it's rather more seamy than naughty. A hand-in-hand shuffle by the Seine and a bowl of onion soup in the small hours is a lot more romantic.

MEDIEVAL BRUGES

An enchanted fourteenth-century town, hardly touched by the twentieth, Bruges is the perfect place for a brief honeymoon. Throw the cases in the back of the car, put the car on a ferry to Ostend or Zeebrugge, and in less than an hour from either Belgian port you arrive at this utterly beautiful medieval burg, where everything new must be built to match its original style. Even the Holiday Inn here is designed to blend into the scenery – though, of course, inside it's as up-to-date as any, complete with swimming pool, sauna, and other universal Holiday Inn comforts. For old world charm there's the Duc de Bourgogne, with its candlelit restaurant leaning langorously over the canal.

Watery Bruges, willows billowing everywhere, is predictably dubbed 'Venice of the North', along with Leningrad and Amsterdam. But this is no living Canaletto – more a living Breughel, perhaps. True, it is threaded with canals. True, the interior of every other public building is covered with wall-to-wall paintings (the Arents House, the Gruuthause, the Groeninge Museum). But Bruges is very much itself, an old Flemish trading city that was a busy Channel port before it retreated from the sea. Woolpacks from England were landed here to be woven into a much sought-after cloth, wines came from France and, in the days of the Dutch East Indies Company, spices from the Orient.

Bruges became rich and enriched. Great art and clever crafts flourished. Woodcarving and engraving inspired William Caxton to set up his first printing press here before heading for Westminster and the Red Pale. Everywhere you wander, Bruges is a feast for the senses – cobbles swirl in circular patterns, the spires of the great Gothic Town Hall soar, the whitewashed gables of the Beguinage dazzle, and beneath the little humped bridges that span the waterways swans drift by in pairs while above them nuns glide by in swan-shaped coiffes.

Take a canal boat trip and watch ivy-clad turrets and towers change places as the carillon of 47 bells from the Belfry echoes across the water and reverberates around the mellow stonework. Shop for Bruges lace in the Markt – you'll spot lacemakers parked in doorways – or stop for a hot chocolate and gooey cake at the Old Bruges Tea Room. On second thoughts, better save your appetite for dinner. All those paintings of paunchy burghers soon make sense when you're confronted with Belgian food . . . shh, it's better than French and the helpings are anything but *minceur*. Don't worry, you'll soon work it off wandering.

Even in winter Bruges is a delight – a lovely place to be in love.

TIPTOE THROUGH THE TYROL

A country where tourism has been a major moneyspinner for over a century, Austria more than measures up to its picture postcard image. It is unbelievably photogenic, hygienic, and the Austrians themselves are charm-bent-over-backwards. What more can you ask for on honeymoon? Romance? It's easy to generate against beautiful backdrops, especially when you know the cogs and wheels of the holiday are likely to turn with the precision of a cuckoo clock.

But don't just moon around. Do something. Try an easy walking holiday. This consists of a few days' ambling up the mossy foothills of the Alps, interspersed with quiet times sightseeing at your own pace.

Somewhere in the Tyrol would be perfect, anchored near Innsbruck, a lovely city with a fretwork of pedestrian streets. In its old quarter the houses are as pretty as marzipan and the rhythm of the place as predictable as a Mozart concerto – appropriately enough, since the great composer's dad was born here. Other notables came to an end in Innsbruck – the Emperor Maximilian, founder of the Hapsburg dynasty, whose tomb is in the ravishing sixteenth-century Court Church.

Above Innsbruck's high turrets, the mountains of the Tyrol reach for the sky. Sometimes, of course, the sky reaches down for the mountains and a shroud of cloud limits visibility – but that only focuses your attention on the greenness of the meadows and the wonderful pine-scented air.

When the snows and the ski crowds have melted away, the preoccupations of the Tyrol are climbing, hiking or merely happy wandering. The latter can be gently organised in small groups with mountain-wise guides who are ski instructors in summer clothing. You don't need special gear for these walks; strong leather shoes with profiled soles or even trainers are adequate when the ground's dry.

When you're not used to it, the first 20 minutes are the worst, since you start climbing at about 5000 feet. After that you get your second wind and a tremendous sense of well-being. Eight or nine miles (13 or 15 km) is an average day's ramble, with plenty of stops to look at the flowers, the birds and the bees. A hearty cheesey lunch in a chalet at halfway stage soon gets worked off on the way down and, back at base, you feel on top of the world!

A centre such as Igls, site of a former Olympic ski run, is ideal – three miles (5 km) from Innsbruck with the countryside on its doorstep. Church bells mingle with cow bells and geraniums blaze on balconies, while a stimulating farmyard whiff emanates from some of the ground floors where the animals are housed.

All hotels, large or small, have shining floors, pristine linen, airy duvets and smiling service. Some have pools. You can't go wrong.

On the days when you feel like climbing no further than up the steps of a coach, there are excursions to Salzburg, Berchtesgaden and Sperzing in Italy via the Brenner Pass. Sperzing is the place to shop for a bit of Italian style – it has some very elegant boutiques – and enjoy a pizza or pasta. Restaurant food is cheaper than in Austria, but not that much. Austria is not as expensive as it used to be – Britain has caught up.

Evenings in Igls are quiet until the band of the civic guard strikes up and the entire village turns out, or your walking guides amble round for schnapps and a yodel. They really do, and the nice thing is it happens spontaneously. In fact, the atmosphere of these 'wander-walk' holidays is so full of that warm and cosy *gemütlichkeit* that loving couples are well camouflaged.

SEDUCTIVE SEVILLE

Background for Carmen, Don Juan, the famous barber and the ballyhoo of the bullfight, Seville might not at first strike you as a place for romantic meanderings. But Seville is not only one of the most dramatic cities in Spain, it is also one of the most sensual.

In the heart of Andalusia, its atmosphere is essentially southern – warm, vibrant, relaxed, and as if permanently in the mood for a fiesta. Walk past any *tapas* bar at midday and you'll be lured in by the ratatatat of clapping to canned flamenco music. *Tapa* is the name given to the snack derived from placing a slice of ham over a glass of wine to keep the dust out in the days when it would be ordered from a cellar and carried through the streets. Today *tapas* come in 57 varieties – everything from chunks of ham and cheese to delicious deep-fried shellfish. In the lively clamour of these bars, which are often lined with vast sherry and wine casks, it's easy to eat such a surfeit of *tapas* you've no room left for a meal – no matter, it's a cheap and tasty way to lunch or dine.

Seville is full of contradictions. One moment it is cramped and picturesquely decrepit as you wander through the narrow back streets where strident señoras shout across at their neighbours and wrought-iron balconies are festooned with as much washing as bougainvillea. Then, turn a corner and it is suddenly gracious and spacious, with shady avenues and wide plazas. In one of these, the Plaza of the Americas, flocks of white doves rise and fall and feed from your hand as pigeons do in other cities. No one knows why they choose only this particular place.

The American continent is remembered a great deal in Seville, for after Columbus sailed forth along the River Guadalquivir to find the Indies and fetched up in the Caribbean, the spoils of later South American colonisation made Seville rich. The Torre d'Oro, or Golden Tower, is an evocative riverside landmark where the goodies used to be unloaded. There is a small restaurant on the other side of the river offering a marvellous panorama of the city.

Dominating the skyline is the third largest cathedral in the world, a massive Gothic structure which is really best seen from a distance. Inside, it is so cavernous and gloomy, it feels anything but a spiritual sanctuary. However, a sight not to miss is the nearby Moorish fortress of the Alcazar with its walled gardens which have more than a touch of a thousand-and-one-nights about them. The old lanes skirting its walls are wonderful to wander in. From Aguas to Judeira to the Patio de Banderas, orange trees are planted. In spring they fill the air with the scent of their blossom and in winter with the zesty smell of dropped fruit. Everywhere you catch glimpses of fabulously tiled courtyards through twirls of wrought iron, and half expect to see the shadow of Carmen.

Perhaps she really did exist. The tobacco factory in which Bizet set his opera is there – though it is now a college – and there's a statue of her across the road from the famous Maestranza bullring which, even if you disapprove of bull-fighting, you must look at. It is the most elegant in Spain, vivid in chrome yellow and white, the colours of Sevillian baroque.

Don Juan may have existed, too. It is said that the unscrupulous Miguel de Mañara was the inspiration for the legendary character and that he founded the seventeenth-century Hospital de la Caridad (Charity) in a fit of repentance for his naughty deeds.

After dark Seville is seductive out of doors and flamboyant indoors as restaurants burst into life, fairly late by our standards, and nightclubs resonate to the sound of flamenco. You'll see the best dancers in Spain here – many troupes come from Madrid. After some Andalusian wine and a good inexpensive meal the passions of the flamenco can be infectious.

STRESA AND THE ISLANDS, LAKE MAGGIORE

Where better to wander hand in hand than through the gardens of a villa built by a prince for his princess? The seventeenth-century Palazzo Borromeo, moored like some fantastic galleon just offshore from Stresa, is at the Italian end of Lake Maggiore. It is actually built on an island, Isola Bella, originally named Isola Isabella by a Prince Borromeo after his beloved wife. *Bella* it certainly is, with or without the *Isa*, though the whole thing is in a curiously overblown style that has been admired by some and ridiculed by others: 'the work of fairies' according to Gibbon; 'one of the most costly efforts of bad taste in Italy', Coleridge's friend Southey called it. The extraordinary tiered gardens, whose statues of prancing cherubs and muses waving lyres seem to change places as you approach from the lake, are filled with the scent of jasmine and roses. White peacocks pose on the gravel paths and lovers intertwine on the balustrades.

The area has long been a favourite stamping ground for the English: nowadays they seem to consist of either older people who prefer the temperature and tempo of lakeside living to that of a beach resort, or of young couples who have eyes for beauty as well as each other. It is simply gorgeous whichever way you turn. From Stresa, where grand hotels drip with Edwardian elegance – conservatories, terraces and striped awnings – you look out upon the lake, its mountainous far shores and the islands, each in a world of its own.

Another is Isola Madre with its own Borromeo palace – the Italian aristos have owned the lake plus everything that's on, in and around it since the Middle Ages. It's set amid delightful landscaped gardens. Isola del Pescatore is just what its name says – the fishermen's island: a village, very simple, where a few small waterside restaurants with pink tablecloths wait to serve you a plateful of crisp *arborelli*, the tiny lake fish which resemble whitebait.

The islands have no traffic and therefore nothing to disturb the peace. The same cannot be said of the lake shore, which has a busy main road running around it. However, an alternative route to divert heavy goods vehicles is soon to be completed and this will restore almost total tranquillity to Stresa. Night-life, by the way, is devoid of discos. There is little beyond lingering over the linguini and listening to palm-court pianists – and perhaps waiting for the naughty bits on late night Italian TV (not for prudes).

In the unlikely event of your tiring of the local vistas, Milan and its designer boutiques are an inexpensive train journey distant (one-and-a-half hours each way), Lugano and Locarno a boat trip to the Swiss end of Maggiore. It's only an hour's drive to the little-known jewel of Lake Orta, said to be the setting for the original Romeo and Juliet story on which Shakespeare based his play (quite believable when you see it).

I THOUGHT IT WAS A BIT OUT OF CHARACTER FOR YOU TO SUGGEST A ROMANTIC GONDOLA RIDE DOWN THE GRAND CANAL.

The real pleasure of Stresa is messing about in boats. Their skippers will sing *O Sole Mio* and regale you with tales of famous passengers like Toscanini and Hemingway, whose novel *A Farewell to Arms* featured Stresa. The romance doesn't end there, for you'll find a hundred claims of the Hemingway-slept-here variety at every stop on the lake shore, most to be taken with a pinch of salt. But who cares what is real or imagined in a place which is itself almost too enchanting to be true?

RAVISHING RAVELLO

If your true love doesn't go dreamy eyed in Ravello, you'll just have to face the fact that you're lumbered with a total non-romantic. This is one of the most picturesque villages in Italy, nestling in the mountains just a few hairpin-bend-filled minutes from the Amalfi coast. From its flower-filled terraces, the views are so stunning that you never stop exclaiming.

It has several obliging, family-run restaurants where you can eat well – and authentically – for not a lot of lira, and boasts some delightful hotels with opulent old-fashioned rooms, ever-smiling old-fashioned service and swimming pools. There are lots of *real* people who don't earn their living from tourism. At night you can walk off at least a little of the mountain of proper pasta you've just demolished by strolling hand in hand in the warm night air through Ravello's winding lanes and alleys.

Hiring a car is far from essential. There's an hourly bus service to the port of Amalfi. In the morning, the buses are packed with kids off to school and grown-ups off to work. The skill of the drivers who throw their buses round those non-stop blind bends is just amazing! From Amalfi, you can pick up connections to all the towns along the Amalfi coast or catch the boat to Capri.

Capri is a very ritzy island. A chairlift ride takes you to the highest point to marvel at the incomparable views. But if you really want to impress your beloved, buy her or him a truly gorgeous item of wildly expensive clothing from one of the exclusive shops.

It's not difficult to be alone in Ravello, but one or two of the organised trips are too splendid to miss. What could be more romantic than a day out in Rome (see Chapter 7)? Sorrento is nearer and, although touristy, has the best shopping of all the Amalfi coast resorts. Naples you'll probably be advised to avoid. Muggers and pickpockets abound and some of the squalor is distressing.

But see Pompeii, a vast archaeological treasure of a civilisation wiped out by volcanic lava. The guide will explain how sophisticated ancient Pompeii really was. For example, it had a one-way traffic system. Vesuvius, the destroyer of Pompeii, is another special trip. You can even walk to the top. It seems so tranquil and safe – hard to imagine it erupting and smothering everything in its path.

Each day trip will end when you catch the evening bus from Amalfi back up into the mountains to the delightful, un-touristy peace of romantic Ravello. It really is a gem.

GREAT PETIT ST VINCENT

For those with low-factor skin types and high spending power, the place to play Adam and Eve is Petit St Vincent, a tiny private island in the Grenadines. Petit St Vincent, PSV for short, is too small to have its own airstrip. So you get there by special charter plane from nearby Union Island, then are propelled by motor launch through the jade surf on the final leg of your journey to what must be one of the most exclusive hotels in the world.

Hazen Richardson II, Haze for short, a charming American with class, brass and imagination, fell in love with PSV, bought it and turned it into a heavenly hideaway. Paradise found? Well, it would certainly qualify in the eyes of the Fleet Street editor who once sent his travel writer in search of 'paradise'. When the intrepid reporter rang from some blissful location to say he'd found it, the editor shouted, 'Paradise hasn't got a phone' and slammed down the receiver.

Petit St Vincent has no phone (top tycoons can really escape), but there's an efficient flag communication system. Raise your flag when you wake up in the morning and breakfast will arrive in no time via room service on little electric buggies.

The food, like you, is flown in and, not unexpectedly, it is delicious. You play all day, swimming out to white sandy atolls, surfing, sailing, scuba diving and anything else you fancy beginning with 's', and at night there's dinner. That's more or less it. A bamboo band flies in once a week for a knees-up, and Haze might move the piano down on to the sands for a beach party. Nothing is too much trouble. But if you hanker after more excitement, you can always be zoomed off to visit Mustique, the island of the rich, famous and royal.

GO BALINESE, IF YOU PLEASE

Bali is the perfect place for a long-haul honeymoon. In fact, Bali is so perfect and so beautiful that if honeymooning were the only way of going there, it would be worth getting married for.

Once upon a time, so they say, Bali was known as 'the morning of the world', a place of enchantment – and on your first morning you'll see why. Bali has long golden beaches backed by drooping palms and facing a warm blue sea. There are great misty mountains draped in jungle and terraced hillsides full of wild flowers, orchids and jasmine. The nights are soft and tropical and you can see shooting stars. As a bonus, Bali is inhabited by the most friendly, smiling people who go out of their way to make visitors feel welcome.

Inevitably, unspoiled Bali has become quite developed in recent years and parts of it have become popular tourist centres, but in most cases this simply means that modern comforts have been added to the island's traditional beauty and charm. From any one of the attractive beach hotels, where the service is irreproachable and the food excellent (whether international or exotic), you can try out a great range of water sports. If you are wise, however, you'll work up a tan gradually, for this is the tropics and the sun can scorch. So take time in between bouts of beachcombing to go exploring.

Bali, which is part of the Indonesian archipelago, is a Hindu island, and therefore full of gloriously carved temples and frequent festivals, with flowers and gongs and classical dances on offer as part of the ceremonies. Balinese classical dancing is light years away from the usual folklore performances. Try to see the *legong*, the Dance of the Nymphs, or the dramatic Monkey Dance, or the fierce Baris war dances performed to beats of the *gamelan* gong.

The spectacle of Balinese dancing – especially when done by bejewelled young women in head-dresses like turreted temples and with sinuous long-nailed hands – is sheer delight. But for something a little different, why not try a funeral? It may sound odd but the Balinese look on funerals as joyful events and visitors are welcome to share in the festivities.

Other less extraordinary excursions might include a visit to the shadow puppet displays, or an outing to the artists' colonies of Mas or Ubed which are places to buy something unusual for a new home. Balinese carvings are very tactile, smooth and round and beautifully worked, and colourfully patterned Bali batik cloth is skilfully hand made. Bali offers an exotic holiday in civilised comfort: wandering about, warming to the people, especially the children; shopping in the markets; lying about on those great long white sand beaches; making side trips to the villages or the capital city of Denpasar, which is packed with markets, or to the sacred volcanic mountain, Batur. If you want a little further excitement on the way out or back, remember that many trips to Bali can incorporate a stopover in the Lion City of Singapore.

IT'S THE FIRST TIME
I'VE HEARD OF A
GROUP BOOKING DISCOUNT
FOR A HONEYMOON WEEKEND.

CHAPTER ELEVEN

The Great Experience

Intrepid travellers with a taste for the exotic have always crisscrossed the remoter corners of the world: on foot through jungle, on rubber rafts down mountain rivers, suspended from hang gliders high above the Andes, on skis across the Arctic. The search for new thrills is ceaseless, and the story goes that traversing the steppes on roller skates is going to be the ultimate trip.

Us lesser mortals with a yen for adventure but not the derring-do prefer to sally forth with civilisation at our elbow and a ready supply of mosquito repellent and anti-trot pills. Happily there are plenty of travel companies specialising in holidays that come into the 'great experience' category without exposing us to too many perils of the unknown. They are, as a rule, the higher priced ones and, for that reason, the kind some viewers criticise the *Holiday* programme for showing. However, these holidays sell. They're part of what's available on the market and many people like to see what's on offer even if they can't afford it. The letters of thanks for an exotic armchair trip usually outnumber the brickbats.

If it's any consolation to those who envy us the job of filming in faraway locations, I can assure you these are often the assignments most fraught with difficulty. To begin with, we have to work at the same speed wherever we go. Three or four days is an average shooting schedule for most *Holiday* films – and it's a lot easier doing it in Kirkcudbright than Kathmandu!

In fact, Kathmandu is a case in point. On a recent trip to

Nepal we spent half a day in the airport trying to persuade customs to let our camera through because an official had inadvertently removed the paper listing it from our carnet. Next, because internal flight times were a bit erratic, we elected to make the journey to the foothills of Annapurna by road – only 70 miles (113 km), but the road surface was so poor it took us seven-and-a-half hours grinding and lurching from one pothole to another. Finally, we all got tummy troubles, even our sound engineer who was a vegetarian! Yet, believe it or not, I can still say it was the most exciting report I've ever made for the programme.

Jet lag is inevitable when travelling half-way across the world on holiday. When you're working, it's slightly more of a problem. At the end of a transatlantic and then transcontinental flight to the western USA last year, John Pitman wasn't exactly wild about the prospect of wrestling with a Winnebago – even though it's only a mobile home and not some grisly beast from the backwoods! With his brain still semi-engaged, John found life in the fast lane on an interstate highway terrifying enough without trying to talk to the camera as well. One of those sneaky high-slung traffic lights turning red took him by surprise, he braked furiously, the cameraman in the passenger seat fell on the floor and the sound equipment hurtled from the seat behind into his lap! Holidaymakers take note. Make sure you rest before you drive.

This final chapter offers destinations that definitely come into the holiday-of-a-lifetime class – ones that in my opinion are worth paying for and going all that way for. I've included a few ideas for adventure too, albeit most of it neatly tailored. Trundling through Turkey by local bus is one for the free-wheelers.

THE ROOF OF THE WORLD

Mysterious and remote, the tiny kingdom of Nepal revs the senses at full throttle. After 135 years of being cut off from the rest of the world, it reopened its borders in 1951 and the twentieth century crept in. Even now, despite an airport, modern hotels and new buildings on its outskirts, the centre of Kathmandu, the capital, is still a culture shock for western visitors. Stepping into its seething street life is like being pitched backwards into the Middle Ages. Under the spiritual protection of age-old Hindu shrines and Buddhist temples, business prospers in the markets. Faded carpets and richly striped blankets flap in the breeze, a treasure of trinkets glitters and fearsome masks glare at you at every turn. Most fascinating of all is the throng of beautiful, small, golden-skinned people wearing clothes as exotic as any you'd find in a Victorian children's book entitled *People of other Lands* – baggy trousers, saris, embroidered shirts. Those who've adopted the basics of western dress still add Nepali accessories like sandals, a waist-coat, or the little *topi* cap that resembles a shallow fez.

In Nepal, images of India and China merge, the divisions between religions are blurred and, they say, the gods mingle with men. The most extraordinary cult is worship of the Living Goddess, a child believed to be the reincarnation of a deity. Tourists can peep at her from the courtyard of the temple where she's closeted. Fleetingly she appears on a balcony, in startling vermilion robes and lipstick to match, almost more demonic than divine. Tradition dictates that at puberty the girl returns to the community, which chooses a new goddess. Precisely what happens to the ex-goddesses isn't terribly clear, but apparently no one will marry them through superstition.

If you can brave the chill of the dawn mists, it's salutary to go down to the shrine of Pashupatinath on the sacred Bagmati River, a scene both sacred and sordid – of wailing mourners and funeral pyres, worship and washing rituals. The participants are either oblivious or indifferent to watching tourists.

Patan and Bhaktapur, other country towns in the Kathmandu Valley, are even more of a time warp than the capital. Forget our standards of hygiene – or anything else for that matter. The people are poor. Yet they're far from poor in spirit and often show their delight – or amusement – at the spectacle we make. Whatever curiosity is at ground level, every now and then you find your eyes drawn upwards, for there, between the curve and curl of elaborate roofs, rise the dazzing white peaks of the highest mountains on earth.

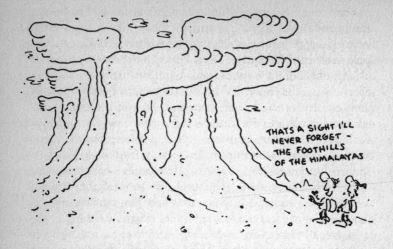

A bit of gentle trekking in the Himalayas is part of what most people come to Nepal for. You leave the valley and fly to a base like Pokhara, one of the most popular centres in the foothills of Annapurna. Already the scenery is stupendous: a Shangri-la lake, hedges of poinsettia blazing against the Himalayan back-drop – fire and ice. After a night's rest in a comfortable hotel, you set out in a small group with your Sherpa guide and his team of smiling, sinewy bearers carrying your gear. You trek, you picnic and you camp, as Prince Charles did, up on the lower mountain slopes, overlooking the beautiful contouring of terraced hillsides below. Along the way, shy farming people come to stare at you, then clasp hands together in the Nepali greeting, 'Namaste' – which means 'I salute your spirit'. You answer the same.

Three to five days' trekking is enough as a taster, but tour companies specialising in this sort of travel will put together anything you fancy. It's hardly roughing it, what with cosy sleeping bags and hot meals prepared for you each evening, but you need to be able to take fairly stiff gradients in your stride at altitudes between 2000 and 10 000 feet (610 and 3048 m). Only the views should render you breathless – and they do, especially at sunrise when the air is sharp and the great summits turn salmon pink against an aquamarine void.

Stage three of a trip to Nepal couldn't be more different: a stay in the Royal Chitwan National Park at Tiger Tops safari lodge. Here, in the Terai plain on the border of India, it's hot, sticky and straight out of *The Jungle Book*. As you sleep in delightful wooden log cabins on stilts, bells ring in the night to tell you a tiger is about. Everyone creeps out of bed to gaze in silent awe at the magnificent beast with his kill. Lured by some tethered bullock due for slaughter, the tiger triggers specially-set floodlights and remains strangely unperturbed by the glare. This is nature red in tooth and claw and not for the squeamish.

In the late afternoon and at dawn, you can go on an elephant ride through grass as high as an elephant's eye. It's a wonderful way to go on safari, for you can enjoy the sounds and the silence of the wild as well as the sights. The prize 'find' is the one-horned Indian rhino, one of the rarest and most dangerous jungle beasts. Of the 1000 that still exist, 300 are in this part of Nepal, and those within the Royal Chitwan National Park are protected. Built like armoured tanks, they are not a pretty sight, but very thrilling to see.

A holiday like this is fairly tough going. There's a lot of travelling involved, and a case of the Kathmandu Quickstep (vernacular for the trots) is almost inevitable. You need to be fit, able to take the rough with the smooth – and you need money. But if you're looking for adventure and the romance of other worlds, Nepal has both in abundance.

TO ANTIOCH BY BUS

There the bus sits in the station, painted in vivid colours like a matron at a garden party and definitely showing signs of age. Luggage on the roof, the passengers crammed into every seat and bulging out of the windows, the driver shouting cheery greetings to the regular passengers behind and then setting off with a great grinding of gears from the centre of Istanbul. Your final destination by this bus and many others along the way is the city of Antakya, ancient Antioch, on the far frontier of Turkey, down on the Syrian border, nearly 1000 miles (1609 km) away.

Turkish buses definitely fall into the 'experience' category of travel. They are not for the faint-hearted. It also helps enormously if you have well-padded hips, sharp elbows and the gift of tongues. Most of the available seats are occupied by gnarled peasants clutching sacks of grain or goats, or large-beamed ladies taking up a seat-and-a-half. So you have the choice of getting on early and being squashed against the windows, or getting on late and balancing on one buttock for most of the way.

On the other hand, there are compensations. Your Turkish co-travellers are invariably friendly, and the driver stops from time to time to offer boiled sweets to soothe dry throats and rosewater to refresh hands and fevered brows. Sometimes he stops just to rescue turtles which have strayed on to the road, looking like small boulders strewn across the dusty tarmac. Given a window seat, there's no better way to enjoy some of the most striking scenery in the Middle East, for very little outlay. As in many other countries, bus travel in Turkey is cheap – about £1 per 100 miles (161 km). Tickets must be bought in advance at the central bus station in Istanbul, so a seat is guaranteed somewhere on the bus. The long-distance express coaches are often air-conditioned but real travellers take the sort of bus used by local people and do the journey in shorter stages, mixing in a few overnight stops along the way.

We're off. The Bosphorous, which divides Europe from Asia, can be crossed by the great Europa bridge or by the numerous ferries which ply across the Sea of Marmara from the Golden Horn, delivering cars, buses and the smaller lorries to the Asian shore of Yalova. From here the bus heads south, through the olive groves, skirting the eastern shore of the Dardanelles, for Bursa, the ancient capital of the Ottoman Turks. Set high above the plain at the foot of Mount Olympus, Bursa is a spa town and, in season, a winter sports resort. It's full of hotels and mosques, each topped with a spiky minaret and the perfect place to ease cramped limbs and brace yourself for tomorrow's journey down the Old Crusader Trail, the route followed by the western armies as they marched to Jerusalem in 1098.

The old military road bursts out of the mountains by Esksehir and then climbs up on to the Anatolian plateau, the great desert that occupies much of the central plain of Eastern Turkey, a place of stony scrub and thorn bush and brilliant blue skies. The bus makes frequent stops – for just 20 minutes, no more, no less – at roadside *lokantas*, where all pile out for mineral water and glasses of *cay* (tea) before flexing elbows and battering their way back on board. A good overnight stop halfway across Anatolia is Konya, once capital of the Seljuk Turks and still a centre for that obscure sect known as the Whirling Dervishes. Actually they only whirl now and again, on certain feast days, and more as a tourist attraction nowadays. Konya has a beautiful green-roofed mosque, wide streets and many good restaurants. It's the sort of town for an enjoyable stay of a day or two.

Many miles southeast of Konya, limping along in the slip-stream of the huge intercontinental lorries that rumble down the E5 en route for the Gulf, still following the Crusader Trail, the road begins to climb and snow-tipped mountains loom above the desert heat haze. These are the Taurus Mountains, the great, jagged range that marks the fringe of Anatolia and bars the road to the coastal plain of Cilicia, once Armenia, on the Mediterranean shore.

The old road has been replaced by a modern motorway here, but the bus drones slowly uphill in a long, long crocodile of lorries, the air turning ever more chill at each bend until the road tilts over through the old pass known as the Cilician Gates and everyone stands up for a glimpse of the Mediterranean far below. The descent from this point tends to be fearsomely rapid. The views may be spectacular, but as most people have their eyes shut, definitive reports on the scenery of the southern Taurus are hard to come by. Once down on the plain, the bus creaks to a halt at the city of Tarsus, birthplace of St Paul and the place where Antony met Cleopatra, so they say.

The road from Tarsus to Antakya follows the E5 through the city of Adana to the northern tip of the Hatay, that strip of Turkey that juts down into Syria. On the way the bus stops frequently, and the passengers climbing aboard now are rather different and rather more Arabic than the ones who climbed on at Istanbul four days previously. Once they recover from the shock of finding a western face on their bus, they are no less friendly. Amazingly, picture postcards of HM The Queen or the Princess of Wales, if distributed at this point, will make you an instant social success.

And so it goes, hour after hour, day after day, across the Plain of Issus, under the looming façades of old Crusader castles, a night in Dortyol, and then another in some nameless village. While the driver and his mates might spend the hours of darkness repairing some fault in the transmission, you will be safely tucked up in the basic comfort of a small hotel or village house. The simpler hotels in Turkey are often better bets than the middle-range ones whose attempts at sophisticated plumbing and decor sometimes don't quite come off. But don't look for frills at either – just clean sheets and the smell of bleach in the showers and loos. Take your mosquito repellent!

And so over the last great pass from the coast to the hinterland, through the Syrian Gates and down the mountain to the wide and beautiful plain of Antioch and into the city of Antakya. There is so much to see in this ancient city: the River Otrantes, the finest Mosaic Museum in the world, the church where St Paul mustered the first Christian community, and a marvellous, very oriental bazaar straight out of *The Arabian Nights*. Here cages of songbirds stand outside every stall, singing their hearts out, while travellers chat and drink *cay* with traders. This is a great place to find at journey's end. No anti-climax. But to enjoy Antakya as it should be enjoyed, you have to get there by bus.

LAND OF OZ

There's a dry, burning heat, the yellow dust sticks in your hair, and the flies aim straight for your nostrils. Suddenly you know exactly why all those jolly swagmen wore hats with dangling corks!

The Kakadu National Park is not terribly far inland from the top end of Down Under, but it's true Crocodile Dundee country – in fact, parts of both Paul Hogan films were shot here. Even when you're whizzed through it in an air-conditioned coach and stay in a civilised motel with a swimming pool, you're aware that out there among the speargrass and the sandstone scrub, life is as rough and raw as anywhere in the primeval outback, and that the only people who can survive in it unaided are the Aborigines.

Kakadu is unique in that it is owned by the Aborigines and managed by the Australian National Parks and Wildlife Service. Only 200 miles (322 km) east of Darwin, its excitements are more accessible than famous Ayer's Rock for anyone with limited time. You travel through infinite stretches of bush to get to the highlights, but they're worth waiting for: Obiri Rock, site of the primitive rock art of the Aborigines; and Yellow Waters, where in September during the dry season (the best time to go) the flood plain shrinks to a thin sliver and the wildlife is so dense you can't fail to spot a crocodile – or six. Safe aboard a small excursion boat, you view the brutes slumbering on the shore, as you catch glimpses of gecko, iguana and snake.

Wherever there are dangerous reptiles, take care. Picnicking in the shade of the paperbark trees on the banks of the South Alligator River is a pleasant option, but one that you'll be able to look back on only if you obey the signs. Stick by the picnic tables and don't stray to the water's edge. People are regularly maimed and killed by crocodiles in Australia.

Billabongs, those peculiarly Australian dead river ponds, don't have crocs and are magical to linger by at dawn or sunset when birds and small animals gather. Only a few minutes' walk from where you stay at the Kakadu Park HQ, there's a billabong so wild and beautiful it could be in the middle of nowhere. As herons and jabiru storks swoop to fish over the glassy pink water, baby wallabies pop out of the long grass and bounce away as if on springs. Sightings of kangaroos are rarer in these parts, but you can be lucky.

Meeting the Aborigines on their home ground is part of the Australian experience. On Melville Island, a 20-minute flight from Darwin, a quiet Aussie couple run a rather special outfit. They've set up an encampment of state-of-the-art tents and established a rapport with the local Tiwi tribe. Each morning, a group of Tiwis turn up to invite you to come hunting or fishing with them. You cannot order events. You simply go with whatever's happening. You might find yourself shrimping in a little boat offshore, clumping through the estuary mud looking for clams or trekking through the forest to flush out a carpet-bag python. The jungle is the Aborigines' supermarket. They eat everything that is edible. Whether or not you sample the resulting cuisine is up to you, but if you accept a clam baked in the ashes of a wood fire, you're in for a treat.

There is a stunning beach on Melville, punctuated by more croc signs. But beach fun is irrelevant here. On Orpheus it is fundamental. Orpheus is one of the Palm Islands scattered along the Great Barrier Reef off the coast of northern Queensland. In this miniature Eden you can shake the dust of the bush out of your socks and unwind in tropical splendour. A number of islands offer similar pleasures – a resort hotel where the guest to staff ratio is one-to-one, the seafood fantastic and the watersports unlimited. If you've never snorkeled before, now's the time to learn, for you simply can't come to the largest coral reef in the world and not look beneath the surface of the water. A sky-hop to the reef itself is a day trip, but you can see just as much off islands like Orpheus. A stay of a few days here is paradise. Longer might fall short of it if you like things lively, for there's no entertainment. The whole charm of Orpheus is that it offers utter peace in a lush setting.

Sydney's the place for high life. Not only is it one of the world's most stunningly beautiful cities, ranged around a series of green hills and blue harbours, it is also now one of the most cosmopolitan. In the last 20 years or so, the influx of Pacific, Indian Ocean and Mediterranean people has broken the British–Celtic stranglehold on the culture. Contrary to what you might hear, the building of the famous Opera House didn't cause the sophistication of Sydney. It merely coincided with it.

The Opera House is nevertheless an asset, a fabulous focal point whose environs are a great draw on Sunday mornings. Sydneysiders flock there to enjoy alfresco pipe bands and chamber music, to climb around the architecture and watch the armada of assorted craft spin by in the harbour en route to lunch in some waterside restaurant.

The eating in Sydney is marvellous too, whether you try the Balmain Bugs (crayfish – fear not!) at Doyles with the span of the Harbour Bridge (the Coathanger) in your sights; or spot the in crowd at Chez Oz; or char your own steak (with spud, salad and glass of vino at low cost) at one of the eateries down in The Rocks. The Rocks is where Sydney sprouted after Captain Arthur Phillip anchored his first fleet of British convicts 200 years back. Old wharfside buildings and warehouses, pleasantly revamped and pedestrianised, abound with galleries, boutiques, theatres and restaurants. Here you can buy everything trendy from Ken Done T-shirts to expensive bush hats, and see The Jolly Swagman show, a nostalgic romp through history. It's a mite touristy, but *Waltzing Matilda* is sure to bring a lump to your throat if the baked potatoes don't!

Sydney is also back-to-back beaches – Bondi, Narabeen, Manly, to mention but three. This is where the surfing never stops and lusty lifesavers get their trunks in a twist – baring the buttocks is entirely practical so they'll get a better purchase on the boards!

So much for the clichés. The unexpected Sydney exists in suburbs like Paddington where streets full of Victorian cottages have been prettied up into the most desirable yuppie territory imaginable; in eccentrics like the cockatoo man who wanders about carrying his birds on his shoulder; in the tramps – an incongruity amid urban affluence – collecting empty beer cans for the returns; and in the decadent squalor of 'red light' quarters. Sydney, like all big cities, can be seamy and steamy as well as smart. But on balance few visitors come away without envying Sydneysiders their up-beat, dynamic and fair dinkum city.

MALAYSIA

Most visitors to Malaysia are surprised by the delightful muddle of it all. This is where the jungle meets the city, the colonial mixes with the industrial, and the Chinese, Malays and Indians live together as Malaysians. Malaysia is armchair orientalism, a judicious mix of the most exotic with the most easily accessible. Here nearly everyone speaks English, but they also speak

Malay, Tamil and Hokkien. Here the population mix endows the country with some of the best eating and most colourful ceremonies in the world.

Running down the spine of peninsular Malaysia is dense rainforest on a ridge of mountains. Wild tigers and *orang alsi* (primitive aboriginal tribespeople) live in these remote areas. Here too are the hill stations of the Cameron Highlands, Frazer's Hill and Genting Highlands – originally created by the British colonisers as cool retreats from the baking plains and necessary precautions against the men 'going troppo' – which usually entailed either omitting to dress properly for dinner or taking a local mistress. With sculpted gardens, tea houses and golf courses, the hill stations are still perfect retreats for the travel-weary.

There is plenty of colonialism still visible in Malaysia: pillar boxes are red and crested, people drive Morris Minors and BSA motorbikes, members of mock Tudor clubs wear pith helmets, swagger sticks and handlebar moustaches, and cricket is still played on the *padangs* of many a Malaysian town.

Malaysia achieved its independence from British rule in 1957. In 1965 the state of Singapore, at that time just a scrubby island with an ambitious port, left the federation of Malay states. Now, gallingly for the Malaysians, their country is a playground for rich Singaporeans, often from Malaysian families, who fill the hotels in the country's offshore islands and gamble at the weekends in the country's only casino in the Genting Highlands (gambling is illegal in Singapore).

Most visitors to Malaysia want to sample Singapore island as well when they come this far, and it's fascinating to explore by tri-shaw what's left of its old Chinatown. This was fast being bulldozed to the ground to make way for the modern city, but thankfully vestiges are left now that the government understand it's what tourists come to see. It's a good plan to start in Singapore, as a number of coach tours do, for in a way it puts Malaysia more in perspective. As soon as you transfer to the mainland, you'll notice how laid back everything is in contrast. But although it may seem a bit behind the times, Malaysia is the only southeast Asian nation to have its own car, the Proton Saga, and a capital city – Kuala Lumpur, commonly known as

KL – like a mini Manhattan surrounded by crumbling old Chinese shophouses.

The west coast, with KL at its centre, is the economic heartland of the country, producing 40 per cent of the world's rubber needs and 25 per cent of its tin. It's alternatively a delight and an eyesore. Rice paddies, dotted with palm-thatched *kampong* houses, alternate with tin mines and the serried marching ranks of oil palm and rubber plantations. Here is the annual Indian ceremony of Thaipusam, in which devotees pierce their skin with scores of hooks and walk over burning coals without apparently feeling a thing, and here grows the durian, the king of fruit, whose taste was likened by one wag to that of old raspberry yoghurt eaten in a French urinal! The locals put it more poetically – they say it smells like hell and tastes like heaven. One of the oldest settlements is Malacca, a trading post that featured in Joseph Conrad's writings, with a distinctive Chinese population – the *babas* – who are a race apart from the other dialect groups.

The east coast, romantic, deserted and traditional, is altogether a different proposition. Mile upon mile of brilliant yellow-white sand is backed by coconut palms and a single highway, where timber lorries are the kings of the road. The coast is speckled with fishing villages and shanty towns, and every year the giant leatherback turtle crawls out of the sea to lay its eggs in the sand.

If you get the chance, don't miss the peace and beauty of the islands that fringe the coast: Langkawi, Penang (see chapter 2) and Pangkor on the west coast, and Tioman, which was the setting for the film *South Pacific*, on the east coast.

THE EARTH'S GREATEST CRACK

The Grand Canyon is without doubt one of the most spectacular of our natural wonders, an unmissable experience for anyone travelling in the western USA whether you're roughing it in a Winnebago camper or living it up in Las Vegas. What adds to the canyon's initial impact is the fact that it lies almost unseen, hidden deep in the Arizona flatlands, until you arrive at the edge of the South Rim. Then it opens up before you, a gigantic gash in the landscape, the yawning 6000-feet (1829 m) deep gorge of the mighty Colorado River. Awesome.

However, it is not size alone that makes the Grand Canyon so, well, grand. Certainly it's huge. It's deep. It strains the eye to absorb. But half of the impact is caused by the serried colours of the rock – reds, blues, shades of indigo and vermilion – a great kaleidoscope which changes throughout the day as the sun shifts across the sky. It becomes even more beautiful as evening sends deep shadows slanting sideways, adding black and purple.

Much of this can be seen from the various lodges, viewpoints and walkways on the South Rim, where visitors can also watch the antics of the little rock gophers which live in crevices in the cliffs. But to get a proper grasp of the Grand Canyon you must either fly over it, raft through it or walk down into it.

The most popular way to see it is by helicopter, taking off from launch pads and airfields round about for a half-hour flight along and into the chasm, with cameras snapping as great views stream past the perspex. Most of the helicopter pilots well know how to make the experience even more thrilling, approaching the rim at tree-top height so that the canyon drops away into a sudden, stomach-lurching void, falling sheer to the narrow brown smear of the Colorado River far below.

A raft trip through the canyon can take up to two weeks. It's a hairy ride on large rubber boats, bouncing over high waves in

the rapids. But there are the pleasures of paddling the quiet stretches, coming ashore to camp each evening and sleeping with the roar of the river still loud in your ears. For the truly adventurous, this is a trip to remember.

The last way down into the canyon is on foot, either your own or a mule's. Most people opt to ride down on muleback, clinging on for dear life as the animals step, sure-footed, round the drops. You stop at the Indian Gardens halfway down for a cookout or picnic before turning back. The trek there and back lasts a full day. Walkers and backpackers can follow the twisting 9-mile (14 km) Bright Angel Trail, one of the world's great footpaths. This takes you to the camp sites by Bright Angel Creek, and you can either complete the 18-mile (28 km) circuit within the day, or camp down there for a night or two, soaking up the marvels of one of the most beautiful places on earth.

JAPANORAMA

After the anonymous road from the airport, the first sight of Japan most people register clearly is the concrete and glass canyons of Tokyo, a city literally risen from the ashes of the second world war. In 1945 it was horizontal. Today it is vertical, full of skyscrapers, traffic jams and people jams – New York with a made-in-Japan label, and you get the same kind of buzz from its pulsebeat.

Then suddenly, in the midst of the inner city hiatus, you find yourself in pockets of pure Japan. The pungent smell of incense wafts along a phalanx of gaudy souvenir stalls, luring you towards the approach to a Buddhist temple. One of the most impressive is dedicated to Kannon, the all-seeing, all-hearing goddess of perception. It's no accident that her name resembles a well-known trademark. Only the Japanese could have a goddess of cameras!

Here, Buddhism and pockets of Christianity coexist with Shintoism, the indigenous religion of the worship of ancestors. So a sizeable part of any tour concentrates on shrines and temples. There are plenty of these even in Tokyo, though smart department stores are the bigger draw. From Gucci to Givenchy to Garrard, designer names litter the counters. To us, Tokyo is excruciatingly expensive, but there are some good buys. Costume jewellery, for instance. Acres of floor space sparkle with copies of the latest western designs. Cameras? Cassette players? Cheaper, yes, but watch out. If you count the duty payable back in Britain, these aren't a bargain.

When you've had enough urban excitement, pause for a moment by the tranquil moat that isolates the Imperial Palace from the outside world, right in the middle of the city. You can barely see the palace peeping above the trees, so the guards in their sentry boxes get all the attention. Most of the sightseers are Japanese. Here, as at every turn of an uptilted roof, they're out in force playing tourist themselves.

On a first trip to the Land of the Rising Sun, the most usual itinerary is Tokyo/Kyoto/Tokyo. This includes a visit to the Hakone National Park south of the capital and a magical boat trip on Lake Ashi within sight of the snow-capped cone of Mount Fuji. The sacred volcano sleeps, but nearby Owakudani splutters – so they take you there, to wander its turbulent slopes which steam and bubble with hot springs and mud pools and pong unbelievably! Inevitably, therapeutic treatments for rheumatism are on offer at the local resort hotel, which is an odd sort of place: a modern hotel with a lovely Japanese garden which nobody seems to go into. The Japanese pad about indoors looking good in the all-one-sized happi-coats provided, while gangly Europeans appear considerably less happi in them. Women tourists enjoy being trussed up in a silk kimono for dinner – a dainty attendant comes to your room to do the gift wrapping. You can also opt to sleep on futons – thick mattresses laid on the floor – reputed to be good for the back.

Part of any journey south to Kyoto is bound to be on the Shinkansen super express, the so-called Bullet Train which was the fastest in the world until the French TGV overtook it. As you speed along at 126 miles (203 km) per hour, staring out at the endless flat plain of central Honshu, you realise how crowded this part of Japan is. Factories, industrial estates, villages and towns run into each other, leaving no space unpopulated.

In Kyoto, the traditional is more in evidence than the modern. There are wonderful old buildings festooned with noodles of electric cabling, there is the exquisite Golden Pavilion of Kinkakuji, a perfect copy of the original palace built by the Shoguns, and there are some amazing Shinto shrines. The bonus of visiting these in November is that you see lots of Japanese children in gorgeous traditional dress, for this is the month when little ones aged three, five and seven – the lucky numbers – are brought to be blessed by their ancestors.

At Nara, a grinding coach trip away through endless suburbs, beats the historical heart of Japan. Its massive temple of Todaiji is a marvel. This houses the great Sun Buddha, the largest bronze statue in existence – or so they tell you, and it seems believable. Incense swirls, unearthly gongs strike, saffron-robed monks aim video cameras and Japanese school parties endearingly cajole blond westerners into joining them in their group pictures!

Perhaps the most unforgettable sight of all is the Kasuga Shrine, inhabited by the ancestral spirits of the Fujiwaras, one of Japan's great ruling families. Painted vermilion and white, the colours of happiness, and entwined with wisteria blossom, it exudes an aura of total harmony between natural and supernatural.

On the lighter side, Japan can be very amusing. You don't have to understand the language to laugh at the hilarious game shows on your hotel room TV set – many surpassing the inanity of Clive James' selections. Then there's the food. Plastic replicas of meals on offer are almost a turn-off in restaurant windows, but at least you know what you're getting. Plump for the raw fish menus of *sashimi* or *sushi* and you're never quite sure! *Teppanyaki* may be more appetising for those unfamiliar with Japanese cuisine. Beef, or prawns, noodles and vegetables are cooked on a hotplate, the *teppan*, at the counter or in the middle of your table. The chef displays the dexterity of a brain surgeon, so it's as fascinating to watch as it is delicious to eat.

Demonstrations of other Japanese arts can be entertaining too. An evening show encapsulating everything from flower arranging to samurai swordsmanship, kabuki to karate, is one way of seeing the lot at one fell swoop. Only the tea ceremony suffers. Truncated to three minutes, it becomes more of an instant quick-brew instead of the prolonged performance designed to induce a state of calm and contentment in tea maker and tea drinker!

Inevitably on a brief trip to a country so different, complex and inscrutable, you come away having merely skimmed the surface of things, but the clash of its images makes Japan rivetingly rewarding: the glare and the glitz of a highly westernised society and the timeless beauty of its eastern rituals.

AFRICAN SAFARI

There's a primitive thrill unlike any other about setting off through the Kenyan savannah before sun up. As your jeep bumps over the lumpy track, anonymous pairs of eyes glow fleetingly in the darkness. Then the sky begins to redden on the horizon and distant herds of wildebeest trek across it like beetles, raising a fog of dust. Elegant giraffe necks sway in silhouette past those typical flat-topped trees, and vultures take off into a mother-of-pearl light. At last, the full face of the sun glares across the grasslands and everywhere you look there are wild animals – Thomson gazelle, zebra, hyena, rhino and even lion at this time of the morning. Somehow it's like being in at the beginning of the world.

To see African wildlife in such abundance, you have to get to the more remote game reserves. This entails quite a bit of flying around within Kenya. Nairobi is the starting point, a pleasant city in which to recover from jet lag and stock up on safari gear. Shops full of khaki are still happily cashing in on the publicity brought to Kenya by the film *Out of Africa*; they use the title as a come-on, daubing it across their windows. The former home of Karen Blixen, author of the original book, is now open to the public. It's exactly as she described it – 'at the foot of the Ngong hills'.

Far beyond the Ngong hills is the Masai Mara game reserve, a huge swathe of southwest Kenya where wandering Masai tribes herd their cattle. From the moment your plane lands – the airport is a mere clearing in the bush – you're in the midst of herds of deer and zebra, and feel totally removed from civilisation. But you aren't. Close by, the permanent safari lodges offer every civilised comfort, and even if you opt for camping under canvas, *Out of Africa* style, there will be staff to look after you, wine in your glass and flowers on the table. The plumbing might be a little unusual. Showers are canvas buckets and latrines a basic hole in the ground with shovel! But these are small inconveniences when you realise the pluses of living *au nature*. Drinks before dinner may be interrupted by a call to come and see the elephants enjoying *their* sundowners by the riverside – then the snort of hippos has you creeping to another vantage point.

A set of binoculars and zoom lenses for your camera are actually more essential on safari than the right clothes. Sartorially, being cool and comfortable is all that matters. The tradition of wearing khaki is founded on the misconception that it blends into the background and doesn't attract the animals. In fact, animals see in monochrome – which explains why zebras are well camouflaged by their stripes. A knowledgeable guide accompanies you on these trips and regales you with this kind of bush lore.

If you can afford to blow the extra £180 (at the last count), a balloon ride across the Masai Mara has to be one of life's all-time highs. The sensation of drifting over Africa at sunrise is unforgettable. You're airborne for almost two hours, floating, soaring and dropping down to take a close look at the animals without disturbing them – perhaps catching a lion with its breakfast. By nine o'clock you're ready for yours. A champagne 'do' is brought out with the recovery vehicles and spread right where you fetch up – in the middle of the bush – with distant hyenas popping up to sniff the bacon and eggs!

Another flight across the country's heartland takes you to the Galana reserve near the coast. On the fringe of a million-acre cattle ranch are a scattering of ranch houses, each with a small cluster of luxury log cabins which cater for a handful of visitors. Here you're welcomed virtually as house guests by the people who run the show, and the main attraction is going for a walk on the wild side.

The excitement of trekking game on foot is heightened after being in the Masai Mara where you have to remain in the jeeps. In Galana, you're on the loose, but in the safe hands of an ex-professional hunter with a gun. There's little need to be nervous provided you do precisely what you're told. Walking groups have been known to wander into lions' dens and come to no harm because they froze in their tracks as instructed until the lions yawned out of boredom and stalked off!

Your luck is really in if the hunter knows the whereabouts of an elephant herd. He'll take you by jeep to within 3 or 4 miles (5 or 6 km) of it. Then, if the wind's in the right direction – crucial, as you must be downwind of them so they can't pick up your scent – you trek, as near as he thinks you dare, maybe to within a few hundred yards of the hindmost. Standing in this hostile wilderness, close enough to count the wrinkles on these mammoth African jumbos, is absolutely breath-stopping – something all those years of watching *The World About Us* doesn't begin to prepare you for.

THE MAHARAJAHS' TRAIN

In the desert state of Rajasthan, the sound of India's famous Palace on Wheels brings people running to the side of the track to wave – small grinning children, wizened old men, farmers' wives with babies in arms. No longer is it the train of the maharajahs, but it still commands respect and is an impressive sight, especially when under steam.

Each of India's rulers once owned a special carriage which would be attached to an ordinary train for travel. When these were obsolete – the carriages as well as the maharajahs – someone had the bright idea of renovating the royal compartments and stringing them together as a tourist attraction. They called it the Palace on Wheels. Now travellers can go intercity in slow motion on a round trip from Delhi, sleeping and eating on board and stopping to visit some of the subcontinent's most exotic mogul cities and palaces. From the rose-coloured spectacle of Jaipur, seventeenth-century capital of the Rajputs; Udaipur and its magical Lake Palace where they filmed part of

Jewel in the Crown; to Jodhpur with its towering fortress and pale blue houses – a visual cooler in the glaring heat. From the golden city of Jaisalmer to Fathepur Sikri and the Taj Mahal.

But does the train take the strain? Palace on Wheels is perhaps a bit of a misnomer. This is not the subcontinent's answer to the Orient Express. It's a marvellous way of seeing a great deal in a short time without the inconvenience of changing hotels, packing and repacking your suitcase and standing in queues at airports, but it's definitely more of an Adventure on Wheels. With carriages of varying widths on a metre wide track, its rhythm is erratic, to say the least, and you don't get a lot of sleep! What's more, during 20 per cent of the journey when it's steam powered (diesel does the rest), a fine film of soot seeps in through every chink. Be warned if you have breathing problems or wear contact lenses.

Aside from these minor discomforts, the Palace on Wheels is a lovable old train, full of idiosyncracies. Each carriage has four tiny double-berthed compartments, communal seating area, shared loo and shower fitting (mainly for show – water doesn't actually come through the showerhead, only the taps; you make do with an Indian bath, operating the plastic bucket!). Two beautifully attired attendants cater to your every whim, keep the place spotless and provide breakfast and endless cups of tea.

Meals on wheels are a great excitement, for the train has no corridor. To get to the bar and dining car you have to wait till it stops in some funny old middle-of-nowhere station and dash along the platform. Ditto to get back again. It's worth the walk, for the food is exquisite. There's simply no other word for it. Beautiful soup for starters, the most delicately flavoured, lightly spiced curries, fresh fruit to follow, and impeccable service. Every meal a gourmet treat. Not all eating is done aboard. During daytime sightseeing (the travelling is mostly done at night), you enjoy the hospitality of salubrious hotels en route, many converted from palaces.

The pace is never too pressured. There's time to wander in the chaotic jumble of city streets where everything is on the move – except sacred cows who tend to sit down in the least convenient places; time to linger by the shores of lakes where the women come to do their washing and gaggles of children crowd around to make friends – they're not always after rupees, often merely want to proffer their addresses so you'll send them copies of the photographs you've taken of them; and time to savour the magnificence of India's past glories.

Every stop seems to be the highlight of the trip – until the next. The Taj Mahal surpasses your expectations. It's so massive a monument and in such beautiful condition, like a building ordered from Aspreys, each semiprecious stone neatly embedded in a filligree of marble. But perhaps the place that most embodies the great romantic pull of India is Jaisalmer, an amazing citadel rising out of the flatness of the Thar Desert on the westernmost border.

Founded by King Jaisal 90 years after the Normans conquered England, the 'golden city' has changed little in the space of eight centuries. Modern plumbing has arrived, sadly spoiling the urban scenery with pipes running across the fabulous sandstone carving of the Jain temples, but the rest is as it was; a library housing some of India's most ancient manuscripts, a labyrinth of streets full of wonderful hangings and carpets and the twanging of a primitive stringed instrument called a ravanhatar. You end up buying one partly to please the sellers.

As the heat of the day subsides, you exit from the city walls and change to a camel train! On a lumbering desert ride blending into the landscape, you imagine how travellers of old would have rejoiced at the sight of Jaisalmer after a long, parched trek across the wilderness. That really *was* travelling – and so is the Palace on Wheels. For all its quirks, it's a great experience. Following in the tracks of the maharajahs, you feel you're travelling in a little bit of history through a land that's baked in it.

SHOP SUEY IN HONG KONG

Its name may mean 'fragrant harbour', but in *Noble House*, James Clavell's epic novel about Hong Kong, one of the characters sniffs the air on arrival at Kai Tak airport and picks up the more distinctive scent of this capitalistic colony – the smell of money. It emanates from the serried ranks of sleek international banks and commercial world-beating names flashing neon on the waterfront, from every poky back street, from the crowded restaurants and from rich Chinese women dripping in crêpe de Chine.

Tourists are said to spend two-thirds of their time in Hong Kong shopping – for cameras, curiosities and Calvin Klein copies. The place to start is the old Wanchai district on Hong Kong Island behind the fence of skyscrapers, a catacomb of narrow streets choked with people and bespattered with Chinese characters. The vegetable market is tossed together with the clothes market in a chop suey muddle: one moment you're marvelling at the piles of arthritic looking fresh ginger root, the next scrutinising smart look-alikes of Italian leather-trimmed luggage at a twentieth of the price back home. The small shops on the sidelines are better still, offering everything from herb tisanes to 100-year-old eggs and 24-hour suits. A letter writer sits, pen poised, on the pavement to serve the illiterate.

All the tourist bumf directs you to spend your HK dollars at the big shopping complexes like New World, the Landmark, Ocean Terminal and Ocean Centre. To-ing and fro-ing between them is the best part of it, on the Star Ferry across Victoria Harbour. Even if the peaks that shelter the Kowloon Peninsula have their heads in the clouds, it doesn't detract from the impact of that skyline. And when a traditional sailing junk billows in among the flotilla of oceangoing ships and yachts, your stomach lurches and the hairs on your neck bristle.

Under the sign of the sailing junk, which means approval by the tourist board, are the Communist Chinese Art & Handicraft emporiums. In these you go cross eyed looking at rattan, carved boxes and bales of silk. Western visitors make odd purchases simply because they're bargains – like cotton vests at 50 pence!

When the flesh weakens and the credit card begins to curl, the rest of Hong Kong awaits. Remember only 13 per cent is actually city. The rest is countryside and islands and beautiful beaches.

Repulse Bay is delightful. So is Deepwater Bay where the

Brits first landed, though both can be as crowded as Brighton on a clear day. The New Territories give you an away-from-it-all feeling with their rolling green hills, villages with duck ponds and rural markets. Tourism has tweaked things up here and there. There's the Sung Dynasty Village, for instance, a recreation of a 1000-year-old village with people wandering about in period costume, but it's too well done to dismiss.

More exciting is to go on a trip to mainland China. One way is by jetfoil via Macau. You spend a day in the Pearl River delta, a landscape far behind the times where there's hardly any motorised traffic on the roads through the rice paddies, the workers wear coolie hats and yokes, geese flock in gaggles by roadside puddles and water buffalo do the ploughing. You visit the home of Sun Yat Sen, the founder of modern China, see a school, eat in a smart restaurant and are free to wander at will through the grubby streets of a poor market town, Shi Kwi, where children are barefoot and puppy dogs in cages are destined for the pot.

Back in Hong Kong, Aberdeen's floating harbour of sampans, junks and houseboats seems less seedy by comparison. If you go by water taxi through its midst, you notice toddlers tethered by ropes to stop them falling in. Once only the boys would have been tied. The girls had no value.

Aberdeen's the place to eat, either at a sampan snackery – you simply go alongside, buy and take away – or in more style at one of the large tiered restaurants that look like floating dragons. Each floor of white-clothed tables is a riot of gold glitter and red lacquer. The food is delicious and tempered to western tastes – no puppy, snake, wild cat or monkey on the menu!

Hong Kong is a tantalising experience, however you spend time there, and the prospect of its impending metamorphosis gives you an extra charge. In 1997, when it ceases to be a British colony and reverts back to China, it will almost certainly never be the same.

Appendix

USEFUL ADDRESSES

NATIONAL TOURIST OFFICES

England

English Tourist Board
Thames Tower, Black's Road,
Hammersmith, London W6 9EL

Regional

Cumbria Tourist Board
Holly Road, Ashleigh, Windermere
Cumbria LA23 2AQ

East Anglia Tourist Board
Toppesfield Hall, Hadleigh, Suffolk
IP7 5DN

East Midlands Tourist Board
Exchequergate, Lincoln LN2 1PZ

Heart of England Tourist Board
2–4 Trinity Street, Worcester
WR1 2PW

London Tourist Board
26 Grosvenor Gardens, London
SW1W 0ET

Northumbria Tourist Board
Aykley Heads, Durham DH1 5UX

North West Tourist Board
The Last Drop Village, Bromley
Cross, Bolton, Lancs BL7 9PZ

South East England Tourist Board
1 Warwick Park, Tunbridge Wells,
Kent TN2 5TA

Southern Tourist Board
The Town Hall Centre, Leigh Road,
Eastleigh, Hants SO5 4DE

Thames and Chilterns Tourist Board
8 The Market Place, Abingdon,
Oxon OX14 3HG

West Country Tourist Board
Trinity Court, 37 Southernhay East,
Exeter EX1 1QS

Yorkshire and Humberside Tourist
Board
312 Tadcaster Road, York YO2 2HF

Local

Cornwall Tourist Board
59 Lemon Street, Truro, Cornwall
TR1 2SY

The Lizard
c/o Kermer District Council,
Council Offices, Dolcoath Avenue,
Camborne, TR14 8RY

Scotland

Scottish Tourist Board
19 Cockspur Street, London
SW1Y 5BL
or
23 Ravelston Terrace, Edinburgh
EH4 3EU

Local

North Berwick Tourist Information
Office
Quality Street, North Berwick,
Lothian EH39

The Oban Tourist Office
Argyll Square, Oban,
Argyll PA34 4AN

Wales

The Wales Tourist Board
Brunel House, 2 Fitzalan Road,
Cardiff CF2 1UY

Northern Ireland

Northern Ireland Tourist Board
River House, 48 High Street, Belfast
BT1 2DS

Isle of Man

The Isle of Man Tourist Board
13 Victoria Street, Douglas,
Isle of Man

Jersey

State of Jersey Tourism Committee
Weighbridge, St Helier, Jersey CI

Guernsey

State of Guernsey Tourist Board
PO Box 23, White Rock,
St Peter Port, Guernsey CI

**Foreign National
Tourist Offices
in Britain**

Sindicat d'Iniciativa de les Valls
d'Andorra
63 Westover Road, London
SW18 2RF

Antigua and Barbados Tourist
Office
15 Thayer Street, London
W1M 5DL

Australian Tourist Commission
4th Floor, Heathcoat House,
20 Savile Row, London W1X 1AE

Austrian National Tourist Office
30 St George Street, London
W1R 0AL

Barbados Board of Tourism
263 Tottenham Court Road, London
W1P 9AA

Tourism Canada (also for British
Columbia)
Canada House, Trafalgar Square,
London SW1Y 5BJ

China National Tourist Board
4 Glentworth Street, London NW1

Danish Tourist Board
Sceptre House, 169–173 Regent
Street, London W1R 8PY

French Government Tourist Office
178 Piccadilly, London W1V 0AL

German (Federal Republic) National
Tourist Office
61 Conduit Street, London
W1R 0EN

National Tourist Organisation of
Greece
195–197 Regent Street, London
W1R 8DL

Hong Kong Tourist Association
125 Pall Mall, London SW1Y 5EA

Iceland Tourist Information Bureau
73 Grosvenor Street, London
W1X 9DD

Government of India Tourist Office
7 Cork Street, London W1X 2AB

Indonesian Tourist Promotion
Board
Embassy of the Republic of
Indonesia, 38 Grosvenor Square,
London W1X 9AD

Irish Tourist Board
Ireland House, 150 New Bond
Street, London W1Y 0AQ

Italian State Tourist Office
1 Princes Street, London W1R 8AY

Japan National Tourist Organisation
167 Regent Street, London
W1R 7FD

Kenya Tourist Office
13 New Burlington Street, London
W1X 1FF

Tourist Development Corporation
of Malaysia
17 Curzon Street, London
W1Y 7FE

Moroccan National Tourist Office
174 Regent Street, London
W1R 6HB

Ministry of Tourism, Department of
Tourism
His Majesty's Government of Nepal,
Kathmandu, Nepal

Netherlands Board of Tourism
25–28 Buckingham Gate, London
SW1E 6LD

State of New York Division of
Tourism
25 Bedford Square, London
WC1B 3HG

New Zealand Tourist and Publicity
Office
New Zealand House,
80 Haymarket, London SW1Y 4TQ

Norwegian Tourist Board
20 Pall Mall, London SW1Y 5NE

Palm Beach Country (Florida)
Tourist Development Council,
35 Piccadilly, London W1V 9PB

Portuguese National Tourist Office
(also for Madeira)
New Bond Street House, 1–5 New
Bond Street, London W1Y 0NP

Seychelles Tourist Office
PO Box 4PE, 50 Conduit Street,
London W1A 4PE

Singapore Tourist Promotion Board
Carrington House, 126–130 Regent
Street, London W1R 5FE

Spanish National Tourist Office
57 St James Street, London SW1

Swedish National Tourist Board
3 Cork Street, London W1X 1HA

Swiss National Tourist Office
Swiss Centre, New Coventry Street,
London W1V 8EE

Tourism Authority of Thailand
49 Albermarle Street, London
W1X 3PE

Tunisian National Tourist Office
7a Stafford Street, London W1

United States Travel and Tourism
Administration
22 Sackville Street, London
W1X 2EA

Yugoslav National Tourist Office
143 Regent Street, London
W1R 8AE

CARRIERS

British Airways
Customer Services, Comet House,
London Heathrow Airport

Dan Air
Customer Services, Newman House,
45 Victoria Road, Horley, Surrey
RH6 72G

British Midland
Customer Services, Donnington
Hall, Castle Donnington, Derby
DE7 2SB

Air UK
Customer Relations Department,
Air UK, Stansted House, Stansted
Airport, Essex CM24 8QT

OTHER USEFUL ADDRESSES

AA Travel Service, PO Box 128,
Copenhagen Court, New Street,
Basingstoke, Hants RG21 1DT

ABTA
55–57 Newman Street, London
W1P 4AH

AITO
The Knoll House, Pursers Lane,
Peaslake, Near Guildford, Surrey
GU5 9SJ

Air Travel Advisory Bureau
Morley House, 320 Regent Street,
London W1

British Activity Holidays
Association
Rock Park Centre, Llandrindod
Wells, Powys, Wales LD1 6AE

British Horse Society
Stoneleigh, Kenilworth,
Warwickshire

British Property Timeshare
Association
Westminster Bank Chambers,
Market Hill, Sudbury, Suffolk
CO10 GEN

British Trust for Conservation
Volunteers
36 St Mary's Street, Wallingford,
Oxon OX10 0EU

The Camping and Caravanning Club
Ltd
11 Lower Grosvenor Place, London
SW1W 0EY

Caravan Club
East Grinstead House, East
Grinstead, West Sussex RH19 1UA

Department of Trade and Industry
10–18 Victoria Street, London
SW1H 0NN

Holiday Care Service
2 Old Bank Chambers, Station
Road, Horley, Surrey RH6 9HW
(provides holiday information for
disabled and elderly people)

Kibbutz Representatives
1a Accommodation Road,
London NW11 8EP

London Transport
55 Broadway, London SW1 0BD

Meon House
College Street, Petersfield,
Hampshire GU32 3JN

National Anglers Council
11 Cowgate, Peterborough PE1 1LZ

National Institute for Adults
Continuing Education
19B De Montford Street, Leicester
LE1 7GE

The National Trust
36 Queen Anne's Gate, London
SW1

Radar
25 Mortimer Street,
London W1N 8AB

Ramblers Association
1–5 Wandsworth Road, London
SW8 2XX

Royal Automobile Club
49 Pall Mall, London SW1Y 5JG

Royal Horticultural Society
80 Vincent Square, London SW1

Royal Society for the Protection of
Birds
The Lodge, Sandy, Bedfordshire
SG19 2DL

Select Site Reservations
55 Avenue Road, Cranleigh, Surrey
GU6 7LJ

Ski Club of Great Britain
118 Eaton Square, London
SW1W 9AF

SNCF
French Railways House,
179 Piccadilly, London W1V 0BA

Vacation Work
9 Park End Street, Oxford

The Wine Development Board
5 Kings House, Kennet Wharf Lane,
Upper Wharf Lane,
Upper Thames Street,
London EC4V 3BH

World Wide Fund for Nature
Panda House,
Weyside Park, Godalming,
Surrey GU7 1XR

Youth Hostel Association
Trevelyan House, 8 St Stephens Hill,
St Albans, Hertfordshire, AL1 2DY

Index